being

40

being 40

The Decade of Letting Go—and **Embracing Who We Are**

STACEY LINDSAY

THE OPEN FIELD / PENGUIN LIFE

VIKING

An imprint of Penguin Random House LLC
1745 Broadway, New York, NY 10019
penguinrandomhouse.com

The Open Field/A Penguin Life Book

THE OPEN FIELD is a registered trademark of MOS Enterprises, Inc.

VIKING is a registered trademark of Penguin Random House LLC.

Set in Frasa with Californian and Texta
Designed by Sabrina Bowers

LIBRARY OF CONGRESS CATALOGING-IN-PUBLICATION DATA
Names: Lindsay, Stacey author
Title: Being 40 : the decade of letting go—and embracing who we are / Stacey Lindsay. Other titles: Being forty
Description: New York, NY : The Open Field/The Penguin Life, [2026] | Includes index. Identifiers: LCCN 2025034877 (print) | LCCN 2025034878 (ebook) | ISBN 9780593831199 hardcover | ISBN 9780593831205 ebook
Subjects: LCSH: Middle-aged women | Aging—Social aspects
Classification: LCC HQ1059.4 .L56 2026 (print) | LCC HQ1059.4 (ebook) | DDC 305.2442—dc23/eng/20260202
LC record available at https://lccn.loc.gov/2025034877
LC ebook record available at https://lccn.loc.gov/2025034878

Printed in the United States of America
1st Printing

The authorized representative in the EU for product safety and compliance is Penguin Random House Ireland, Morrison Chambers, 32 Nassau Street, Dublin D02 YH68, Ireland, https://eu-contact.penguin.ie.

Dear Reader,

Years ago, these words attributed to Rumi found a place in my heart:

Out beyond ideas of
wrongdoing and rightdoing,
there is a field. I'll meet you there.

Ever since, I've cultivated an image of what I call "the Open Field"—a place out beyond fear and shame, beyond judgment, loneliness, and expectation. A place that hosts the reunion of all creation. It's the hope of my soul to find my way there—and whenever I hear an insight or a practice that helps me on the path, I love nothing more than to share it with others.

That's why I've created The Open Field. My hope is to publish books that honor the most unifying truth in human life: We are all seeking the same things. We're all seeking dignity. We're all seeking joy. We're all seeking love and acceptance, seeking to be seen, to be safe. And there is no competition for these things we seek—because they are not material goods; they are spiritual gifts!

We can all give each other these gifts if we share what we know—what has lifted us up and moved us forward. That is our duty to one another—to help each other toward acceptance, toward peace, toward happiness—and my promise to you is that the books published under this imprint will be maps to the Open Field, written by guides who know the path and want to share it.

Each title will offer insights, inspiration, and guidance for moving beyond the fears, the judgments, and the masks we all wear. And when we take off the masks, guess what? We will see that we are the opposite of what we thought—we are each other.

We are all on our way to the Open Field. We are all helping one another along the path. I'll meet you there.

Love, Maria S

For the wild women in our lives who have saved us,
often invisibly, through lifetimes.

And for my mother, Tai-Tai, Ava, and Maura.

I want to believe that the imperfections are nothing—that the light is everything—that it is more than the sum of each flawed blossom rising and falling. And I do.

—MARY OLIVER

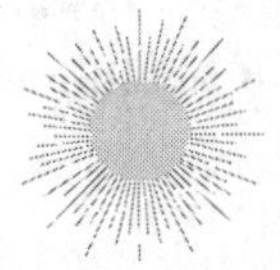

Contents

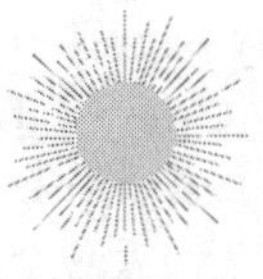

A Note on Words and Community

I HOPE YOU FEEL SAFE WHILE TUCKED INTO THIS BOOK. UN-judged and free.

The purpose of sharing our stories in a book like this is to crack open new portals—portals to feeling, seeing, and growing. But I have to say something before we continue: This book is filled with words (as books are!), and words can be limiting, at times. Language is one of our boldest instruments; it's the tool that sets us humans apart from other creatures. But just as language can heal and unite, it often lacks what's needed to embrace the open sky of being alive. It can keep us stuck and alone in our heads.

I write this because of four words I use throughout this book: *woman* and *women*, and *she* and *her*.

I use these nouns and pronouns to refer to myself and the people I interview (with their consent), and to explore and interrogate the ideas of what it means to be a woman in her forties today. But I do not intend for these words to be absolutes. The goal of this book is to shed light on the possibilities this life holds for each of us, no matter how we identify and wherever our sex and gender fall on the infinite spectrum.

I anchor this book in my experience. I am a cisgender, physically nondisabled woman living a relatively heteronormative existence. (I say "relatively" as I loathe qualifiers when it comes to our sexuality and how we connect.) I am white, in my forties, recently married, and do not have children. My identity is one of countless identities around what it means to be, feel, and live as a woman today. I also share the stories and sentiments of many women whom I interviewed for this book—women who are married and unmarried, have children and do not have children, are partnered and unpartnered, and are of varying races, ethnicities, faiths, religions, and sexual orientations. My intention was to include as diverse an experience of women as possible to explore the decade of our forties, but I know, inevitably, I will fall short and there will be unconscious biases in what I present. I hope you will forgive me for this.

My deepest passion is to write about and for women. Every opportunity to illuminate a woman's complexity and beauty gives further reason to why my voice in journalism exists.

There is no right way to be a woman. There is no right way to be a person. There is only who we are—and we can learn all we're meant to by honoring this truth and listening.

being
40

introduction

An Intersection

THIS ALL FEELS DIFFERENT.

I kept thinking this after I turned forty.

I had been living with the idea that forty would look and feel a certain way. This age had loomed with the promise of a neat "arrival." I held the assumption that I should and would enter my forties with all the societally informed boxes checked—kids, spouse, career success, self-worth, owned property, status, togetherness. By forty, I thought I would have outgrown that tug on my mind, the one that whispered incessantly through my twenties and thirties, You sure about that?, and instead I'd be free from disorientation and anchored in immaculateness.

But my reality was far from this story.

I arrived at forty without a spouse or kids. I didn't own a home. An accumulated nest egg was a mere daydream, despite decades of breaking myself against the walls of other people's dreams. I was still wrestling with my worth, battling an internal legacy of feeling like I had to be good for everyone. When I looked into the mirror, the soft lines starting to map my face belied the teenage girl still kicking inside me. I kept looking over my shoulder for approval of my life choices, conditioned by decades of society saying I must care about others' opinions more than my own.

In truth, I wasn't gunning for many of these things, like children and marriage. (We'll dig into this.) And I had been filling my adult years with experiences enriching to me (or I had been trying to).

Still.

Why did everything feel so different?

Like most if not all women, I'd learned that being a woman in this world requires a certain dexterity, a habit of putting on a cloak of armor to attempt to shield yourself from the world's opinions while you fulfill all your prescribed obligations.

Part of me felt like an outlier, even a little duped. It was as though I had turned forty having whizzed by the information booth handing out the guides on how to "be" forty. My head was a snow globe of questions. My body a heat map of curiosity and yearning.

What if a woman turns forty without any of the conventional markers checked—by choice or not? What if a woman doesn't want or can't have these things because of family expectations, social or economic factors, or life or health circumstances? What if a woman turns forty and still feels thirty-one or twenty-two? What if she doesn't know who she is or what she wants? What if she struggles to find time for herself because she's caring for children or aging parents, navigating an abusive relationship, facing gutting loneliness, hiding her sexuality, juggling several jobs to pay for health insurance, yearning to move away from the life she has, or traveling nonstop for her work?

What if a woman is scared and confused, or excited and curious, or feeling all this and more?

As these questions throbbed in my throat, a deeper tension pressed against my chest: an urgency to explore the truth. I was experiencing a feeling that I was somehow "behind" when I turned forty, but when I looked around, I saw that I was in no way behind. Women near and far were in their forties living lives of unique designs. They were blossoming, changing, leaving, returning, expanding, questioning, grounding, quickening, slowing, and evolving.

Women in their forties were screaming, "This is me!"

As my lens widened to the realities around me, I started to take notice of something primal happening within me, something I can explain only as a thirst to get closer to myself, to gain a proximity to my true north in a way I never had. I wanted to release old stories, be truer to myself, and take better care of my spirit and body. I wanted to let go of the desiccated rules and rip into the juicy cantaloupe flesh of being fully me—an ever-blossoming, unfinished, wildly complex woman in her forties.

I began to see how this age is a season that evades the myopic, privileged, all-encompassing idea I'd let soak my mind. Being forty today is complicated and vibrant. There is no right way to be in this decade, as this is a time that brims with different meanings, places, and possibilities for women.

And there was even more. A universe more.

The reason I thought everything felt so different was because it was so different.

Being forty is different.

Complex and layered, messy and unique, our forties are a period far too potent to consign to expectations. A gorgeous force of creativity, learning, and unlearning comes with this age.

And you and I will explore it all.

What Is It About Forty?

What's wild about this decade is how it marks an intersection. It is a time of spiritual, mental, physical, and emotional changes for women. We face massive evolution inside ourselves and our lives, juxtaposed with scrutiny—and with all of this come obstacles and revelations.

One obstacle is how society always has something to say about forty, as if entering this decade were an embarrassing pox on our lives. It's an age where someone is either in front or behind, and if you're a person who has been socialized as a woman, being behind can turn you into a punching bag, even amid today's evolving pro-aging landscape. There's a long-held fallacy claiming that this decade marks a landslide in our desirability and vitality. It's a "push-out year," says my friend, journalist and historian Janus Adams, as much as it is a sticky qualifier.

I've absentmindedly picked up on this punitive rhetoric my entire life. Most of us have. Comments get lobbed around like beach balls, ranging from the passive-aggressive observations—"You still got it!"—to ridiculous gossip—"So-and-so celebrity is getting married after forty"—to the banal-but-harmful headlines—HOW TO AGE GRACEFULLY IN YOUR FORTIES. (Age gracefully? Seriously?)

Like a banana peel, these reductive, biased ideas interrupt our stride, causing us to slip and question ourselves. One time at a friend's wedding, a guy (a friend of a friend) blurted to a small group of us, "Did you see all those forty-year-old women dancing?" In half a second, I went from smiling to having to remind myself to breathe. (I was fresh into my forties at the time.) That comment is symptomatic of society's tendency to reduce this age, making it out to be some arbitrary tipping point. It's as if forty were a piece of toilet paper on my shoe after I'd left a public bathroom with my hair brushed and lips glossed. "You look gre—oh, wait, you're dragging something. . . ."

Then there is the pressure. My gosh, the pressure. As I mentioned earlier, when I turned forty, I started to worry about not meeting the expectations that seem to circulate women like flies on fruit. The world continues to perpetuate the idea that we must do this, by this time—kids, career, marriage, you name it. I worried about losing my relevancy in my work and whether I was where I "should" be in my life. Am I behind? Am I ahead? Should I be further along? On the cusp of her fortieth, one of my dearest friends, Amanda, emailed me and a few friends sharing similar turbulence. She wrote how despite having a life filled with things that give her joy—a dog, an apartment she loves, close friends—she still didn't feel as "settled" as she'd expected or hoped to. "Somehow, I feel so old and exhausted by the world, and still exactly the same as I felt when I was 15," Amanda wrote in her email. "How is this possible? What does it mean? Does everyone feel this way?"

I summon these stories not to lament but to interrogate the seeds from which they grow. Patriarchal narratives feed so much of our angst around this age. Even when we give a middle finger to society's rules, we still feel we must justify our choices. It's tough.

All the while, we face a giant shift in our forties: our changing bodies and fertility. Perimenopause comes into the fold for many of us, demanding that we double down on taking care of ourselves. We may start thinking differently about the well-being and needs of our families, from growing children to aging parents, and our relationships and sexuality may be revving up or waning. There's also a brighter light on our mortality. As much as the term *midlife* irks me, because none of us has the privilege of knowing when we're in the middle of our lives, it is a fact that if the modern average lifespan for American women is approximately eighty, our forties are a midway signpost.

So, there's a lot thrown at us. Still, our forties are a time when things bloom. This is a decade filled with messiness, adventure, and discovery. And if you're like me, tons of full-throated screaming. (The number of times I've let a lion's roar out into the ocean or a forest . . .) We face change and opening, confrontation and letting go, realization and surrender. We recognize new parts of ourselves. Chianti Lomax, a women's life coach and author, said it precisely. "Something just awakened in me," she told me about when she turned forty. "A whole new level of Chianti just unlocked. And I'm, like, y'all better watch out."

Meeting Our Autumn Queen

Lomax's passion gives words to what is missing in our cultural storytelling about women in their forties. Despite society's attempt to reduce this chapter and mitigate its messiness and fullness, leading us to believe we're on a downward decline, the truth is that this time is when something cracks open. A fire ignites. A y'all-better-watch-out carnal energy explodes.

Our forties are when we meet our inner Autumn Queen.

I learned this term from women's coach and author Steph Jagger. I recall feeling a thud in my chest when Jagger first uttered the words.

"We're the Autumn Queen," she told me over the phone.

"Autumn . . ." I wanted Jagger to say it again.

"Autumn Queen," she said.

Jagger has a passion for weaving mythological and archetypal storytelling into her writing and coaching work. When she mentioned the Autumn Queen, she was discussing the three common female archetypes found in ancient narratives: Maiden, Mother, and Crone. These three archetypes are models of unconscious energies and traits that loosely correspond to the cycles of a woman's life. The Maiden correlates to a young woman, representing fertility, youth, and beginnings. The Mother embodies the energies of nurturing, stability, and caregiving. And the Crone represents an older woman who holds profound wisdom and knowledge. (It's important to note that the archetypes are combinations of energies, qualities, and behaviors and can link with anyone regardless of sex or gender identity, and if they are or are not mothers. They also can transcend age.)

There is immense beauty in each of these three archetypes. Still, Jagger believes there is one missing: a fourth phase situated between Mother and Crone that represents a fresh chapter of our raw power, totality, and creativity. This archetype symbolizes the essence of our forties when we experience a newfound clarity and conviction. We are not yet in the Crone stage, contrary to what narratives may suggest, but we are evolving into something newly potent. This is our Autumn Queen.

What is striking about this phase is how it transcends gendered expectations and roles. Our Autumn Queen illustrates our autonomy and trueness of self, and she challenges old narratives. This audacity can be intimidating to systems that center men, believes Jagger. "It's no coincidence that there isn't storytelling around us," she said about women in their forties. "It's one of our most powerful ages."

Months after Jagger and I spoke, therapist and author Dené Logan offered a similar take on our Autumn Queen. Logan refers to our time of entering and growing through our forties as the Enchantress phase. This is the phase when a woman plunges into her deep intuition and her connection with nature, she told me. It is when a woman unapologetically comes back into loving her body, claiming her sensuality, and fully being herself.

"She starts to remember her Enchantress, which ultimately is her witch," Logan told me with smiling eyes. "But what's really happening is she's remembering how powerful she is."

I want this book to help you remember how powerful you are.

Whether you're looking ahead to forty, are fresh in this decade, or are in its later years, my hope is that it awakens your inner Autumn Queen and ignites your Enchantress.

As we move forward, I want to invite you to envision your inner Autumn Queen—your strong, wise, exquisitely powerful self in your forties. She is whole, proud, and grounded in herself. She gives her attention to her values. She embodies her autonomy and sensuality. Picture her: How does she hold herself? What is she wearing? How does she handle tough situations, say, when someone is speaking over her or when she witnesses injustice?

Embody her. Feel her. Channel her. Know her.
She is gorgeous.
She is you.

What You'll Find Ahead

I subtitled this book *The Decade of Letting Go—and Embracing Who We Are* because I want it to be a resource and a gentle guide to unlearning and discovery. Women have been denied agency and shamed for living in their wholeness for so long that it can be hard to delineate between what we want and what society tells us we should want. My hope is that in these pages you will learn how to get closer to discovering and satisfying your desires in your forties, first by realizing the stories that may be holding you back and then by seeing that there is no perfect path for this time, only an embodied trail that is yours.

The chapters in this book explore the significant life topics of work, beauty, relationships, mothering, and our changing bodies and health, unpacking how each of these areas is unique in our forties. You and I will embark on an epic trip: In the beginning, we'll go far out into the world to help you discover how its stories have shaped you. Then we'll make stops in various ports, each one closer and closer to the inside of you.

We'll take a macro look at how women are conditioned to feel bad about their forties and growing older. As author Sharon Blackie writes in *Hagitude*, "How we think about aging women depends on the images we hold of them." You and I will examine the images we hold. We will look at how our patriarchal world is a system of made-up ideas mandating the ways a woman "should" be. By seeing this system for what it is—totally made-up—we naturally loosen our grip on its expectations and instead seize the opportunity for the self-discovery our forties have to offer. (In contrast, when we try to counter ageist ideas only with positive reactions—"Embrace getting older! Love middle age!"—we rob ourselves of fully understanding why we feel and respond the ways we do.)

From there, we will examine work life, which is a significant part of a woman's identity and one of the main ways we tend to define ourselves. We'll explore how career-building expectations can be exclusionary, how our passions ebb and flow, and how our forties can present an opportunity to delve deeper into creativity, meaning, and personal power, both inside and outside work.

You and I will then move closer to self and explore beauty in our forties. We'll interrogate why the world always has something to say about a woman's face and body. We'll examine beauty culture and ideals, as well as the relentless pressure to cling to our youth as we age, all to reveal a more inclusive, expansive, and joyful embodiment of beauty—one that is an experience waiting for every woman.

Next, we'll delve into our lives with others. We'll examine our relationships, exploring the ongoing pressures surrounding conventional partnerships and marriage, the far-reaching ways women are and are not partnering today, and how we can find love and freedom beyond binaries and traditional romance.

Then we'll jump into the soul-stretching energy of mothering. We'll take a journey through the constellation of feelings surrounding having and not having children and the ways that influence how we see ourselves. We'll also explore the labor of caring for aging parents and how harnessing our maternal energy can manifest in all aspects of our lives.

Finally, we will come home to caring for ourselves. We'll look at the wild terrain of perimenopause, how women must continue to advocate for their well-being, and the habits we can lean into to deeply care for our minds and bodies in our forties and beyond.

We will move through stories and exercises to help you find clarity in your values around these subjects and cultivate bravery to live in alignment with them in your way, no one else's. You will hear a lot of my story and those of women of various backgrounds, most of whom are in their forties with several nearing or on the other side of this decade. You will also gain counsel from doctors, therapists, coaches, healers, and artists. At the end of each chapter, I include gentle reminders about the truths of this decade, pulled from my research, interviews, and learnings. These moments are not meant to be prescriptive but rather are there to offer you a little squeeze so you can open your heart and move forward into your forties with compassion, power, and excitement.

You could say that I chose to analyze these specific topics, but in truth, they kept coming to the forefront. When I started writing this book, I was a confused woman fresh in her forties, desperate for deeper conversations about the realities of this age. The stakes felt extremely personal. Then I started interviewing women and those stakes felt collective. I talked with women in line for coffee, at doctors' offices, over phone calls, and across screens and kitchen tables about their angst, excitement, and confusion around being forty. I asked: What is inspiring you? Scaring you? Maddening you? What do you want to let go of? What do you want to grab? How does your body feel?

Their answers felt like tracing the inside of a rose. So many turns and curves; so much color and density. And every one of our conversations touched on work or beauty or partnership or children or health—and oftentimes they touched on several or all these topics. We can get twisted over having to face prescribed ideas about how we should be actualizing giant areas of our lives—ideas that have permeated our culture and hurt us.

In every conversation, I felt as though I were being let in on electric secrets—because these areas of my life have always felt like magnets for scrutiny, teeing me up for a constant game of justification. I've heard whispers in my head that say, What's going on with my career? Maybe I should get filler? Why does everyone ask if I have kids? Did I get married "late"? What is happening with my body?

Maybe you've heard these whispers too, or something like them. I hope that these chapters will stir curiosity within you, helping you to see you don't need to justify any part of your life—not to your family, your friends, or the world.

Of course, no book on our forties can offer some supreme model of this age. Gosh no. Such an attempt would miss the point, as there are infinite ways to be in this decade. What is most important to me is that this book allows more space for our hiccups and questions. I hope it casts light on the truth that, as women, we're always in conversation with one another in our minds, bodies, and hearts. I hope these pages serve as an addition to that conversation and as a reminder that when we generously listen to ourselves and one another, we see that we have the choice to tap into our intuition and live like the wind—strong, wild, and free.

A Little More About Me

I'm curious where you are in relation to being forty. Maybe you just entered this decade, have been in it for a while, or are "staring" it down, as my friend put it recently. I am nearing forty-four as I write this, looking out to the Pacific Northwest sky that overlooks Lake Washington, my rescue pup, Andi, snoring beside me.

I am a longtime journalist, so talking with people is how I find purpose. And digging into narratives—their histories, fallacies, and truths—is how I orient myself. When I'm presented a tale that claims absoluteness, I dig: Who claimed this was true? Clarity comes from pulling threads, especially when the world's harshness causes our personal morale to tear, a truth that runs through the lives of too many women and marginalized people.

My work has spanned the media spectrum, from magazines to newspapers to TV news. I love sinking into the layers of why people feel and live the way they do. I am expanded by the wells of love and perseverance people hold. In my late twenties, I earned a master's in journalism (a feat that stretched my soul despite the financial debt it created) and spent the following years chasing writing and reporting jobs, exhausted by how the close of every damn month opened the need to pay rent. I ached for more—more purpose, more interactions with different people, more fast-paced journalism experience. Eventually, I landed a gig as a news anchor and reporter in the Midwest's four-state region. I filled a tiny U-Haul and drove halfway across the country to terrible pay and a lifetime's worth of journalism adventures. I'd spend hours driving throughout southeast Kansas to speak to farmers and veterans about their rights and to parents about school bonds before racing back to the station to swallow three bites of dinner, package my interviews into a story, and go live for the evening news. Other days, I'd sit in people's living rooms across Missouri, Oklahoma, and Arkansas, asking small-town locals how corporate America had changed their once-thriving city and about the sacrifices they made to pay for health insurance.

I've reported on tornadoes and murders, food prices and water crises, spiritual awakenings and colossal personal feats. I've interviewed celebrities and politicians, therapists and healers, children and centenarians. I've asked questions of people on the front lines of euphoria, including a professional runner right after he flew by the Boston Marathon finish line, and the depths of despair, including a father who'd lost his baby to gun violence. I've asked Reese Witherspoon about dreaming big, former combat reporter Sebastian Junger about near-death experiences, and author Pico Iyer about paradise. I've chatted with writer and artist Julia Cameron about creativity, late self-help author Melody Beattie about anxiety, late lawyer-psychologist Sietze Vanderheide about conscious uncoupling, and therapist Nedra Glover Tawwab about personal boundaries.

Exploring how humans transcend adversity is the wind that propels me, and nothing has fueled me more than reporting on women and our relationship to this brimming, complicated time during our forties.

What's especially fascinating to me are these times in which we live. Here in the United States, when I look around, I see an eclectic and evolving plane of existence for women. A growing number of us are single today. Those of us getting married for the first time are doing so later in life. There are more households headed by same-sex couples. As for motherhood, more women are delaying having kids, causing a rise in the average age of first-time moms, and more are doing so unpartnered.

We're also living in challenging and changing times. Artificial intelligence is advancing at a velocity impossible to keep up with. A cloud of financial insecurity looms in the United States. Wealth gaps cast shadows. As I write this, our current administration is making efforts toward historic budget cuts that would severely impact people's access to social services, food, and health care. Critical incentives to give marginalized people access to opportunities are ending. Regressive legislation is puncturing the freedoms of people in the LGBTQIA+ community and the safety of trans teens. Women are losing their lives as a result of being forced to carry pregnancies, as some governmental forces attempt to exert more control over what we do with our bodies. (I say "attempt" because we will never give up the fight for our bodily autonomy.)

Education and awareness around perimenopause, menopause, hormone therapy, reproductive rights, and what happens to our bodies are growing yet are still not mainstream enough.

There is a collective interstice among us women: We are living in a tough, changing, and expensive world. We are existing amid circumstances wildly different from those of generations prior. We are tired and misled. We are hungry to chuck stigmas for good. We are eager to claim our whole rights forever.

And we are charged and excited.

Our forties are the time of hyper-clarity, incredible strength, and fire. They're a time to protest. We look back at all that we've done—all those years *lived*—and use that as fuel to tackle the now and what's ahead.

This is when you start to lean into what a meaningful, rich, fulfilling life is for *you*—no matter the stories or obstacles you face.

Alyssa Nobriga, a psychotherapist and women's coach, set the meaning of our forties aflame.

"I genuinely feel really grateful and excited about my forties," Nobriga told me. "I'm no longer trying to prove myself. And I'm no longer willing to participate in things that I'd been letting myself do that I didn't want to do. This number actually gave me that permission slip—and I'm excited."

You and Me and All of Us

Writing this book expanded me. For one, it introduced me to my Autumn Queen. And I'll tell you, she is strong and stylish. She wears a white hemp T-shirt, a Montana sapphire on her hand, and well-worn orange-tab Levi's—clothing and adornments that make her feel beautiful. Her eyes are open wide, and her hair is air-dried and messy. She is impenetrable when it comes to others' comments, deeply kind, embodied, and sensual. She never compares her life or light to others'. (Come to think of it, my Autumn Queen is not on social media.)

I ask for her counsel every day. When I'm down and weak, I close my eyes and let her lead me, surging my whole self with strength. I check in with her when I feel the scalding heat of anger, the sharp tang of resentment or frustration, asking her how to release my thick emotions in creative, sexy, healthy ways. My Autumn Queen comes with me everywhere—to meetings, gatherings, doctors' offices, weekends with friends. I am so grateful to have met her in my forties, to know her, to live with her.

This book also allowed me to spend time with someone else who expanded me: you.

Hundreds of you.

Many of you I've known personally and professionally for years. I've had the honor of watching as you give the middle finger to anyone blowing ageist stereotypes your way. You have shown me that you can have a choose-what-you-like life by getting married, finding soul-stretching partnership, getting divorced, embracing being single, and finding deep love in friendship—all in your forties. You are opening your bedroom to different lovers, sexualities, and desires and closing doors to be alone. You are having kids in your forties, not having them, or gifting your maternal energy to unrealized projects and plans. You are entering and exiting the work world, leaving positions, starting companies, moving places, or channeling your ambition toward vocations and hobbies that holistically fulfill your needs.

Many others of you I met recently, thanks to this book. Your stories and admissions came into our conversations burning and luscious. You shared so many things:

You are afraid of turning forty.
You are excited to be in this decade.
You think this is the best time of your life.
You hate how parts of your body are "loosening."
You are facing health obstacles in your forties.
You want to take better care of yourself.
You wish you had more children.

You are resolute that you don't have any children.

You wrestle with feeling suffocated and overjoyed by motherhood.

You grieve over not being a mother.

You love the silver hairs peeking through your strands.

You wonder if you should get Botox.

You loathe the lines on your face.

You love the lines on your face.

You wish you earned more money.

You wish you hadn't worked yourself to the bone.

You worry about the future of your work.

You wonder what leaving your career might look like.

You suddenly want sex all the time.

You suddenly don't want sex at all.

You want to be held only by a woman.

You want deeper friendship.

You worry about your aging parents.

You cannot believe how fast forty came.

You love being forty.

My body is filled with your stories. This ongoing dialogue we have had over the last several years has been the honor of my life. We have all held space for our differences and honored our similarities.

I believe we all are seeking orientation within ourselves—day-to-day. I wrote these pages for myself and for you. I wrote them for us seekers and dreamers tired of justifying our lives and ready to walk down our true paths with open hearts. Our forties are when an electrical charge for life starts pouring through our skin.

No matter if you're excited, scared, confused, exhausted,

pissed, sad, curious, rageful, hungry, or a bit of it all, what's ahead is for you.

If I had it my way, you and I would be sitting next to each other, shoulders brushing, hot mugs of tea in our hands. I hope for this one day. But at this moment, before we move forward, I have something urgent to say: This life, your life, belongs to you. The days are short, years more so. Your forties, whether they're here or in front of or behind you, are yours. It's a bounty and beauty to love them for what they are, just as it is a glory to rise from the dregs of expectation, pull yourself from the flames, and let the depths of your insides pour out—showing the world a complicated, beautiful woman who is embracing the waves of her infinite ocean.

Until we can understand the assumptions in which we are drenched we cannot know ourselves.

—ADRIENNE RICH

chapter one

Losing and Finding Ourselves

Our critical world, societal expectations, and the gorgeous possibilities here and ahead of us

WHERE DO WE LOSE OURSELVES? WHEN DO WE HAND OVER the key to our flame and take in its stead a script for how to be? At what point does that little girl start to cede and say okay more than her own name? You know that girl, the sassy one shouting with glee in the home video, the one blowing out candles at her seventh birthday party with a smile bigger than the sky, the one rubbing dirt out of her eyes as she plays wild with her friends on the last days of summer vacation, gulping the August air. When did she lower her voice? How did it happen that she started to sit in the cheap seats in the back when she is meant to be courtside?

For years, I wondered where I'd gone. It was as if the world had chipped away at me, slowly taking bits of my life in my teens, twenties, and thirties, rendering me in a strange out-of-place existence that I now can describe only as a perpetual homesickness for my truth.

I wonder if you have felt this: a gulf between who you are inside and how you present on the outside.

As my forties marked a primal drive to get closer to myself, I have wanted to better understand the roots of the deeper subconscious stories that tell women it is okay—actually, that tell women it is right—to quiet the voice inside us in service to the world around us. You and I know we're sold scripts consistently telling us how a woman's life should be lived. But what are the true costs of those scripts? And better yet, how can we rewrite them?

In this first chapter, you and I will journey back. We'll examine the legacy of the ageist ideas and sexist rules that have held women captive. We'll look at how these parameters influence us, weaving pain into our days. And most importantly, we'll explore how we can transcend to something deeper, richer, and more beautiful—in our forties and at every age. I'll share more of my story with you, and we'll hear insights from other women, as well as from therapists and healers.

If reading about these roots feels too intense or if it doesn't interest you, I understand. Take it slowly or skip ahead if that feels best. But if you choose to stay here, I promise you'll end this chapter stronger—and less likely to suffer societal fools. Your inner Autumn Queen is ready to care for that wild girl inside you and let her roar again.

An Invisible Battle

One of the toughest realities of being a woman is facing the lie that we must follow suit. That we must let go of our wildness to service everyone else. Whether we live in the most regressive or progressive of places, there are threads in the fabric of our existence that make us feel second. There is an unspoken memo (or spoken, in some cases) that says we must say yes.

No matter where we land on the vast gender spectrum, every person is subjected to conditioned ideas about how a life should be lived. But there is a fiery orange blaze that scorches women. The narratives around us are steeped in expectation. Society's cacophony of opinions causes us to fight an invisible battle, all the damn time. Even with our heads held high, these expectations hurt us. Even when we're living lives filled with joy, these ideals cause harm. We're expected to fit into confining boxes, follow codes, and contort our bodies, minds, and dreams. And all the while, we think that whatever we're doing isn't enough. "Or that it isn't impressive," as Kara Loewentheil told me. "Or that there are reasons for our success that aren't our own ability."

I met Loewentheil for lunch to interview her for a story about her 2024 book, *Take Back Your Brain*. She's a brilliant feminist coach who was previously a reproductive rights litigator. In her book, which I swallowed in two sittings, she points out the crux of what women have faced for so long: We absorb messages that tell us our worth is based on what the outside world thinks of us—our looks, the boxes we check, and the care we give to others and others' agendas. "Your brain has been programmed by society to always be criticizing yourself," Loewentheil continued.

There is no tangible memo for women, but still, something

lands in our inboxes. It tells us we're expected to marry, have children, build a career, and look "good." These messages may or may not come to us directly from our families, but their whispers carry. There's the additional message—whether or not we believe or follow it—that we must do these things in a certain way by a specific time. And no matter how we conduct our lives, whether or not we do what's expected of us or, heaven forbid, "take our time," as society likes to say, we find ourselves in an interrogation room.

I've felt the walls of this room my entire life. I've fielded comments and questions from people asking when I'm going to do something (marry), have something (kids), or build something (a career). If my skin had been see-through in my twenties and thirties, you'd have seen a knot twisted with the world's opinions.

Oh gosh, our twenties. Do you think about yours? Mine feel so far away and right behind me. I remember Sunday mornings spent over pancakes with my girlfriends, wearing jeans so tight they chafed my thighs. We'd ask one another existential questions—Why is this so hard? When does this get easier? Is it weird that I don't think I want to get married?—so loudly over the café table that our words created an emotional smog thicker than what loomed over our California city.

In my thirties, the noise got louder. This was a decade of increased nonstop work and newfound pain. Taxing relationships, growing debt, workdays that bled into nights and work nights that bled into days. Many of my friends were getting married, having kids, and buying homes. I was doing none of those things and started to face pressure about whether I was doing this life—my life—the right way. Like a match in a desiccated forest, an innocuous comment from a stranger—"Think you'll get married?"

or "You want kids?"—ignited a blaze of questioning inside me, fueling my inner critic. I'd wonder: Should I? Am I behind? Am I on track? Am I letting the world down? Am I weird? Am I worthy? Am I beautiful? Am I too much? Am I enough?

When I became a journalist, I started to direct my questions toward others. As I told you earlier, I am endlessly curious about what pushes and pulls the human spirit. I love telling stories about what ignites someone to leave, stay, dance, follow, tear up, laugh, escape, hide, and heal.

When I was a news reporter, I covered a tornado that ripped through a small town in Oklahoma. Seconds before going live, I looked to my right at a half-demolished apartment complex. The tornado had sliced it like an apple, leaving one side standing, the other in smithereens. I could see into a small kitchen where a table stood. On top were two glasses filled with orange juice. I still wonder what happened to those people. How did they move forward?

After I left TV news, I leaned into print journalism, focusing on issues that impact women. I became invested in seeing how the countless facets of our individual and collective stories beg for more air. I have written for and been on staff at publications created for women, and much of what I saw left me empty. Articles touted binary thinking, fueled capitalism, or underscored patriarchal ideals. (And I wrote my share of these!) Stories about flawless skin or wellness protocols pushed forward the same antiquated agenda to look perfect in a man's world. (Do this, in this way, in these steps!) And superlatives reigned. (The best way to rid yourself of crow's-feet.) Stories about career success and taking leaps fueled the constant message to build and achieve and do do do. The narratives about having it all always included kids and marriage. Or if a woman rejected the socialized realm of kids and marriage, she must then be building a giant career, right?

I've always seen these elements as valid and important, but they're not the only ones that make a full life. Where were the ideas that touted other paths, say an unpartnered life in which one focused their ambition on friendship and deep soul care?

Karin Brummell, a dear former colleague of mine, reflected this frustration to me. She was near forty when we spoke. She told me she felt pressure around the choices she has and hasn't made. "My life hasn't gone the way I expected it to go," Brummell told me. "When I was a kid, a lot of those expectations weren't really steeped in me personally. It was a lot of just, well, this is what society tells me I'm going to do. But now, I am unmarried and have no children, and I'm happy about that for myself right now. But I do sometimes think, Does the world see me?"

A knot formed in my throat when Brummell told me this. I felt her question in my chest because I've lived and breathed it. This tug of feeling not enough and the reality of seeing how we've bargained away parts of ourselves are evident in journalist Rainesford Stauffer's book *All the Gold Stars*. As Stauffer writes, "What we want and what we're supposed to strive for—be it because of cultural expectations, fear of taking a wrong turn and it all going wrong, or what's structurally reinforced as good dreams, a good life—are like melted-down crayons, increasingly indistinguishable from one another as we search for where our ambitions end and expectations begin."

Like melted-down crayons.

It's true: Where our agenda ends and society's begins can be impossible to detect at times. The lie that we're supposed to follow suit causes us to lose ourselves. And I remember the first time I witnessed this lie. I was very young, and it ultimately broke the two people closest to me.

"I Did Everything I Was Supposed to Do"

When I think about my childhood, an image claims the forefront of my memory: reading under a blanket in my room as my parents argued downstairs.

"All I do is work, and you're never happy," my dad screamed, often. At the time, I didn't have the guts to shout to the adults in my life, "Stop fighting! This is bullshit! Go live the lives you want!" But I knew things were wrong. Life at home felt stifled.

By all accounts, my family was normal. If society had handed out a memo about how to be a middle-class white family in 1980s New England, we got it. My mother stayed home to raise me and my brother. My dad worked. He was my model of how to hustle. When he started his asbestos-removal business, we were living in a small house on a horseshoe-shaped street. Soon after his launch, thanks to the capitalistic contractors from the Industrial Revolution, demand for my dad's business went into overdrive. We moved into a bigger house in a "nicer town," as he and my mom said, where my brother and I wanted for nothing. We had food and safety, friends and birthday parties.

From the outside, I was a happy girl, smiley and playful. But there was a heat inside me. A deep sense of worry that something was always about to crack. My parents seemed unhappy—my father thirsty for connection and relief, and my mother starving for adventure.

I lacked the vocabulary at the time, but I knew the concern I felt was linked to what was happening in our home. Words about money and drinking ricocheted off the walls at night. Fights between my parents were as normal as brushing my teeth.

Sometimes I felt like I had two dads: One goofy and alert, who would kiss my cheek in the morning before he left for work. Another subdued with bloodshot eyes, who would eat dinner with us before passing out on the couch, beer in hand. I would find big square bottles of brown liquid tucked into crevices throughout the house—between couch pillows and in random drawers. Sometimes I emptied the bottles and refilled them with iced tea; the sour tang of alcohol would sting my nostrils as the amber liquid pooled in the sink. My dad never said anything. The bottles always appeared.

Books were my escape. My mom would take me on weekly library trips so I could refresh my stack. I'd throw my head into the pages as soon as I got home, the paper slicing the tip of my nose. I could not get enough of women's stories and women writers. In sixth grade, my teacher Mr. Holmes, a gangly man who loved reading to us, knelt by my desk and slipped a copy of *Little Women* into my hands. "I think you'll love this, Stacey. Read it at your own pace." It was as if he had hugged my mind. After dinner, I'd lie on my belly and consume the news like ice cream, raptly watching women journalists Diane Sawyer, Maria Shriver, and Christiane Amanpour report from faraway places. I wanted to be where they were and do what they were doing. I wanted to meet people, challenge ideas, and ask *why*.

"You're going to make a man very happy one day," I remember one of my parents' friends saying to me in our driveway when I was ten or eleven. It took me half a second to retort, "I'm going to be a journalist." There was no room for make-believe husbands or others' motives. The lives so many of the adults around me led, filled with stress and pressure, felt confined. I wanted something different.

I was fifteen when I asked my mother if she liked her life. She and I were driving in the car—I wish I could remember where we were going. My concern for my parents had ballooned, and my mother never seemed joyful. She was always doing—cleaning, organizing, making lunches, cooking—for all of us. She'd started working part-time for a contractor in town, cleaning the new properties before they were listed on the market. We had moved three times over those last few years, each house smaller in size until we'd settled into a condo. My mother claimed it was because smaller spaces were easier to maintain. The nightly shouting about bills told a different tale.

"Are you happy?" I asked my mother.

She was quiet for a few seconds.

"You make me happy," she said, clutching the steering wheel.

"What about your life? You're always talking about going to Montana."

"One day. I'll get there one day."

A lump filled my throat. I kept at it for another minute.

"Do you think you and Daddy will ever stop fighting?"

"We don't fight that much." The air in the car felt dusty. She continued, "I want you to be happy, sweetie. Keep reading, keep writing. Don't lose your identity. Never lose your identity."

She seemed to drip with yearning. She'd checked the boxes—the kids, the marriage, the house—but her light was gone.

I didn't think about this brief conversation much until about a year later. It was the summer before my junior year of high school. My dad's drinking had worsened along with his declining work. The energy in our home felt desperate. Thankfully, I was distracted by my life during the day—high school, soccer, reading, homework, horseback riding, babysitting, and a boyfriend.

One afternoon, my boyfriend dropped me off at home after he and I had spent the weekend away with his parents. I walked through the door of the condo my mother, dad, brother, and I were living in to find my dad on the couch. His hands were in fists next to him, pushing up his body to take the weight off his hips. His face was flushed. He looked like he was in pain. I glanced around the condo and saw furniture missing.

"She left," he said.

I stood there. Through the window behind my father's head, I saw my boyfriend's truck grow smaller. I wanted to say something. Anything. I wanted to ask "What happened?" But before I could, my dad put his head in his hands and started to weep.

"I did everything," he choked. "I worked hard to give her everything. To give all of you everything. I did everything I was supposed to do."

That night, my mother called. She had gone to live somewhere else.

"I'm sorry, sweetie," she said. Her voice was tinny and distant, as if she were calling from a landline in another country. "I needed to take care of myself."

Happily Ever After

It took me years to understand what my mother faced. And I'll never be able to see the entire picture. Every one of us contains a universe of feelings and desires. What I know is that my mother was up against the tough force of my father's drinking. She was trying to fit into a life that did not entirely fit her. All of this was camouflaged by her heart that pumped bright-red maternal blood. She loved me, my brother, and my father. Doted on us. Wanted the best for us. And she never wanted to cause anyone pain. (Her constant apologizing to this day expresses this truth.) But she had to make an excruciating decision to step toward herself.

Somewhere along her path, she lost herself. And this happens to so many of us, even when we do it all "right."

"We're sold this idea of happily ever after that comes with a checklist," Deepa Purushothaman told me. "We get the credentials, get the husband, get the kids, and get the picket fence. Yet I know a lot of women who have all those things, and they're still miserable because they haven't figured out who they are and what they want."

Purushothaman and I met over Zoom to talk about the gendered limits and expectations placed on women. It's a topic of fury for her. In her book *The First, The Few, The Only,* which holds a permanent place on my shelf, she guides women from marginalized communities on how to confront the toxic messaging and microaggressions they face in their work lives, offering them a roadmap for creating cultures of belonging and thriving. Beyond her book, she advocates for women to listen to their voices in any situation, be it in the doctor's office, the boardroom, at home—anywhere.

Purushothaman's insight "Because they haven't figured out who they are and what they want" hit me. We spend countless hours, day after day, hearing society's message that there's a "right" track that we must get on, stay on, and never veer from.

All this energy gets pulled away from us learning about ourselves, especially when we're young, and put toward what we think we should do. But it is hard to know what we want when we spend so much time and energy trying to satisfy others' expectations. And no matter what we do, our choices will never satisfy society, Purushothaman continued.

"The message to women is: If you don't have kids, you're not enough. If you have kids, then what are you going to do about work? You're too heavy, you're too thin, you're this, you're that. It's almost like death by a million paper cuts."

I leaned toward my screen to get closer to Purushothaman, as if we were in the same room. I would have squeezed her arm if I could. As much as I didn't want her statements to be true, I felt relieved by how her fervor matched mine. Society puts women in an impossible paradox. We're too qualified or not qualified enough, too early or too late, too young or too old. We see this come up in all the big-box areas of our lives. As Purushothaman explained: "When women are young, we tell them they need more experience. But then you get to your forties, and I'm hearing a lot of women feeling that they're aging out. So, then, when is the right time for women? What is the message? What are we saying to women?"

I was about to say yes for what felt like the thousandth time. Then she dropped one more sentence that landed as if ice-cold water had been poured down my back.

"Have we even stepped back to question what we are told and taught? All the assumptions and myths?"

Purushothaman's reflections haunted and fueled me. They illuminate the irony women have grappled with for ages. We're pushed to do and be so much yet confined by the thick-lined boundaries of a restrictive society. We're told to do this, this way and by this time. Then as we grow older, the world dangles a ticking clock in our faces.

While these standards for women stem from heteronormative, cisgender, white, able-bodied men, they transcend the male-female gender binary and hurt everyone. The pressure and expectations hurt my father as they did my mother. They also pit women against one another, often fueling judgment and scrutiny among us when we do things differently or in our own way.

Kameko Grant told me about the judgment she's felt from other women. "I was in same-sex relationships for thirteen years before I met my husband, and I heard all this then!" said Grant. "We're chastised for not having kids and chastised for having too many kids. You're a slut if you sleep with a lot of people; you're a prude if you don't. You're too late for this or too early for that. If you're a stay-at-home mom, well, your life must be so unfulfilled. But if you go to work and you leave your kids with someone else, then people think, Why did you have kids?"

Grant paused before she continued. "It's like we can't win."

As these three women—Grant, Purushothaman, and Kara Loewentheil all point out—we must stop and look at the messages thrown at us. And most importantly, we must consider what we should be asking ourselves instead, especially now as women in our forties.

You and I will get to this question. But first, we'll dig deeper for a few more pages to look at the damage caused by the patriarchal world as we've known it.

A System That Has Hurt Us All

From an emotional perspective, patriarchy and the oppression of women may seem unidirectional and absolute, as though it were human nature for men to dominate women. But a historical perspective shows the roots of the patriarchy to be varied and mired. There is no one theory behind how it started—but we know it is about authority and influence. Science journalist Angela Saini refers to what we call patriarchy "as a set of factors" in an ongoing conflict around power. "It's about people looking to assert dominance over others through claims to nature, history, and the divine," she writes in her book *The Patriarchs*. "They are inventing and reinventing these claims all the time, sometimes succeeding, sometimes failing."

Saini has traveled the world studying different cultures and narratives around why men have controlled women—and her findings are as stunning as they are hopeful. I say "hopeful" because, counter to what it may seem, the hierarchy of male dominance is not humans' natural biological state. Historical research shows countless examples of egalitarian cultures over time. Anthropologists have also identified matrilineal societies, those based on a kinship with the females, finding over 160 across the Americas, as Saini reports.

Patriarchy has varied across time and place. (Note that Saini titled her book *The Patriarchs*, plural.) While locating the exact starting point of male dominance would be like trying to find a navy thread in a black quilt, Saini points to the rise of empire and colonialism as a formative factor in changing life across the Americas (as well as in Asia and Africa) and spreading patriarchal practices.

Many of the male-dominated customs that grew across the world, including women leaving their families of origin to live with their husbands, were steeped in the oppressive practices of slavery and ownership. Women came to be seen as property, things to be owned and controlled, and systems and laws expanded to overlook their rights and needs.

Over time, in certain cultures, these practices fueled the falsity that women are less than and meant to be only in certain places and standings—at home, in a marriage, with children. In the United States, patriarchy lands at an egregious intersection, crossing lanes with racism, sexism, and ableism. As author and scholar Anna Malaika Tubbs outlines in her critical book *Erased*, American patriarchy has been "the guiding story and system of the United States" since the drafting of the Constitution. Tubb writes:

"While patriarchy is present around the world, it is unique in the United States as a result of the heterogeneity of our population, which has been used to further build on a gender-binary divide. In the United States patriarchy places men in a higher position of the hierarchy of humanity and also organizes race, ability, class, and other identifying factors as reasons to separate some of us from the gender binary."

Tubbs's work is so critical because it spotlights how patriarchy in the US is a defined system that has told us there is one right way to be—one right way to be a man and one right way to be a woman, thus leaving out the nuances of what it means to be a complex human beyond a constructed binary. This system, she argues, has excluded most if not all people and therefore has hurt most if not all people.

Patriarchal practices have also perpetuated the idea that a

woman's worth declines once she is past her procreative years. Within the context of American patriarchy, as a woman grows older, beyond her ability to reproduce a certain type of manhood, her desirability and contribution to society begin to dissolve. As novelist and global women's advocate Isabel Allende says, a woman's age is seen as a "character flaw" through a patriarchal lens, as this system interlocks our value with our youth. "For any woman, it is difficult to navigate those waters," Allende writes in *The Soul of a Woman*. "For most of us, it's a shipwreck."

Allende's language makes me shiver. Patriarchal advantages hurt us. They have been one giant gaslighting campaign that has created tactics to make women think we're naturally the lesser—and we've been further conditioned to think that we're unsafe and doing something wrong by growing older. We get pushed out, and the age of forty has long marked a tipping point.

As I write this, my mind goes to a radiant woman I met several years ago. A bunch of people had gathered at a mutual friend's house after spending the day outside on the lake. Everyone's hair was tousled and skin tender from the sun. It was a happy vibe, and it felt natural when someone pulled out her phone and said "Get closer" to take a photo. That was when I could feel the woman's body retract next to me.

"No," she said sternly, dropping her head. Her discomfort was palpable.

"I get it," I said. "We're gross from the water. Let's take a photo later."

"No," she quietly responded to me. "I don't want my picture taken. Ever. I look old."

Water was about to spill out of my eyes. I wanted to say, "Get in the photo! You're beautiful!" but I didn't. I understood. I've worried many times, more so over the last several years, how a camera would spotlight what the world might critique—the crinkles around my eyes, the changes in my body, the fact that I'm a woman in her forties, getting older, all in the face of a hypercritical world.

In the thirtieth edition of her bestselling book *The Heroine's Journey*, Maureen Murdock writes that it continues to be natural for women to fall victim to what she calls "the myth of female inferiority" because we live in a society that has viewed and continues to view the world from a masculine perspective. Conditioned ideas permeate us deeper than we realize and cause us to jettison parts of ourselves. Think about how many times you've tried to take up less space. Maybe you've physically sucked in your stomach or metaphorically pushed aside your needs or dreams. Maybe you've lowered your voice or been quick to think you had to "fix" something about your appearance. (Note: You don't ever have to fix anything.)

It was Valerie Rein who opened my eyes to how much we contort ourselves to fit into society's expectations. A psychologist who coined the term *patriarchy stress disorder*, Rein has studied the ancestral and collective trauma women have experienced because of patriarchal systems. She told me of her concept "the invisible inner prison," the unseen chains inside us that keep us from embodying our full authentic power and presence.

"The more we reach for and claim what has historically been prohibited for women under the patriarchy, the more our nervous system goes into overdrive," Rein told me. "Our subconscious sounds an alarm that tells us we're unsafe, so we're held back from going after what we desire."

What's bone-chilling is how an invisible inner prison intrudes on our lives without our knowing. "We think life looked good on the outside because we were fulfilling all these expectations, checking off the boxes, getting the right education, growing the right career, starting a family, and doing everything society tells us," Rein continued. Then something massive happens, maybe a health scare, a loss, or a fortieth birthday, that causes us to stop and question why we feel stagnant, frustrated, or lost.

We look around and think, Where did I go?

But as painful as it is to think about this, it is also freeing. By looking closely at the grips of the system in which we live, we can untangle ourselves and move toward something new.

The Cherry Blossoms

Stories of how we "should" be start infiltrating our minds as early as preschool. Girls are socialized to be good, compassionate, and subservient, while boys are socialized to be wild, powerful, and bold. Researchers from NYU and Princeton found "brilliance" to be a particular marker of avoidance for girls, showing that by the age of six, girls are less likely than boys to think of themselves or other girls as brilliant and are more likely to avoid activities said to require brilliance.

This research mirrors Rein's invisible inner prison. As we grow older, a schism forms between who we are and who we present ourselves to be. This divide grows up with us, deepening between the part of us that is authentically expressed and the part of us that conforms "to be patriarchy-perfect" in how we speak, look, act, and fulfill roles, believes Rein.

Consciously, you may reject these ideas. You may not believe them and you may revolt. Still, this pressure to be perfect becomes lodged in our subconscious and passed down. To support this, Rein pointed me to a study where researchers encouraged mice to smell cherry blossoms—sweet, inviting, fragrant—while simultaneously zapping the animals' feet with electric shocks. The researchers then bred those mice. Now get this: The offspring were never shocked, but when they smelled cherry blossoms for the first time, they became anxious and fearful.

"It gives me chills every time," Rein said. "These mice were not telling stories to the next generations. This was an epigenetic intergenerational transmission."

As I listened, I felt a surge, which I could only guess was adrenaline—a physical response that often happens when I get mad. This patriarchal conditioning is why we face a lack of fulfillment, ease, even happiness. It's because we're always in trauma activation. It is ingrained in us to lose ourselves, feel second, quiet our voices.

I looked at Rein with my forehead scrunched like putty. I needed to know how we break this transmission.

"We resist, right?" I asked her, feeling no shame for my leading question.

"Yes." She smiled. "We resist."

It Begins with Us

I want to check in with you. It can be heavy to talk about the systems that oppress us. If you feel this or frustration or the need to take a break, I invite you to put down this book and move your body if you're able to or go outside to breathe.

The idea that we can resist and break free from the tug of always following suit first seemed like an unfathomable dream. But when I talk and write about it, I feel stronger. I feel clearer. Looking deeper at these roots allows us to see that these oppressive practices are manufactured. They've been built, which means they can also be dismantled. Not easily. But it's possible, especially when we start in our immediate lives.

When I asked Rein how we can begin to move away from the tough world we live in—patriarchy, expectations, the need to keep up—she took a deep, long breath and closed her eyes. Her energy anchored me. A warmth filled my work nook.

"We start with these conversations," she replied. "We start with making the invisible visible."

Rein told me that research shows we can change culture. We can shift ideas and spread new patterns of thinking and living. "We know from epigenetics that not only is trauma genetically transmitted, but healing is too," she added. "Healing is passed down."

For us women entering and in our forties, the first step toward healing and breaking from old systems is to listen to ourselves. Listen deeply to what you feel and need, suggested Rein. Pay attention to when your body wants to rest. Notice when your body wants to move. Reach out when you are craving connection. "And listen to when your body wants more pleasure and joy or space for sadness, anger, or connection."

Rein's insight speaks to self-compassion—treating yourself with support, consideration, and warmth. I originally learned about self-compassion from Kristin Neff first through her popular books *Self-Compassion* and *Fierce Self-Compassion* and then more intimately when I interviewed her for a story in 2022.

Self-compassion is simple but can be extraordinarily difficult. Neff posits there are two reasons for this: The first is that human beings are designed to respond to negative information and threats with the fight-flight-or-freeze response. We see a lion, and we bolt. But what often happens is we turn that fight-flight-or-freeze response inward. "We fight ourselves, we criticize ourselves, we judge ourselves, thinking somehow that's going to keep us safe," Neff told me. "We feel it won't hurt so bad if we beat ourselves up before others do." The other reason is cultural. "Most cultures give messages that self-compassion may not be such a good thing," said Neff. We confuse it with self-pity or self-indulgence or think it will make us weak.

What Neff wants us to see is how self-compassion is a radical act of strength. It helps us move through this world with more resilience and joy. She believes there are two types: tender and fierce. Tender self-compassion is nurturing and warm, aimed at accepting ourselves and life's imperfections. Fierce self-compassion ups the ante. It is about speaking up, taking action, drawing boundaries to care for ourselves, and motivating change in the face of injustice. "It might mean knowing our values and needs in the face of the patriarchy," added Neff.

As women, we need to practice self-compassion—for ourselves and one another. Again, this can be tough. Neff said to start here: Consider a dear friend who needs support. Picture what you would say to that friend. What would you ask them? How would you counsel them? Now, turn that kindness back to yourself. Be there for yourself. Speak to yourself kindly. Tap into your intuition. Show yourself warmth and compassion.

I have practiced Neff's exercise countless times since navigating this journey of my forties. I'll look to myself like I am a dear friend, sometimes even my own child, and gently bestow kindness and counsel. Other times, when I am stuck in the jungle of feeling behind or not enough, I'll practice my own exercise of putting my hand on my chest and saying to myself, "Trust." It's a quiet whisper that brings me out of my head and into the present moment. It allows me to unlock the power of my Autumn Queen and reminds me that I am enough—and that all I need to do is trust my wisest, most compassionate sage: myself.

I wish for you to do this for yourself. I know in my bones you're holding this book because you want to tap into more of the real you. You want to start feeling freer. Begin by giving yourself compassion. Tell yourself how far you've come and be open to dreaming. Whisper "Trust" to yourself as you squeeze your arm. Envision your Autumn Queen and what she wants you to know and feel and be.

These are small acts, but they are radical. Pausing to see the tough world around us and the harm it can cause offers priceless information. When we do this, we see the old messages society has been telling women, as Deepa Purushothaman challenged earlier in this chapter, and we give ourselves the capacity to flip the script. Instead of wondering if the world sees us, we see ourselves.

This changes culture. As Rein told me, "When each one of us touches something on our journeys of exploration and healing, we bring those precious pearls back to the community."

Comparison Breaks Us Down

To expand our lives beyond the grip of oppressive practices, we must also recognize the tactics that erode our worth. Our work lives and the beauty industry are often rife with cryptic (and not-so-cryptic) tools that break us down, and we'll explore these in chapters 2 and 3. Right now, you and I will look at something that has saddled my heart for decades—and I'm guessing yours as well. Comparison.

One of the cruelest legacies of the system under which we live is how it has taught us to look outward. We've been conditioned to ask others for directions to places in our lives only we know how to get to. It has gaslighted us into thinking messiness is a fault. And it has taught us women to live in a mindset of scarcity, causing us to compare ourselves with one another and think that one woman's gain is another's loss.

The social media soup we live in today is ground zero for comparison. Whether we scroll every hour or vow to scroll only once a week, these platforms seem to come with an invisible force, pushing us into a mental corner of feeling not good enough. As women in our forties, we are not exempt. While most of the research about social media's impact on female body image has focused on younger women, one study noted that growing pressures around appearance for women forty and older are associated with social media use. I'd be horrified if I could somehow count how many times I was feeling good only to have my confidence shattered as I landed on a post of a woman appearing to do it all better than me. It can be anything: a writer touting how she landed a byline in a huge magazine; an influencer swinging her freshly highlighted hair as she bakes bread in her pristine kitchen; an old friend traveling through Europe, seeming not to have a care in the world. It feels like a cruel clown is laughing at me, yelling, "You're not even close to having any of this."

I know social media is not real life. I also know it has benefits.

Still, when comparison takes the reins, it can feel impossible to see anything beyond the glassy glow of my screen. These platforms kick up the inky depths inside me that scream that I am not enough and do not have enough. Every post I see, every accolade sent into the social ethers, makes me feel as though something was being taken from me.

One of the frankest conversations I've ever had about social media was with Jen Gottlieb. She and I have known each other for years, and although we haven't spent much time together, I've always felt close to her. And when we're together, I feel close to myself. Gottlieb is the best kind of company: engaged and genuinely kind, with her full attention locked in. As a motivational keynote speaker, she travels constantly, getting onstage to help entrepreneurs unlock their self-belief. When you watch Gottlieb, either via social media, where she has an enormous fan base, or onstage, you see that performing is in her DNA. (She's also a former actor.) But there's no sugarcoating in her approach. She brings human stories—the struggles, the fear, the reality of it all. She's real. And she admitted that, at times, the platforms and all the perfection they project can get to her.

"Back in the day, all the societal demands and the things we thought we should be like were in the magazines," Gottlieb told me. "You'd see the celebrities in *Cosmopolitan* or *Vogue* when you were waiting in line at the grocery store, or the magazine would come to your house. Or maybe you'd turn on E! News. But it wasn't around you all the time. It wasn't in your pocket. But now it is, so for every second you're waiting, you're scrolling and seeing all the highlight reels—and not just of beauty, but of the type of house you should have and the vacations you should be going on."

Gottlieb doesn't think we're all looking at our feeds and explicitly thinking, This is what I should be doing, but she believes we subconsciously feel a need to keep up—especially when we consume one curated reel after another. "When we're out there living our own real life, and we have all the experiences of being a forty-year-old woman and have real life shit going on that most people don't share about publicly, we can feel very, very alone."

She makes it a point to counter this on her feed. Every morning, she goes live on Instagram to answer people's business questions while she gets ready—removed from all the stage lights and dazzle. My insecure, hypersensitive social media self loves it, because she lets you in.

"So, if I have a zit, you're going to see it. If my dogs are running around like crazy and my house is a mess, and I've got a big stripe of makeup on one side of my face, you're going to see that," Gottlieb told me. "If I can at least create one hour of somebody's day where they can feel less alone in their real life, I want to do it. And it also helps me feel more normal with being an imperfect human and a woman that's aging."

Still, Gottlieb says that nothing compares to talking openly with another woman, face-to-face, in person. Just as Valerie Rein told us that connecting and sharing our truth is how we resist, Gottlieb believes this too. When we share the hard stuff—fears of aging, work pressures, loneliness, the relentless pressure to be perfect—we grow.

"Every single time I have one of these conversations, I want to cry, because we're all going through this," said Gottlieb. "We're all in this together. We're all feeling like we need to play this game. So, it's about: How can we be more kind to ourselves and to each other in this world that we live in?"

It is impossible to have a conversation anchored in eye contact without considering the incalculably massive debts we incur when we consume passively—which is to say, when we compare ourselves without a thought or never stop to consider the history that weighs on us. We live in a world soaked in social media; that will likely not end—and, again, there are great aspects to these platforms for building awareness, making connections, and having fun. But what we can be proactive about is how we engage. We can employ more discernment—with one another and ourselves—about how social media impacts us for better or worse.

A small-but-mighty step I have taken in my forties is to never check social media before 8 a.m. or after 8 p.m. I honor this rule. While I still struggle with that make-believe clown who jumps from the screen to laugh at me, I don't need to let these curated ideas into my bedroom and safe spaces. When I have the urge to look, I swear I hear my Autumn Queen inside me speak up: "Your real life is here," she tells me. "It is gorgeous, it is real, and it is worth all your attention."

It Is Hard and Messy and Freeing

Like many, I read the memoir *The Tell* in one sitting. Its author, Amy Griffin, tells of how after decades of living a life that looked perfect, she excavated a horrific secret of sexual abuse from her past and shared her story first with her family and friends and then with the world.

The Tell is swift and rich. Despite being a memoir, it reads with the urgency of a thriller. That's because Griffin, who is in her forties, is a brilliant writer. But there's more: I believe so many women read the book voraciously because we have an appetite to hear one another's messy, complicated stories. We want to know our darkness and pain are not exclusive to us. We want to feel united in our healing.

I felt powerful reading Griffin's book because I was in the presence of her bravery. Of her willingness to change. For decades, her body was telling her something was wrong. She faced chronic physical pain and deep feelings of disconnection. She ran miles and miles every day, all while saying yes and following rules. (She also did incredible things from her heart, like marrying a kind man and building a family.) As Griffin writes, she struggled with "something unexplainable, something deep, but something that I couldn't touch." When she finally gifted herself the chance to get still, call for help, and listen to her gut rather than everyone else, she found freedom—and she ran home to herself. It was not neat. It was brutal and hard, as her writing reveals. But it was worth it. Doing so opened the door to her freedom and the path toward herself.

Hearing the raw journeys of women opening their lives and digging into themselves invites us to see more perspectives and support women in whatever change they yearn for or take.

When artist and sexologist Brigit Ritchie told me about her leaps, she shook with passion. Ritchie left her marriage and dazzling friend-filled life in Los Angeles to move halfway across the country with her two children. She sought peace, nature, and a deeper connection to her body, as well as radical honesty in her relationships, all of which she said she had been sacrificing. She found solace and stoked the fire inside her to further her education in psychology and sexual well-being and lean into her art.

As she described it, she came home to herself.

"What surprised me most about meeting myself is that it meant really understanding my values," Ritchie told me. "And through a certain threshold and a dark night of the soul and a lot of letting go, I've come into this cycle—because women, we are so biologically cyclical—of an absolute, unapologetic commitment to loving my nervous system and loving myself in a quiet, nurturing safe space."

Ritchie did "literally everything" to get to where she is now. That meant giving up things that were important to her—her life as she knew it, her connections, her work. She pushed herself to face multigenerational fears of reclaiming her sexuality and the reality of how that would impact her identity and family. She went on a journey of consciousness, exploring what psychedelic medicine could help reveal to her and looking at all she'd carried from her fundamentalist conservative Christian upbringing.

"These journeys have been super messy," she said. "I was worried that if I stepped into living from this place where I could feel the most honoring of who I am, I might lose my friends, lose some of my influence, lose some of my career opportunities—and all of that happened."

But even with the costs, she would do it all again. "And I'll continue doing what I need to do to be there for me," she added. "And that doesn't just mean loving me. I want to love my kids. I want to love my partner. I want to love my community. But never again will I make the best of things at the cost of self-betrayal."

As Ritchie told me her story, I felt protective of her. Why must women make such bold sacrifices to live how we want? Why do we have to leap and choose and do such tough things? But I realize that this is part of our resistance. Her story proves that in the messiness of change, we find a beauty that is too often hidden.

"It's a level of not just loving myself," Ritchie added about her life now. "I genuinely respect myself as a person."

Respect is the apt word. It encapsulates how I have felt listening to every woman for this book. It takes gumption to make these changes, to see that we are worthy of all that we yearn for. We just need to look.

Deepa Purushothaman, whom we heard from earlier in this chapter, showed me the beauty of looking. Purushothaman worked relentlessly for decades in a high-functioning, corporate, male-centered world, ultimately gaining a highly revered position at Deloitte. She smiled and worked. She hustled and nodded. Then a health crisis came, and with it a reason to stop and question it all. Purushothaman found herself at an intersection: She could stay or leave. She made the radical decision to leave Deloitte and all the accolades that went with it and to do what she wanted to do, which was advocate for women.

She has done all that and more in the time since. She's become a bestselling author and a true embodiment of her Autumn Queen. She also got married at forty, which was a break in tradition from her Indian heritage, where there are strong expectations around young arranged marriage.

Purushothaman says she wants women to challenge expectations. She also recognizes this is hard work. Maybe we don't know we can. Maybe we're afraid. Or maybe we're mired in situations that won't allow us to. But we can try by starting small, listening, and recognizing that any arbitrary rules do not apply to us.

"I find women are often like, 'Wait, I was a "good girl," and it didn't work out for me. So why am I following the rules?' " Purushothaman told me.

"And you did this," I responded. "You followed your heart."

"Yes" came her reply. "It was like I rewrote who I am."

"It's a De-layering"

The questions at the heart of this book—Why do I feel different in my forties? What do I truly want? How can I grab my truth?—can be challenging to answer. And that we must ask them implies a greater complexity. These questions (and this book) would be inconceivable if we lived in a society that included and honored every person. But the reality for women is that for so much of our lives we have been served manufactured rules that have pushed us aside and made us swallow our desires. We are enmeshed in this system, which can make the start of letting go and leaning toward our truth seem insurmountable.

So, the question, then, is Where do you start?

I love Carrie Hammer's advice: Think of the process as a de-layering.

"None of us have ever been taught this internal self-inquiry," Hammer told me. "It's work to go backwards, maybe at forty or forty-two or whatever our age. It takes courage."

A designer and women's activist, Hammer is a force—and this is no platitude. The woman sees inequities and charges toward them with the antidote, not out of spite but out of healing. She garnered global attention in 2015 when she featured women of varying sizes, ableness, and professional tracks to model her spring collection. She coined her decision "Role Models Not Runway Models," and it's now a trademarked movement credited with kickstarting body inclusivity in the beauty and fashion worlds.

I admire Hammer's confidence, self-love, and vulnerability. She recognizes that it takes work to move beyond old stories, but she focuses on all that we gain when we do. We make room for our truth. "It really is like a de-layering," she said.

Hammer's insight offers a visual. To make room for the new, we must first let something go. I picture myself removing physical layers that stand for the "shoulds" and all the rules—too-tight jeans, suffocating dresses—so I can breathe. When I'm in the shower, I imagine the old stories pooling around the feet of my forty-three-year-old self before they rush down the drain. In the water are ideas that hurt me in my twenties, stories that pained me in my thirties, and opinions that dig at me still in my forties. I take steps to reduce social media in the mornings and nights to lessen the grip of comparison. I de-layer.

I invite you to try this. Close your eyes and consider what you do not want to hold any longer. Maybe it is the feeling that you need to keep up. Maybe it is the story that you look old or feel unseen. Maybe it is the sensation that you do not fit in or feel at home. Maybe it is a job, a partnership, a habit, or an ideal. Acknowledge it, then picture physically letting it go, into the air or down the shower drain. De-layer it from yourself.

This practice requires you to slow down, and it makes way for a clearing, creating room for the next hard-but-essential step.

The Most Critical Questions to Ask

"We become so good at attuning ourselves to other people that we're out of practice attuning to ourselves," Vanessa Cornell told me.

A mom of five, writer, and connector of women, Vanessa founded NUSHU, a community for women to gather with, share with, and nurture one another. Through her workshops, retreats, and courses, she helps women learn (or relearn) how to listen to themselves and, equally so, how to share what's on their hearts—how they feel, what they want, what they need—in the company of others. Spending time with Cornell feels like sitting in the grass on a late-May afternoon with the sun on your back. Things are warm and feel possible. No subject is taboo. She intends to help women know that they're not alone—and she herself admits that she can't help but say the things out loud that we're not supposed to say.

Cornell holds space for many women in their forties. In her newsletter, *Voicenotes from a Friend*, she talks with disarming humor and candor about all aspects of being a woman in her forties. When we connected over Zoom, she told me that she sees this age as a tipping point in exploration. We spend several decades trying to figure out who everyone else wants us to be "and getting really good at that," she said. Then forty comes, and we may not know what we need or want because we've spent so many years "practicing how to ignore it."

Cornell faced this head-on in her mid-thirties. Raised to never share anything outside her family, she learned to keep everything about her internal life tucked inside. "I used to be a total liar," she admitted to me. Everything came to a head when she came clean with herself that she had been living in "a deep loneliness," despite having a life that seemed full on the outside. So, in her late thirties, she decided she would start doing the opposite. "Now, my daily practice is to tell the truth," she said. "I tell the truth about how I feel to my friends. I tell the truth to my husband. I tell the truth to my children. I tell the truth on Instagram. I tell the truth to myself."

Because she sees this as work that is both hard and daunting, Cornell invites women to join one another in sharing their truths. Her workshops and gatherings are about radical honesty. Women come together and let go. These gatherings offer a place to say, "This week sucked." "I feel disconnected from my husband." "I am scared." "I am lonely." "This is all too much."

It takes practice to be vulnerable in the company of others, Cornell told me, but when we are, the payout is tenfold. An expansion happens. Too often we worry what people will think when we say what is inside us. And while it is possible to push people away, and even to lose people, more often love and hope await us when we speak our truth. As Cornell witnesses, women get closer to one another when they share things tucked deeply inside them. By revealing the human truth that we are messy works in progress, we create more connection. "We realize, 'Oh, wow, no one went running into the night because they thought I was a terrible person because I said that,'" said Cornell. "You start to see how being honest and sharing yourself is the way toward more love and connection."

It is important to note that not all of us can gather with women to tell our story. You may live somewhere where you do not have this option. Or you may be shy or scared. That is all okay. What I hope you can allow yourself to see, though, is that the critical part here is the radical honesty. Saying aloud—to yourself in the mirror, to a journal, to the sky, in a meditation—what is digging in you or pulling you is how you can start to break open your truths.

This brings us to the question we all must ask ourselves in our forties: What do I want?

For me, this has been the hardest question, I admitted to Cornell. Stopping to ask myself this can feel like I am moving toward a stone wall. Then when I do ask, a mix of feelings percolate in my chest—relief, grief, excitement, sadness, rage, and joy.

"That's why we have to keep asking ourselves," she replied. "This is our work."

Cornell explained that our work as women in our forties entails asking these questions:

How do I feel?

What do I need?

What do I want?

These "are the only three questions you need in your midlife," she stated. "They are very difficult questions. They are very confronting. But just the asking is powerful because it implies how you feel matters, what you need matters, and what you want matters."

I invite you to ask yourself these questions.

How do you feel?

What do you need?

What do you want?

Consider reflecting on them first thing in the morning, when your mind is clear. Or present them to the air when you're moving outside. Ask when you feel safe. Share these questions with a close friend and ask together. Jot down anything that comes up in a notebook or voice note. The answers may not be concrete. That is okay. As humans, we crave certainty. We wish to know how things will turn out and yearn to make giant changes happen instantly. That is why the internal asking can be so daunting: We think the answers need to arise immediately. But the asking is movement—and movement opens our capacity to align with something bigger.

As Valerie Rein showed us earlier in this chapter, paying attention to what we crave and need is the way through the patriarchal maze. Asking is an engine that can yield so many other things—joy, love, community, decency, freedom—in our forties and beyond.

It can be messy, of course. I think of my mother. It's no coincidence that she was in her forties when she started asking herself deep questions. She was in pain. She left abruptly, and it hurt. Change often does. But she saved herself, and in turn, she saved me. She showed me the consequences of staying in something that isn't right for us and the beauty that can come from leaving, an act that deserves more credence. To go away from something is often marked as a weakness, when leaving is sometimes the very act that gets you closer to the woman you're destined to be.

And it all starts with inquiry.

"You may not know the answers," said Cornell, "but asking the questions is revolutionary."

Moving Forward: Reflection and Action

Nearly twenty years ago, when I was in my mid-twenties, my dear friend Noa brought me to a Double Winners meeting, a recovery-support gathering that functions simultaneously for Alcoholics Anonymous and Al-Anon. The Al-Anon side was calling to me. My father had just died. Those brown-liquid-filled bottles I told you about earlier eventually killed him. He faced liver failure and sepsis from decades of guzzling. I held him as he released his last breath, an honor that left a hole in my spirit that will never close. Months after my father's passing, my brother fell into life-altering addiction. I was searching for water in a desert. I was nervous to go to the meeting, mostly because I was afraid it would require energy from me that I didn't have to give.

When we parked at the venue, Noa looked at me.

"Listen," she said. "These meetings can be a lot. There can be a lot of pain, and people talking and talking. It may not be for you, at least not all of it. Take what serves you and leave the rest."

Leave the rest.

Never could I have imagined the impact Noa's words would have on me two decades later.

Being in my forties has taught me to "leave the rest" in so many ways. There are simply facts, stories, and ways of being that do not fit me any longer. Maybe they never did. Part of my work is seeing these, de-layering them, and letting them wash down the drain.

This age has also shown me the gift of surrendering. This does not mean giving up, nor does it mean giving in. Surrendering. Understanding that there are giant forces—culture, societal ideals, patriarchal rules, people's expectations—that we cannot control and may not even ever fully understand. We can acknowledge their deep roots that have spawned forests of self-doubt and caused us to do things (or not do things) because we thought they were "right" or expected. And then we can move forward, at a pace that is best for each of us.

Our self-evolution is not linear and does not happen all at once, my friend Camille Styles told me. "Rarely do we wake up one day and feel totally transformed, evolved to the next level of who we are. It's a slow growth, usually the result of small steps that, over time, add up to something bigger. I'm very much still on that growth trajectory," she told me.

Styles is in her early forties and has viewed this decade as a "call" to listen to her intuition and go after what she wants. For so long, she pushed off doing things—spending more time in nature, taking up a new hobby, saying what was truly on her mind—thinking she would get to them when she had more time. No longer. Now she pays attention to what is true in her life and what she wants to go toward. "There's no practice round," she told me. "If there's something I want to do, someone I want to be, I want to step into that now and I want to be her now. Turning forty opened me up to this."

Before she continued, Styles paused to take a deep breath. "You know," she continued with a smile, "one of the biggest shifts I've noticed in this decade is how much less I care about what other people think. For most of my life, I wanted to be bolder and fully myself, but I'd still catch myself double-checking how I was coming across or overanalyzing what others thought of me. Something about turning forty gave me permission to let that go. I started trusting myself more—and in those moments when I've really gone for it, I feel really proud of that woman I've become. It's the ultimate freedom."

This is the bounty of our forties at its best: urgency, rawness, candidness, possibility, and wisdom fueled by the awareness that this gorgeous life is not to be lived passively.

I felt this joy in my conversation with Brigit Ritchie. "What comes up for me is this Big Magic energy," Ritchie said, referencing the famed Elizabeth Gilbert book about embracing curiosity and creativity and letting go of needless suffering. "Not to be cheesy, but it's so exciting that we're still at the beginning of this conversation. Women in their forties are living uniquely designed stories of their own choosing."

What is essential is that we see that each of our stories can be messy and hard, wavy and nonlinear. We may even "fall flat on our face," continued Ritchie. But it's in the looking, the doing, the process that we encounter ourselves.

"I feel like I'm twelve-year-old Brigit on a swing with a popsicle and her middle school friends. I feel here and now in my body and a quietness in my mind and in my spirit, because, again, I literally did everything I knew how to do to get here."

Our forties mark a conversation with ourselves that will last the rest of our lives. We are growing, unfolding, evolving—always. How you choose to live this chapter is up to you. There is no right way to squeeze the most juice out of your days. But I urge you to consider the tools of embodying compassion and kindness, looking within, and de-layering and letting go. You hold everything inside you necessary to release old stories and reveal your authentic self in your forties. Be courageous in doing the work only you know you must do.

Let your inner Autumn Queen take hold. Imagine her—her smile, her beauty, her incredible strength. She's looking to your younger self, grabbing her hand, and saying, "There you are. You were always here."

This time in your life is a calling. It is up to you to listen.

CONSIDER THIS:

You never have to follow suit.

You can de-layer old stories and expectations, one by one, piece by piece, in your own time.

You can make major, messy, complicated changes. Even if you think you cannot, you can.

You hold the power to ask yourself: How do I feel? What do I need? What do I want?

At some point we have to understand that we do not need to carry a story that is unbearable. We can observe the story, which is mental; feel the story, which is physical; let the story go, which is emotional; then forgive the story, which is spiritual, after which we use the materials of it to build a house of knowledge.

—JOY HARJO

chapter two

The Work of Our Lives

Untangling the career maze, reevaluating our jobs, and exploring new paths toward peace, creativity, and fulfillment

AT THE AGE OF FORTY-SIX, CLAUDETTE MONICA POWELL changed her life. The one she had been living was brimming: She'd attended acting school in New York. Worked the comedy scene in Los Angeles. Married a man. Juggled a career and built a network of friends. But nothing fit. She rose every morning and stealthily ignored her soul's yearning in the face of her hustling. She felt like she had to apologize for herself everywhere she went.

So she left—and became a nun.

In the decade-plus since, Sister Monica Clare, which she now goes by, has found a community in her Episcopal convent. She has created an existence so aligned with her soul, her life sparkles like Sirius in the night sky. She tells her story with a Technicolor brio in her 2025 memoir, *A Change of Habit*.

I sat to read an advanced copy before I was scheduled to interview Sister Monica for a story. I dog-eared pages, scribbled notes, inhaled audibly, circled words, and wrote *Yes!* next to them. I skipped dinner that night to finish it. Her sentences quickened my heartbeat, the way the Cure's "Just Like Heaven" does every time I hear it. "As I got older, I felt like the world kept presenting me with an imaginary checklist: one that required me to be beautiful, smart, obedient, and then have a job, a husband, and children," Sister Monica writes. "But I resisted that idea."

Sister Monica details how she broke herself for long hours and for jobs that never seemed to meet her needs. Chaos ruled. Her marriage was bloodless. Throughout it all, the monastic life had always intrigued her. She yearned for that peace and belonging, free from the rat race. Now as superior of the convent, she lives with passion and a giant smile. Her new chapter has presented hard days and unique challenges, but it's more so opened new portals of hope that she'd dreamed of for decades.

When we spoke, Sister Monica told me that years before "coming out of the closet as a nun," as she described it, she dove into therapy, attended Al-Anon meetings, and did the work of pulling the threads of pain and taking responsibility for her part. As she did this in her forties, she inched closer to what she wanted. There were dark moments, but it all slowly led her to a new trail.

She moved toward the once-far-off concept of true agency as she learned to set boundaries and then, ultimately, take her leap.

"It was around the time that I went into perimenopause, and all of a sudden, I had a little bit less tolerance for people talking down to me," she told me. "I had a little less tolerance for [others] treating me like I was dumb because I'm a female. I started to learn how to fight back and defend myself after years and years of frustration that built up through my thirties. I think in our forties, for a lot of women, you get to a point where you're like, I gotta try something new because that other stuff is not working."

Sister Monica paused before she continued.

"The forties were one of the best decades of my life."

I have thought of Sister Monica often since we spoke. This is a woman who, in her mid-forties, having lived a lifetime trying to fulfill others' expectations, made a change—solely for herself.

Of course, leaving one's life for the convent is drastic, and the logistics may not appeal to many of us. But what screams to me, and I'm thinking it also does to you as you read this, is her courage to look. To ask the questions. To see her patterns. To take strides into the unknown.

She gave herself the gift of seeing that, unlike in the sky, the stars in our internal universe are not fixed.

Itching to Start a Fire

Sister Monica's gumption could be fodder for exploring countless expectations we face as women, from partnership to family legacy to abuse. I find it a most fascinating study of how work sanctions our lives. Much of what kept her stuck was her vocations and the struggles they brought, just as so much of what gave her light on the other side was her grabbing a role that mapped her heart.

We do not talk enough about the moral nature of our working selves, of the fragility our jobs can exploit. We do not explore enough how if we're not careful, the churning can turn into a sheriff, arresting our spirit, putting us in a jail of callousness, noise, and disdain.

We also don't talk enough about the joy and peace we can find when we adopt new perspectives on the role work plays in our lives.

In this chapter, we'll unravel how work can feel different in your forties and can take on new meanings and shapes. We'll explore the opportunities this decade can offer to reevaluate how you spend your time and show up for yourself, and the ways you might want to delve deeper into creativity and meaning.

My feelings about work and my career—or at least my engagement with work and my career—shifted when I entered my forties. I started thinking more about how work shows up in my life, how the people I work with make me feel, and whether spending so much damn time in Zoom meetings (spoiler: I do not like too many Zoom meetings!) is worth my soul, my separation from loved ones, and—to be frank—the money it delivers (and often does not deliver) to my bank account.

I love to work. And I must work, like most of us. But there's been something deeper going on for me in my forties. A desire to release my identity entanglement with my job and break from the legacy of the hand-around-my-throat, pleasing-everyone stress that punctuated my twenties and thirties.

I also hear a little robin in my ear chirping, "Do it." The "it" I have yet to figure out, but I know it includes letting my personal markers of ambition expand toward more creativity, care, and peace. This is why Sister Monica's story dazzles me. I feel the same when I see any woman making a shift to nourish her spirit.

"Your forties can be a deeply creative time," women's coach Rae Leslie told me. "But patterns of overachievement often foster the belief that you must do it all and all alone."

She was right. I have always felt alone in my career. So, I wondered, where do we start to let go and find ourselves and one another in this chaos? How do we get off this treadmill moving us toward building other people's dreams? These are questions you and I will explore in this chapter.

On that note, I will not attempt to toss you a follow-your-dreams tagline. As much as I love this narrative, it falls into a privileged pond. So many of us work to support ourselves, and often that truth requires us to simultaneously hold our dreams and face the grittiness of capitalism.

Before we dig in, I want to ask you: How do you feel about work? Is there an urge to change things, maybe your role or career or routine? Maybe you yearn to have your work life take less and give more. Or, heck, maybe you want to transcend the socialized concept of building a career altogether and shift from letting work dominate your worth to finding a place of deeper compassion—and fun.

I am with you. However you feel right now, I can see your Autumn Queen. She is moving through the forest, gathering tinder, itching to start a fire.

Always Feeling Behind

My work has always landed at the intersection of euphoria and exacerbation. There have been moments of phantasmagoric joy—going live on TV, working alongside a legendary actor, getting my first article published. But sums of all my energy often fell like raindrops that fed others' lakes. I have lived on the adrenaline of overbooking, over-*yes*ing, overworking.

And I could never crack the feeling that I was behind.

I think back to an afternoon when I was twenty-six. I had just walked into my boss's house carrying a fresh haul of vitamins and prescriptions for him. I was the assistant to the late movie star James Caan, and my role was a kaleidoscope of bizarreness, from pharmacy and kid pickups to traveling to film sets. I worked what felt like a million hours a week and kept at it for several years because Jimmy was incredible and grew to become a second dad. (I'll tell you the job also delivered novelty like wind. Once, while we were traveling on a private plane, I heard "Excuse me, darlin'" and turned to find Jack Nicholson looking for me to pass the potato salad.) That afternoon, in Jimmy's hallway, I tripped, and the bottles of vitamins and pills splattered across the floor. As I was on my knees picking them up, my chest felt heavy.

Is this what I'm meant for? I thought.

I can't say that I loved that job, but I loved Jimmy and reveled in the excitement and people. I was in my twenties, making just enough money to afford my apartment and buy pancakes with my friends on the weekends. Still, I carried this feeling that I should be doing more, that I was wasting my time pleasing others, running around in fantasy lands, working nonstop hours in a role that was light-years away from a corporate gig with benefits and a title. I poured every ounce of myself into what was expected of me, answering calls at 9 p.m. on Sundays, reading scripts on the way to film shoots, and playing an impromptu mediator between producers and agents. I worked earnestly and endlessly.

But pressure started to bubble.

A few weeks after that entryway flub, my father died. I was in my apartment in Los Angeles when my dear friend Tiffany came knocking. I opened the door to see her frowning, just as my phone started ringing. It was my mother. She had called Tiff the minute before so Tiff could be there when she told me the news.

"Daddy's in the hospital. It's not good, honey," my mother said.

It had been ten years since my mother left us. Steadily, over that decade, she and my dad had built a new friendship that was gorgeous to witness.

I flew to Massachusetts the following day to sit with my father. He'd gone into a coma: sepsis and liver failure related to alcoholism. I stared at his skin, his hands, his hairline as a machine breathed for him. Ideas about life and work swept through me as I oscillated between looking at my father and out the window. I'd always wanted to work in journalism. I'd always wanted to interview people, write stories, and dig into facts. Why wasn't I doing it?

I didn't need my father dying in front of me to tell me that I was scared—scared to say out loud what I wanted to do. Scared to follow the vocation that excited me since I was a girl. There, sitting in that sterile hospital room, I decided that I would take one step, then another, toward becoming a journalist.

A few days later, I squeezed my father's arm as he gulped his last mouthful of air. When I got back to Los Angeles, I applied to journalism graduate schools across the country. Those months applying and working felt as though I were treading water in an ocean of grief, with my stability at risk of drowning. Sleep was unattainable. I woke up on my couch soaked in urine and sweat. A hole seemed to open every few seconds to let in more of depression's grip. The only reason I got out of bed was to work. Work was my reprieve, my identity. Being busy was a drug. And I was determined to get into grad school. On film sets with Jimmy, I would find quiet corners to chip away at my applications.

I got into graduate school. The following year, I moved to Colorado to earn an MA in journalism. (Jimmy, being the man he was, had invited me to live with him and his family for months to save up for school.) A feeling of doing something, making it, coursed through me. I got a master's degree and spent the following decade working, from freelance writing job to freelance writing job—hustling, scraping, grinding, fretting.

I'd feel out of breath when rent was due, a feeling exacerbated by taxes and incoming electric bills. Around me, near and far, many of my friends were getting married and buying homes. Some were having kids. I was working.

Thirty came, and I didn't think much about the age. I was too stressed about starting to pay grad school loans and rent. When I landed the role as a news anchor and reporter in the four-state region, I grabbed it. I yearned for something different—geographically, societally, fundamentally different. I wanted to sink my teeth into on-the-ground reporting. I packed a U-Haul trailer and trekked twenty-three hours to a wintery Midwest and a job that paid me less than I'd made when I was twenty-four.

But I felt something I had not felt in a while: freedom.

As I went out into the world as a reporter, I gained a bit of small-town stardom, as local reporters do. People recognized me from my newscasts, so they often leaned in and asked questions. I didn't expect some of the inquiries to come brazenly.

Do you have kids?

Do you want kids?

Are you married?

Do you want to be married?

I heard these questions in the field, at dinner, in the studio. They never felt malicious, but I'd always chafe. The impact started to accumulate. The man I was dating at the time said marriage and kids "should" be top of mind. "At your age," he said, his heels scuffing the floor as he walked away.

It wasn't that marriage and kids were not on my mind. There just didn't seem to be space for anything when I was squeezing every paycheck, working six to seven days a week, and cobbling together another box—a career—that the world seemed to expect every woman to check. I was feeling friction against something more profound: a do-it-all-by-this-time structure. The "right" time to build a career, the "right" time to marry, the "right" time to buy a house, and the "right" time to have kids all seemed to be swirling around, leaving me feeling as if I were caught in a perpetual windstorm, unable to find a branch to hold.

Then, around when I hit forty, I felt a current of conviction, mixed with some fiery rage. For two decades, I'd worked nearly every day. The proving and scraping started to feel . . . wrong. In fact, it never felt right. It doesn't for any of us women, which is why so many of us may get sick from our work lives.

Entering my forties put a spotlight on things. I started to grow tired of giving away my writing to people's brands and platforms (often with no credit), seeing my bank account hover over zero after rent was due, and gritting my teeth. I thought, Why can't I stick up for myself?

I've come to see so many of us women harbor this merciless echo of judgment. It's the byproduct of being caregivers in a world that measures worth with a ruler created by men.

"I've always measured my success on being self-sufficient," Meredith Baird told me. "That being said, I have not always been a good advocate for myself, especially financially."

Baird's words surprised me. From afar, she oozes success. She's a certified health coach, the founder of a beautiful skincare line, and the author of several cookbooks, among other things. When she admitted to failing to demand more money for herself, it took me aback. It also made me feel less alone.

"I have a ton of confidence in my talents and abilities and know that I'm really good at the things that I do. But I've not been as financially successful as it may look or as I have expected from myself," she added. "So now looking at forty, I anticipated that I would be a little bit further ahead."

What is gutting about Baird's admission, and about looking back at my younger self, is the discovery of our fragility. Women are powerful. We have the capabilities to do anything we seek in and out of our work lives. But we can find ourselves overmatched by the giant patriarchal and ableist-fueled career world around us, unaware of how we generate to please, often leaving our well-being and desires in the wake.

Messy, Embodied, Uncharted Experiences

Work is vital. Our existence depends on our ability to work in the most basic sense—to feed ourselves and our families, care for children, provide homes, and create art and inspiration. Laboring for our survival, which in our capitalistic world means working for economic gain, anchors our lives.

I have always enjoyed working. Since I was young, I've enjoyed feeling like I've earned my sleep at night. It came after a day of babysitting in middle school, teaching horseback lessons in high school, or tending bar until three in the morning while in college. Earning my own money was an electricity that fed the buzz of autonomy. That buzz morphed into angst in college as the need to work steadily grew in my life. Still, I liked it.

What I have never liked is the expectation that one has to create a body of work to fit into society. "You want to build a career, something you're proud of," I remember a college professor telling us red-eyed first-year students. It was a compelling comment, but it left me confused. This thing loomed in front of all of us like a binary choice—you built a career or you didn't. You had one or you didn't. A career seemed like an exclusive club to which we should all vie for entry.

As I've grown older, I've seen how ableist this is. The concept of building a career, especially one ignited in the expectational time frame of postgraduation, strips the nuance of what it means to be human with a range of desires, needs, abilities, and resources. It overlooks the noble act of simply working, be it one job or many, to survive. As empowering and incredible as a career can be, the neat lines of it can be taxing. Building one often requires skills obtained through higher education, whether that be vocational training, college, graduate school, certification, or something else. Additional learning calls for time and money (colossal amounts these days), which can be out of reach. In tandem with financial means, building a career requires physical and mental ability and is structured around the idea that it must be shaped in a linear, constant fashion.

Time is also a necessity. I think of the woman raising children on her own. Or caring for her aging parents. Or navigating health treatments. Or struggling to exit an abusive relationship. Or living with disabilities. Our lives can be filled with many other demands that creating a career, especially one within a society-mandated time frame, falls down the ladder rungs—or may not even be on the ladder at all.

The pressure to build, build, build, and stay on track is exhausting, as is the *Merriam-Webster*'s definition of career being "a permanent calling." This leaves little (if any) room for self-exploration, let alone true self-care.

Natalie Silverstein always felt this pressure. As the daughter of immigrants, she imbibed a heads-down picture of work as she grew up. Her parents "came to this country with nothing, no money, no language, no resources, and they built a life for themselves," she told me. So being gainfully employed and successful in a career "was the ultimate thing from that immigrant perspective."

That perspective fueled Silverstein. By the time she was a late teen, she'd chosen to go into health policy and administration after spending time in the hospital as a kid and watching "all the cool, smart people," from those in administration to the doctors and caregivers. She applied to college, earned a degree in health policy and administration, and became, as she calls it, "a working girl at twenty-two." Since then, Silverstein has never stopped. She earned a master's degree from Yale, wrote two books, launched a popular podcast, and started a nonprofit. She's proud of it all, she told me, but the expectation to always be optimizing and building loomed over her like a storm cloud.

Today, Silverstein sees this pressure land on her own kids. She told me how her stomach dropped when a school administrator asked what her daughter, then a first-year high school student, wants to do. "I was like, 'I don't know, *summer camp*? Make *friendship bracelets*?'" she told me. "She's fifteen! We just have this mentality that you must know what you want to do and have this goal in mind. It's a lot of pressure."

As we spoke, I kept thinking about that pressure and how I felt that I needed to define my career. It's a daunting expectation that starts getting us quite early. I've felt angst around this and talked openly with my friends about it over the years, sometimes feeling better and other times worse.

When I picked up Satya Doyle Byock's book *Quarterlife* a few years ago, I felt as though I'd exhaled decades' worth of stale air. Byock, a Jungian psychotherapist, writes about the existential qualms of Quarterlifers, people roughly between the ages of twenty and forty. "As much as my peers and I have been led to believe that life is a tidy, incremental staircase toward certain goals—career advancement, marriage, home ownership—at some point, we discover that it is not," she writes.

I was forty when I first read Byock's words, and they gave me the solace I didn't know I needed.

Byock believes that Quarterlifers are simultaneously in search of two things, stability and meaning, with some people being initially more aligned with one than the other. Stability Types, as

Byock refers to them, strive to meet society's prescriptions, but in doing so often find themselves unfulfilled and feeling empty at some point. Meaning Types balk at the prescribed path—building a career, making money, getting married—but often feel they're lost within society's expectations or less than. "Quarterlife is not a sterile journey," Byock writes. "It demands the gathering of *experiences*—messy, embodied, uncharted experiences."

Now, you may be thinking that this is about Quarterlifers and not women in their forties. I argue that Byock's theory stands true for those of us in our forties too. Our work lives—heck, our entire lives—are a spectrum on which everyone lands in their own unique spot. Liberation comes from seeing this truth.

Two years after first reading her book, I reached out to Byock to test my theory. I asked her if this gathering of "messy, embodied, uncharted experiences" continues after we turn forty. More so, I wanted her confirmation that I wasn't alone in my messiness.

"There is no question that that continues past the age of forty," Byock, who is kind and present, told me, smiling.

Quickly into our conversation, I realized she and I were touching on something transcendent. No matter our age, we are always on a journey, seeking a life rich in self-actualization, free from the restraint of others' demands. We are always blooming, always finding our way through the topography of challenges, mysteries, and magic that make up our lives. We bloom into a new time of discovery—and, often, nothing quite brings this journey into focus like our work lives. Like a teacher, our work calls our name, looking for us to ask questions and offer new perspectives.

"It really is a deep psychological and spiritual question of Why are we alive?" added Byock.

As we will see in the pages ahead, this existential quest begins to take a new shape in our forties.

A Time to Look Inward

"It started to emerge suddenly."

As I listened to Kathy Caprino, I felt like I was in her living room, even though we were three thousand miles away and two computer screens apart from each other. Caprino embodies a natural warmth with a willingness to delve deep quickly.

What "started to emerge" for Caprino was a new clarity when she turned forty: a deeper discernment around her work. She had spent the first twenty years of her career in corporate publishing, marketing, and product-management roles, advancing to a VP-level position. She liked many parts of her career, but she started to struggle. Work began to feel "false and inauthentic," she told me. She had little time for herself or her family, which haunted her as a mother, and she faced harassment, politics, and biases in her work environments.

"I remember hitting forty, and there was this urgency for meaning," Caprino continued.

It was a brilliant therapist who turned her toward a glimmer of hope. Caprino had just been laid off and was reeling. "I was in his office crying, and he said to me, 'I know this looks like the worst crisis you've ever faced in your adult life, but from where I sit, it's the first moment you can choose who you want to be in the world. Now, who do you want to be?' "

Caprino followed the nudge of her counselor to consider studying therapy, a field that would allow her to help people. She became a therapist, a vocation she leaned into for several years before becoming the sought-after women's career coach, writer, and podcast host she is today. Given her history, she is passionate about helping women explore their work choices sooner, and more deeply. She anchors her work and book *The Most Powerful You* in what her research has shown to be key barriers that interfere with women's confidence. These barriers, which include failing to recognize our true talents and passions, reluctance to ask for what we deserve, and giving up on a dream because we feel it's out of reach, can keep us feeling stagnant, stuck, or overlooked. Caprino calls these barriers "power gaps" and posits that they can cause "leaks" in our confidence, keeping us from building meaningful work lives.

Another power gap Caprino sees happen with women is that many of us operate from fear rather than strength. We receive messages from patriarchal stories or our families of origin or authority figures who say we must stay in our lane and be diminutive and we shouldn't go confidently toward what we want.

"I made so many decisions, so many moves, that were faulty for me, and they were based on beliefs or assumptions, some of which came from my childhood," she said. "Growing up, I somehow sensed I had to pursue high-level corporate work because my father forged a successful career at GE for thirty years and found it so rewarding and fulfilling. So that shaped me. And I'm also a singer, and I realized later that I never even remotely considered saying to my parents, 'Can I go to school to study music and theater?' "

Caprino sees the forties as a time when women look inward and ask: Does my work have meaning? Is this what I truly want to do with my talents and abilities or is it what the world (and others) expects me to do? This age brings with it a keener awareness of our mortality, she added, which can prompt the question How am I spending my precious time and energy?

Lesley Jane Seymour told me the forties for women today look a lot different than when she was this age several decades ago. These days, many of us are more curious about exploring unique career paths, creating new roles, and fighting for schedules that allow for room to live, care for ourselves, and care for others. "I think you're going to be less programmed into thinking it has to look this way," she told me.

Seymour, who is in her late sixties, said her thirties and forties were a time of endless hustling. As part of the second generation of women who entered the workforce full-time, she had built a life that consisted of working nonstop: She was constantly thinking about work, getting ready for work, attending work-related events, and doing more work, all while raising her children. She was building a coveted—and highly public—career covering women in the zeitgeist as a journalist, writer, and editor at famed women's magazines, including *Vogue*, *Redbook*, *Marie Claire*, and most recently *More* (she became editor-in-chief of the last three). She loved it—but all the work took a ton from her.

After *More*, a lifestyle magazine that spoke to women over forty, closed in 2016 (news that gutted me), Seymour launched and ran a popular podcast and platform focused on women forty-plus reimagining their careers and lives—essentially making changes and creating career autonomy that was once unheard of.

So many lessons came out of all her years of hustling—some good, some not so good. But there's one that stands out: all the energy she spent following the rules and caring about what others thought.

"My daughter asked me, 'What do you regret the most about those careers?' And I said, 'All the time I wasted!' I think about the years I spent at *Vogue*—nine years—and every morning when I would walk into that coffee room, I would worry if the women liked me. Now, I look back and go, 'My God, who cared?' But still—all that time I wasted!"

As Seymour continued, I heard the fire in her voice. Our forties mark the time when we start to get really comfortable with who we are, and we jettison the excuses.

"You start to say, 'I know who I am, and not everyone's gonna like me, and that's okay.' You start to let go and work on the things that matter. You're at the beginning of this incredible transition—and I believe your cohort today will be doing it differently. You're going to find a better path than we did, and that's exciting."

We Must Pay Attention to Our Needs

Seymour and Kathy Caprino touch on a work issue that can continue to haunt us in our forties: the constant hustle, the need to please, and the politics. There is a growing awareness of how unforgiving work can be, how it's a system that often takes a ton and gives very little, thus enticing many people to opt out of or change jobs or careers.

We must also consider the times we live in. Americans face a crisis of affordability around rising costs for food, housing, and other living essentials. Three out of four adults who participated in a 2025 CBS News poll stated that their incomes cannot keep pace with inflation. Gas and grocery prices are skyrocketing. If you're not a millionaire or linked to family financial support, buying a home can feel like a pipe dream. All the while, our governmental high office has been dismantling infrastructure for critical social and health services and the arts, harming our nation's morale.

Now, the reality is that costs will always rise. Still, life today demands immense resources just to live, and this reality impacts some people more intensely, depending on socioeconomic status and partnership standing. A 2024 analysis by the Center for American Progress illuminates the particular economic hardships faced by single mothers in the US today.

At the state level, we have few social safety nets. We have no guaranteed paid family or medical leave at the federal level. We still face a gender pay gap, with women averaging 85 percent of what men earn. All of this illuminates why we must pay attention to how we respond to the world's relentlessness. If we don't, we "can get caught in a tornado of neglecting our needs, relationships, and health," as Rae Leslie told me.

The word *health* is critical. While our forties mark shifts in our focus, desires, and creativity, they also welcome changes to our physiology. Many of us are in the land of perimenopause, a time of wild hormonal changes, which can make us feel a host of things, including tired, erratic, unsure, and anxious—all of which and more we will explore in chapter 6. We don't feel like ourselves, and this impacts both how we work and how we feel about work. For some of us, our sense of capability, confidence, and eagerness may be all over the place.

Research is starting to illuminate this truth. In 2021, Mayo Clinic invited more than thirty-two thousand women to participate in a survey study evaluating the impact of menopausal symptoms. Of the more than 5,219 women who responded, 85 percent reported information about their employment, and the overarching result was "self-reported adverse work outcomes related to menopause symptoms," the study stated. Two years later, research from the United Kingdom surveyed two thousand working women between the ages of forty and sixty. The report found 67 percent of the women had experienced menopausal symptoms that were detrimental to how they felt and performed at work.

There is also a growing conversation around middle-aged women and attention deficit hyperactivity disorder (ADHD). Experts in the medical field are increasingly recognizing that ADHD symptoms, which can begin in childhood, may remain in adulthood. Some studies show women are more likely to be underdiagnosed earlier in their lives, and fluctuations in hormones due to perimenopause may exacerbate ADHD symptoms.

I deliver these facts to ask you a question: If society will not support your evolving needs inside and outside work, who will?

You.

That is why you must reevaluate the ways in which you care for yourself, including how you relate to your work.

"I want you to remember this in your forties: There. Is. No. Finish. Line," said Rae Leslie. "All this racing is collective. We must break the cycle."

So that brings us to the operative question: How do you start to "break the cycle"?

Look at Your Discomfort

As I shared with you earlier, the first two decades of my working life were punctuated with fear that I'd always be behind and that

I'd never be enough. In my forties, that fear is being replaced with the stark reality of mortality. Our forties show us that time is finite. This finiteness acts as a direct line to reality, putting light on how we feel in our day-to-day. Are we stressed? Trapped? Joyful? Engaged? Sad? Pissed? Fulfilled? Aching?

And most importantly, are we working to satisfy ourselves or societal expectations?

I was in my mid-thirties the first time I considered this question. I had worked in TV news for a couple of years and knew it was not a path I wanted to follow long term, despite the highs it delivered. I wanted to put my energy toward writing and interviewing. When I received two back-to-back offers for anchor positions in bigger markets, one in Arkansas and the other in California, I froze. Both studios promised me more—more airtime, more mentorship, more exposure to hone my brand as a journalist. From the outside, these were incredible career-advancing opportunities. On the inside, my guts were a pretzel.

"You are craaaazy if you turn this down," a news colleague told me. I was sitting in my car with my phone clutched in my sweaty palm, looking at one more night before I owed the stations my answer. "Stacey, if you don't take this, you will regret it," he continued. "You only get so many chances in this business."

I turned down both positions.

Years later, in my late thirties, I received the opposite advice from my friend Barbara Stamis. I was feeling suffocated in my job as an editor. The position I held fit the classic a-million-people-would-kill-for-that-job trope. My days were filled with bright rays, including working with brilliant women, some of whom are my dearest friends today. But there grew an unease in me. Despite the benefits, I still had to take freelance jobs on the weekends to make ends meet. I felt empty and confused. During company-wide meetings, I would often step outside to walk off what felt like a Hulk hand on my chest.

"Leave," Stamis said to me. "Listen to your body, your heart. You don't need that. There are so many other things you can do."

"Yeah. . . . No. . . . I can't just leave. I have . . ."

"What?" she replied.

"I just can't . . . I can't leave."

The stress from my bills, student loans, rent, and dependent boyfriend all bubbled in my throat. But Stamis, a deeply intuitive somatic healer and breath work coach, knew all of this. She wasn't telling me in literal terms to leave at that moment. Rather, she was nudging me to open myself to possibility and to move away from the idea that I must stay in a role that satisfied others' ideas of success. She reminded me of my agency and, in doing that, invited me to look deeper at my discomfort.

Tara Mohr believes that discomfort can be one of our greatest teachers. Instead of pushing it down, we can lean into it and listen to what it's telling us.

"I've started using the term *the disillusionment upgrade*," Mohr told me. "When you're feeling disillusioned, that is actually your signal that it's time to upgrade your ideas about what's relevant and what's meaningful. It's a cue."

Mohr is a women's leadership and well-being coach who wrote *Playing Big*, a book I have turned to for years. She believes it can be our natural inclination to grit our teeth and keep going with the status quo. But in Mohr's world, the growth happens not when we look away from our disquiet but when we face it. "We want to lean toward this feeling of emptiness," she continues, "because it's pointing us to the question, 'What wouldn't feel empty?'"

That question makes me emotional. It can stir compassion and agency, especially when your work world feels like a concrete block thwarting you from choice. It also opens a portal that allows your truth to emerge.

But most of all, that question signals a turning point. It shows us that we can keep going down the path of hustling and obliging or, instead, we can consider a new direction—one that welcomes our singular desires and creativity.

Rae Leslie taught me that the first step toward taking a new path forward is to observe ourselves—our stories, habits, tendencies, and fears around work. To do this, she suggests three critical steps: Ask. Notice. Act.

First, ask yourself:

> What am I chasing?
>
> Why am I chasing this?
>
> Where did this chase come from? Is it from a fear of failure? If so, whose definition of failure?
>
> Am I seeking others' approval?
>
> Am I competing with someone? If so, whom and why?
>
> What or who evokes envy, be it a person's work or creative life?

You can ask yourself these questions while journaling, driving in the car, or being out in nature or anywhere you feel calm and safe. This stage is not about making change. It is about exploring.

When you feel ready, lean into step two: Notice. Pay attention to how you respond in your work setting or around the idea of work. Leslie suggests asking yourself:

> What about this job—or role or career—makes me feel good? What about it makes me feel bad? (And if you are not working, what about that makes you feel good or bad?)
>
> How do I feel around the people I work with?
>
> When am I most stressed, hypervigilant, or shut down?
>
> Where do I feel open, creative, and alive? For instance, is it collaborating with people? Writing alone? Researching out in the field?

Dig deep into these questions. Let yourself follow a stream of consciousness as you jot down your answers. "Over time, asking yourself these questions and making room for self-reflection leads to clarity," said Leslie. "It encourages more self-belief and more self-understanding, which moves you toward change."

These two steps have been immense for me. Witnessing how and what I feel about my work has proved to be a quiet revolution. Getting it out—physically out—on a notebook or journal page (or in a voice note when it just comes to me) has lightened a heaviness in my body. (I once scribbled: *I worry I'll never live up to my ex-boyfriend's parents' expectations of me.* Whoa.) Rather than endlessly venting to a friend, jotting down what I am chasing and how I am feeling—even for one minute, a few times a week—allows me to see my fears and blocks.

Now, it is time for the third step: Act.

You may think this means making a huge change, like leaving

your job or asking for a raise. And it could. But such drastic measures may not be feasible for you at this moment, and that is okay. This exercise is about nourishing your agency. It is about showing yourself that what you truly feel and desire matters. That is why Leslie suggests making this step small and deeply personal. Consider one thing you can do immediately to give yourself more peace and agency in your work. It may be imperceptible to anyone but you. It could mean leaving to go home five minutes earlier. It could mean speaking up in a meeting. It could mean blocking out an hour every Wednesday for therapy, meditation, or brainstorming a new work life. It could mean turning away from email an hour earlier. It could mean doing a spiritual practice to help you physically part from the energy of an annoying colleague. (I used to pretend to cut an invisible cord that linked me with a pretty mean work superior. I would "snip" before heading home, and I swear it helped keep thoughts of them from coming into my apartment.)

Whatever it might be, act in the most immediate, deeply personal way for you. Your inner Autumn Queen loves these quiet shifts because they are quiet revolutions. They feel good because they are powerful.

For me, acting has meant putting up guardrails. As a freelance journalist, I have lived on the brink of not having assignments, gripped by the need to secure work. Such precarity has caused me to always be on my phone, ever willing to respond to an editor or client in the wee hours of the morning. But after years of doing this, I saw how counterproductive it is. I was always reacting, passively allowing my energy to go toward defensive modes instead of putting that effort into creating more of what I wanted to nourish—an interview series, long-form journalism, this book.

In my forties, I've employed a strict personal policy of no work messaging or emailing before 8 a.m. and after 6 p.m. (like my social media rules). I stick to it. It is a small act, one I don't think anyone else sees, but it has granted me the room to better care for my biggest work asset: me.

Often the most impactful changes we can make in our work lives start with caring for our hearts. Work can range from vibrant to excruciating. Our careers or jobs might be inimical to our nature, filled with having to bend to someone else, follow rules, work horrific hours, and say yes in instances where we want to say no. The push to sell and perform is real. Most of us avid to be seen, and the best way to explore something beyond work hardships is to give ourselves the room to pause—even for a few minutes.

In doing this, we expand.

You Get to Decide

One of the roots of pain around work is the feeling that we're never enough—never good enough, smart enough, promoted enough, producing enough, successful enough. This jungle of uncertainty affects women both in and out of the workforce. It came up in my conversation with Stephanie Long.

Long and I connected when I put a message on Instagram asking to interview women for this book. Over the phone, she generously talked about motherhood, aging, and her winning fight against breast cancer. Warm and affable, Long is a natural conversationalist, so it surprised me when she admitted to being nervous to talk.

"I'm like, Oh gosh, she is probably going to expect me to have this great job and to be doing all these things," she said.

That was when Long told me she didn't have a career. She'd attended college and law school, but rather than work in law, she had her children and "many things going on" in her life, she said.

I hated how Long felt she needed to justify her decisions. What she has been doing with her time is noble—and hers. But I understood why she felt the need. Our patriarchal world valorizes work and career building.

"I'm happy with my choices," Long continued, her voice clear with conviction. "It shouldn't be 'Oh, I went to law school, and I got pregnant, and my life stopped.' It's not all about that. My life started in so many different ways. But it is funny, the societal expectations or even just the expectations that we put on ourselves."

My close high school friend Lauren shared something similar. When her second child, Griffin, was born, she stopped working. At first, it was to spend more time raising her two children, an opportunity she grabbed, as her husband's job could support the family. But then Griffin was diagnosed with diabetes. "It was a realization of our new life and the way we had to do things," Lauren told me about her son's diagnosis. "Motherhood is the centering thing of my life. I don't say that in a sad or negative way, but it wasn't what I had planned for myself."

I told Lauren she always seemed self-assured and happy, never looking to her side for validation. I admired this in her in high school and still do today.

"Thank you, buddy," she replied, laughing. "I always knew I wanted to be a parent, but I thought I would also have a career, that I'd be a lawyer. But then it just didn't happen. I'm at peace with it, but sometimes you meet women who are so accomplished in their career it does make you feel less than."

This raw vulnerability underscore women's need to justify their worth in the face of work, all the damn time. This truth becomes even darker when we consider how society lacks respect for all labor, whether paid or unpaid, and continues to venerate the labor of men over women. The COVID-19 pandemic illuminated this gap. As the world plummeted into a vortex of loss, fear, and disorientation, and millions of essential workers put their lives on the line, millions more lost their jobs, with a greater number of women losing employment than men. Additionally, schools closed and many facilities offering childcare shut down, causing droves of working mothers to leave their jobs to both homeschool and care for their kids. (The closure of childcare facilities also meant colossal job losses for those employees, a large percentage of whom are women of color and poorly paid.)

In a 2020 article for *The Cut*, Claire Lampen described the situation as a "perfect storm of intersecting circumstances," from balancing around-the-clock care to juggling homeschooling, that pushed women out from their jobs and prevented them from looking for new ones. I remember being on the phone with my best friend, Maura, around that time. "This is impossible. It's too much," she told me about trying to work and care for her family all at home. I could hear her two young daughters running wild in the background.

The pandemic's repercussions on our work and personal lives continue to ricochet throughout the nation. The impact rattled a ton, and what settled to the surface were haunting questions for women: What am I doing with my time? Why is there still no system of shared care? How will I juggle all of this? Why must what I do to feed myself and my family take so much from me?

Following the pandemic, workforce movements, many with trendy names like "the great resignation" and "quiet quitting," happened, reflecting the boiling frustration with how extractive work can be and our collective desire to revolt. And while some research showed that women's post-pandemic employment, particularly that of mothers, eventually surpassed pre-pandemic levels, much of which experts credited to more flexible remote work offerings, more recent data suggests that women are losing a foothold in the American workforce. In an August 2025 article for *The Washington Post*, journalist Abha Bhattarai reported that the number of working mothers with young children had fallen "to the lowest level in more than three years," according to data she analyzed by economist and author Misty Heggeness. Bhattarai noted that among the dozen women she interviewed who had recently left their jobs, many cited various reasons for leaving, including layoffs, a lessening work-from-home flexibility while caregiving, and a "discernable shift in workplace attitudes, including return-to-office mandates and discarded diversity policies, that made it feel like they were less valued at work." Additionally, approximately 300,000 Black women left the labor force in mid-2025. "This isn't a coincidence," gender economist Katica Roy reported for MSNBC. "It's the result of federal policy changes—most immediately, sweeping job cuts across public sector agencies where Black women have long held the strongest foothold in middle-class employment."

All of this is to say that it is jarringly clear how tough the world of work can be on women. Society puts an unjust reverence on certain types of labor and overlooks and undervalues others, just as it venerates certain working people based on gender, race, and socioeconomic status.

The idea of building a career, one that is fueled by the idea that we must always be ascending, can also eclipse the nobility and necessity of many types of critical work. How is it that a person running a hedge fund can receive a paycheck that is millions of dollars more than that of an elementary school teacher? Where is the societal support (and reverence) for the woman who spends her energy caring for her elderly mother or growing child?

Angela Garbes captures these inequities in her critical book, *Essential Labor.* Garbes, a writer and mother, writes powerfully about how the United States, a nation of immense wealth, relies on "an invaluable force of women, most of them brown and Black," to perform the most critical work of caring for people "for free or at poverty wages." Garbes argues how American society places value on how much we produce and, instead, reveals an alternative approach. "If we were to think about work in terms of our humanity—making people feel dignified, valued, and whole—then caregiving is the most important work we can do with our time on earth," she writes.

Seeing how there are no cultural accolades or social support for one of the most critical ways we can spend our time—caring for ourselves, our families, and our communities—is a clarion call to untether ourselves from feeling like we're never enough. Because the truth is, we are enough. You are enough. Society valorizes certain types of work and overlooks others. This is a harsh reality. But we must not let it infiltrate our lives and rob our worth. As women in our forties, we must put our attention toward our well-being, our worthiness, and the expressions of our care, energy, and passions—and how those do or do not fall within the traditionally defined confines of work is up to each of us.

We also must cleave ourselves from the idea that our personal interests and work must neatly align. In *The Trouble with Passion*, sociologist Erin A. Cech argues that modern society idealizes the pursuit of fulfillment in one's career, while the truth is that doing so may be attainable only for a few, mainly those with financial safety nets. Cech explores how striving for passion-centric vocations can leave out swaths of people, overlook various types of meaningful work, and feed into a culture of hustle and overwork.

Cech's insight illuminates the importance of finding meaning outside of our jobs and to center our inner passions, whether through engaging in hobbies, community work, or other efforts. I now know that in my forties, I want to make room for finding this meaning. I want to put my *ambition* toward finding fulfillment outside the confines of a job.

"We used to think, particularly in the girl-boss era, that work had to be everything," women's executive coach Amina AlTai told me. "We used to think that our identities were intrinsically tied to it, and if work wasn't everything, we had a bit of an existential crisis."

AlTai would know. Before becoming a coach, she spent more than ten years kowtowing to late capitalism. She put in every ounce of her being with her head down, building a company and white-knuckling it. "I felt like my work wasn't just a job but my whole personality," she writes in *The Ambition Trap*. It was a never-ending uphill trajectory that cost AlTai relationships, peace, and her sense of self.

The relentless hustling also took a toll on AlTai's health. The morning she received a call from her doctor telling her she was "days away from multiple organ failure" was when she knew she had to expand her story. AlTai put her work ambition "under the microscope," as she said, and she stopped chasing the next milestone and began putting her energy toward wholeness, deeper meaning, and joy.

Today, AlTai is a clarifying voice helping women care for themselves both in and out of the workplace. When we spoke, she told me that one of the biggest hurdles she faces, and that many women face, is operating from a place of fear. (Yup!) We often think we are never enough and that there will never be enough for us. This feeling of scarcity pushes us to have what she calls "painful ambition"—a tendency to cling to perfectionism, work ourselves to the bone, and operate under the fallacy that we are what we do. AlTai believes that our "core wounds" of rejection, abandonment, humiliation, betrayal, and injustice drive our painful ambition.

Painful ambition makes sense, given how ableist and taxing our patriarchal society is. But we can turn it around, AlTai told me. The key lies with our beliefs. When we work to shift our mindset from one of scarcity to one of abundance and recognize the truth that we are always enough and worthy, regardless of our actions, we can move forward with greater strength to claim what we want.

"Our beliefs are so important," she added. "Our beliefs drive our thoughts. Our thoughts drive our actions. Our actions drive our experiences and reinforce our thoughts. And round and round we go."

AlTai said a good place to start shifting our beliefs is to examine the stories we tell ourselves about having our needs met, getting paid, feeling joy, maintaining good health, and experiencing connection. "Many of us have stories running in our minds like an operating system, telling us we have to *earn* the right to have our needs met," she said. "But we don't. It's our birthright."

Prioritizing our well-being is our right—but this takes effort, individually and collectively. As women, we must learn to speak up for ourselves and one another. We must remind ourselves of our worth, advocate for closing the gender and racial wealth gaps, and prioritize care and community.

And we must see work for what it is: a beautiful part of the multitudinous journey of being a woman.

"It can be connected to our purpose, or it can be the good-enough job," AlTai added. "You get to decide."

Cultivating Your Power

We can be cryptic when talking about work. And it's no wonder, as any truly deep, meaningful discussion of it requires acknowledging a quilt of feelings that may include fear, regret, resentment, confusion, joy, excitement, boredom, and longing. We may wish that our work situations were different, so when people ask "How's work?" we tend to answer with overarching comments, avoiding how we really feel.

"Whatever work we do, we want to be satisfied," women's therapist Patty Bechtold told me.

I told Bechtold about the work frustration and angst I had observed in the women I'd spoken to for this book. Here we are in our forties, many of us feeling a creative spark but also a sense of heaviness. We wish we had taken better care of ourselves in our work, asked for more money, and pursued certain opportunities and hadn't overexerted ourselves to the point of exhaustion.

Bechtold nodded and put me at ease. She said it is natural for women in their forties to start deeply inquiring about what they have done and what they want to do.

"We start asking ourselves, Am I doing enough? Am I doing the right thing? Am I wanting more? Am I wanting less? All those questions are there," she said. "So, around this time, it's natural to be saying, 'Hmm . . .' "

Bechtold cited a practice called "inner relationship focusing" that she weaves into her therapy sessions with women. The practice requires us to observe our feelings with compassion and a sense of curiosity, to notice and listen rather than try to conquer them. Doing this can be helpful, she added, because it allows us to witness and learn.

If you face a sense of unease, frustration, or doubt around your work, lean into Bechtold's insight. She suggests sitting with that feeling for a few minutes. Pay attention and notice what occurs in your body. "Can you listen very kindly and compassionately and see if it has something to say to you?" she said. "Or can you see if you have something to say to it?"

Her counsel prompted me to think of what Tara Mohr shared: Your discomfort can often reveal something important. It might reveal what you want to change, let go of, or heal. Therefore, we must listen deeply and keep our hearts and minds open. "Doing this is the deepest form of self-care," Bechtold added.

One morning, as I was working on this chapter, a new memory on my phone popped up. It was a photo of me at age six. (Technically, it was a photo of a photo.) I was sitting at the dinner table next to my maternal grandmother, Tai-Tai. I am wearing thick glasses with my hair half pulled back, staring into the camera—a piercing gaze. There is neither a smile nor a frown on my face. Only the depths of a little girl with boundless curiosity.

What struck me when I looked at myself was how I felt responsible for that little girl. I wanted to make her proud. To stick up for her. To give her peace. I felt my Autumn Queen come to the forefront, in all her strength, and say, "You're safe now. I got you."

That photo made me see how our feelings about our work lives in our forties are different and new because *we* are different and new.

We are growing and evolving. We are stronger and fierier. We are no longer saying okay to old ways and instead are stepping into new paradigms. Therefore, we must show ourselves more compassion than we ever have, whether we want to downshift, step back, step in, or step up. Whichever it may be, we owe it to our younger selves to listen.

"What calls to us requires us to be different," Kathy Caprino told me. "Our dreams need us to become more confident, self-loving, and resilient."

So I asked Caprino, "How can we listen to what is calling us? How can we step toward our dreams?"

"We need to cultivate our power and self-trust," she responded.

To cultivate your power, Caprino recommends taking three actions:

Lean into what excites you. "Follow every morsel of excitement to the fullest degree you can," she said. Listen to your inner fire. However, she warns against attaching your excitement to one specific outcome or number. "For instance, I have heard so many women tell me they want to become writers and they must have a bestselling book," she added. "But I say focus on the book you're meant to write."

Practice asking for what you deserve around money, benefits, time, respect, and exposure. Caprino said you must dig into how you truly feel about reaching for what you deserve. Look at patterns and old stories you might have around money, freedom, the spotlight, "success," or autonomy. Notice your blocks and take the necessary steps to release and heal them. "Regardless of what the ultimate stretch goal is, if you don't examine and shift any limiting mindsets, beliefs, and behavioral patterns, they will often keep you from creating and experiencing what you most deeply long for," she said.

Make brave connections. Caprino told me that too many women tend to isolate themselves from support and go on the journey alone. (I am guilty of this.) Doing this only holds us back from our full potential. "We need people in our corner to help us do the things we want to do and open doors that we can't on our own," she added. Reach out. Ask for help. Be vulnerable. And be there to support other women and ask for their support in return.

Ultimately, when it comes to honoring and fulfilling our desires, "the journey requires a deep and clear understanding of both what you want more of and what you want less of," said Caprino. "And it's about understanding that you are far more capable than you may realize to shape it. The world needs your great talents, energy, brilliance, and capabilities, now more than ever."

Maybe This Is Modern Feminism

One day, in the early weeks of writing this book, I found myself on the phone with Anne Campbell. She and I met several years prior at an editors' gathering in Austin, a wonderful few days hosted by our mutual friend Camille Styles. That weekend, we went deep into a few conversations, which left me feeling as though I were wrapped in cashmere. Campbell is refreshing, open, and eager to dive into the moment and talk about what is real.

She reached out when she learned I was writing this book. Campbell is in her forties and had been thinking a lot about this age and what it means for women.

"I had this epiphany," she told me in her buttery Texan twang, "that maybe modern feminism is doing whatever you want to do, whether that's stay at home, go to work . . . just do whatever the fuck you want to do!" There was a charge in her voice, and I pointed it out to her.

Campbell went on to tell me how she'd recently decided to take a sabbatical from work—a colossal decision for her, given that she'd spent the previous two decades working and working and working more. She'd managed projects for an interior design firm, cofounded and run a landscape architecture firm with her husband, written design columns for magazines, and raised her three children. Her worth felt tied to her endless output. All she knew was to be on and working, all the damn time.

"It takes an emotional toll when you're trying to do the mom thing, and your phone is blowing up, and I'm like, I'm not even supposed to be on the clock right now anyway!" she said. "And I was like, I'm not doing anything well. And I'm barely making any money."

I told Campbell I was grateful for her honesty because, although I'm not a mom, I've lived through all the other things she was describing: the endless hustle and relentless need to perform. She admitted she was wrestling with the identity aspect of not working, feeling like she didn't measure up to the women around her who were running public businesses. But then, she added, that was part of why she'd decided to pull away.

"I'd had enough of people-pleasing my entire life and of caring so deeply about my ego and having to be ahead of this and that," she said. "I'm really trying to shirk all my labels. If you're friends with me, you're friends with me because you like me for me, not because I started this company or am a creative director for that company."

Campbell's conviction brought to mind my close high school friend, Kerri. I FaceTimed with Kerri and Lauren, whom we heard from earlier in this chapter, at the same time to talk about our forties. Kerri is usually goofy and open, but she was a bit reticent during our call, especially when we got to talking about work and identity. I sensed something bubbling in her on the video, but I didn't pry.

But later that night, Kerri texted me. She told me how it had taken her years to find herself. She'd had to take time to look within and face some dark truths from her childhood. She was able "to finally start the process of healing" by letting go of the expectations around her—expectations to look perfect, be perfect, and have a perfect career—and embracing the things that really make her happy, like making art, gardening, and digging in the dirt every day. These pastimes are not for anyone's gain, nor are they part of a career, but they bring her joy.

"I look at finding my hobbies as something wonderful that came out of the distress," Kerri texted. "I feel more accomplished now that I know ME rather than trying to be someone making millions of dollars."

Taking the time to stand back and consider that work is not

the definitive measure of who we are can be clarifying. It can show us who our people are and what makes us feel truly alive.

When I was on the phone with Anne Campbell, I told her how entering my forties helped me shift my perspective around work. That young woman breaking herself to build a career in her twenties and thirties is gone. I am no longer her. Now, in my forties, I've become more tender with myself. I no longer feel the need to constantly prove my worth to the world.

Looking around, I see so many of us women wanting the same—and grabbing it—like Campbell, who told me again about her idea of modern feminism.

"Maybe," she said, "we can start accepting each other for who we are versus what we put on our résumé."

Everything Goes in Cycles

Though I have been working for three decades (if you count my early babysitting jobs), my work life now feels like it's nearing its first bloom. For the first time, I am putting my health and creativity at the forefront. Much of this feeling stems from my taking better care of myself—which is the most essential thing we must do in our work.

Rashel Hariri reminded me that one critical form of care women can show themselves is to see that we do not need to continue miming how men work. Hariri, a longtime marketing consultant, discusses this on her podcast, *She's Interesting,* which focuses on women entrepreneurs. She started the show because she was exhausted from seeing men continue to dominate the images of conventional success.

"I always joke about them wearing Patagonia vests and being in the start-up world," she told me, laughing. "But it's a certain persona—and most of the attention and funding still goes to them."

The funding goes to men, but so does the structure of work. These eight-to-five schedules we're so used to were not only built by men but also cater to men's physiology without even a nod to women's needs. A growing body of science reveals the cognitive and physiological differences between women and men, as well as how these differences impact the rhythms of our work energies. The long-held average workday tends to complement men, as their levels of testosterone, which affect energy, peak in the morning and decline in the evening, on average. Our testosterone levels, however, fluctuate depending on our menstrual cycles and on whether we may be experiencing perimenopausal changes in our hormones. All of this impacts our energy and how we may or may not want to engage with work on any given day. Rather than break ourselves against this hypermasculine image of what a powerful workday "should" look like, it behooves us to know that we are biologically unique from men and, therefore, our work capacities may be different too.

"It just doesn't make sense to me that we would want to lean into this type of hustle culture when we know, biologically, we're different," said Hariri. "We can still work hard. We can accomplish great things. We can run for president. We just don't have to do it the same way as men. There can be a better way to work."

Hariri's message landed: A better way is our way.

It is your way.

Like life, our work worlds are personal and deeply unique for each of us. The story that career ambition is a linear trajectory that always moves upward is false, and it sets us up for disappointment. How you choose to be in or out of the working world is up to you. What is critical for you now, in your forties, is to direct your ambition toward your care and passions. Toward the people you love. Toward your life. And the messier your constellation of experiences, the better.

Kameko Grant embodies this. A self-described "jane-of-all-trades," she's worked as a fashion designer, private chef, postpartum doula, entrepreneur, and writer.

"It's been a wild ride, for sure," Grant said of her work life, admitting that she got "a lot of pushback from people" when she made drastic changes in her career, like leaving coveted jobs with health insurance. "Some friends told me, 'That's so irresponsible,'" she said. But change was never a question for Grant. Having grown up in a "hyper-religious home" in rural Virginia and with interracial parents, she faced intense scrutiny and pressure when she was young. She learned to trust her instincts early on and never follow the rules. She followed passions and new opportunities, steering away from a linear line. "There were tons of expectations on me," she said. "But the older I got, the less and less I gave a shit what people think."

Now in her forties, Grant said she has "never felt more creative." She's writing a book while raising her three kids and leaning into all her project visions. There are hard days, she admitted. But she feels alive. And her Autumn Queen is on fire.

Amina AlTai told me that when women enter their forties, there is a more natural honoring of who we are—in and out of our work lives. And she believes our ambition is cyclical. "Nature goes in cycles, so it's a much more generous way to think about ambition in our careers as going in cycles too," she said. "We'll have these quiet moments underground where we're getting clear on where we want to grow or not. Then we nurture both our inner and outer environments, and we experience a beautiful growth spurt—a peak in the sun. Then the seasons change, and we wind down and go back underground where we rest—and perhaps the ground is even fallow for a while—until we are ready to grow again."

As you grow into your forties, I want you to honor your natural cycles. I hope you can shrink the imprint of needing to build a career for others and instead focus on doing meaningful work, however that looks for your soul. It could mean writing a book, starting a company, leaving a company, taking a less stressful job to allow more time to think, laugh, play, or simply be. It could mean entering a new industry, reigniting a beloved pastime, stopping work altogether, caring deeply for your family, implementing new boundaries, or finding some new realm that creates a tangible shift in the world. Whatever it is, be audacious in caring for yourself and fueling that fire inside yourself.

And know this: Work is a part of you, not all of you. Your work does not have to make sense to the world, only to you. I hope you can de-layer, as we touched on in chapter 1, and remove the story that you must hustle and grind and prove yourself. You do not need to prove anything. You only need to care for yourself so you can care for those you love and radiate that energy to your community.

Be bold and surprise yourself, honor your energy, listen deeply, and make yourself proud.

Let your Autumn Queen take the reins, because I know she leads with kindness, strength, and empathy. She has boundaries like no other, responds to emails within her schedule, and never allows work to take her self-worth. She always finds the sunshine.

Your Autumn Queen makes room for the wild, creative, only-makes-sense-to-you feats that can be accomplished anywhere you choose, outside the realms of the metaphorical office, in the wild woods of your messy, complicated, beautiful life.

CONSIDER THIS:

You can break free from society's relentless pressure to "build" a career. Your work life needs to make sense only to you.

All work—paid and unpaid—is valid and deserves respect. The same goes for creative passions and caregiving.

Your health, time, and personal space deserve guardrails, always.

Listen to your discomfort and lean into your powerful Autumn Queen intuition.

Beauty seemed to mean something else entirely to them, something deeper, more internal. They were free.

—SISTER MONICA CLARE

chapter three

On Beauty in Our Forties

Moving beyond industry ideals, tapping into wisdom, and feeling what is real and transcendent

I HAVE BEEN IN THIS LIFE FOR MORE THAN FOUR DECADES, and for three of those, I wished the doughy flesh of my body to be different. I have longed for a gap between my thighs, lamented over the bumps and blotches on my skin, yearned for thick hair and spidery eyelashes, daydreamed about sucking away ponds of fat from my waist, mapped each pore on my face, tilted my head over the size of my breasts, and attempted to suck in my major organs when someone was looking at me.

I have wanted to be taller, thinner, lighter, darker, bigger, smaller, rounder, straighter, and curvier.

Nearly every surface of my exterior has been victim to the knives of my mind and the daggers of the world.

"We can do something about these," an aesthetician said to me a few years ago, pointing to the skin around my eyes that resembled a cat's whiskers. I was there for a facial.

Through this entire book, you and I will see this: fabricated ideals claiming how women should look or be, creating false models against which we compare ourselves. And our appearance gets the harshest gaze. The world focuses on aspects of our exteriors, insisting they must look a certain way rather than appreciating what our physical bodies do. Skin that protects our organs is seen as "wrinkly" or having "fine lines." Thighs that carry us forward are viewed as "too big." These false narratives, weaponized by systems of oppression, plant seeds that grow into trees of self-doubt and later forests of self-loathing.

When I turned forty, I started to feel the weight of these untruths more intensely. But I also began to experience something more profound: a curiosity and expansion peppered with a good dose of rage. Exhausted from playing by the beauty rules and being told I must "age gracefully," I was ready to reallocate the energy I spent worrying about the skin around my eyes to other things. I wanted to divest from feeling like I must do all the "shoulds"—the tricks, procedures, products—as I age and instead lean into what makes me *feel* beautiful. Intensely, wholly, untouchably beautiful.

I'm guessing you've felt this weight. The judgment that can come from comparison or social media. No matter what you feel right now—maybe you fear how your face and body are changing in your forties, maybe you yearn to let go of beauty ideals, maybe you're curious to try filler or a new treatment, or maybe you want to shift your perspective—you and I will explore it all in the pages ahead. We will interrogate the relentless messages that say you must cling to the face you had at thirty, and explore practices to bring you toward what true beauty in your forties is: gorgeous and free and transcendent.

Who Defines Beauty?

Merriam-Webster defines *beauty* as "the quality or group of qualities in a person or thing that gives pleasure to the senses or the mind."

That makes sense. But then I keep reading.

"The quality of being physically attractive."

Okay. But who deems what physical attractiveness is?

In the Western world, women have been sold a story about physical beauty. It's specific: thin, curvy, symmetrical, and kissable with dewy, unwrinkled white skin and an able body. We've seen the variations of this look, this face, this shape a zillion times in movies, TV, and ads. This market-driven, white-centric ideal is a brick wall against which we break ourselves. It's vicious, gendered, ableist, and racist.

It doesn't matter how we look or even if we share physical attributes with this ideal (and I share physical attributes with it). Since we were young, every one of us has been accosted with a standard of beauty. Yet when we worry about this code, when we put energy into how we look, we're called "superficial," as psychologist Renee Engeln writes in *Beauty Sick*.

How can we not worry? We're expected to be time fighters as we fend off absurd ideas that at forty we must cling to the faces we had at thirty. We're expected to be smaller, tighter, younger. With this comes a casino-size buffet of suggestions to suck, freeze, drain, lift, tighten, tone, and sculpt. And if a woman is growing older or is wrinkled, disabled, fat, or bigger than the ideal, she's thought to be less than—or, worse, society mocks her and casts her out.

Our faces and bodies are not barometers of supposed correct or incorrect actions. Yet everywhere we look, from our phones in front of us to the billboards above us, we're told otherwise. "Maintaining our physical desirability is one of our jobs," author and philosopher Elise Loehnen reveals in *On Our Best Behavior*. "We love to judge the worthiness of women on the basis of factors we can apprehend with our eyes, and, in my lifetime at least, that worthiness has been pegged to litheness, a body under control."

To borrow Loehnen's word, my "job" got harder as I grew closer to my forties. My body started expanding more readily and my skin lost some of the manufactured glow I had put copious dollars—dollars I hustled to make—toward trying to achieve. Another reason is that I, like every woman, started to see how the obligation to conform is a job I never applied for but was pushed into. I yearned to let go of all the energy and stress around how I looked. I wanted the angst to be gone. But it wasn't. It was still there, and acknowledging this made me feel like a hypocrite. How can I write about female empowerment when I continue to feel directed by these standards?

I admitted my tension to Carmen Cool, a therapist and body-justice activist. I first learned about Cool and her work while writing my graduate thesis paper on the media's portrayal of women. Back then, the gas in my grad-student tank consisted of anxiety and coffee. I was hungry for sustenance, and Cool's work, which she describes as landing at the intersection of eating disorders, weight stigma, love, and resistance, injected me with the vitamins of a new perspective. The same thing happened when we connected again years later for this book.

Cool told me she has witnessed a tension like mine in her practice. There is a growing awareness of the societal beauty expectations placed on women. However, this awareness can come with shame if someone is unable to break beyond the ideals. We may know the stories are ludicrous. We may know that it's powerful to resist. But it is still. So. Damn. Hard. "There is a lot of 'I think I'm supposed to be a good feminist role model and a body-positive person, but if I don't feel okay, then I feel guilty about the fact that I don't feel okay,'" said Cool.

Her words rocked me. I look around and do see a world pushing against beauty norms. I see women giving a middle finger to the standard by letting their hair go gray, showing their wrinkles, and uncovering their aging, larger, or disabled bodies. And advertisements include a more diverse range of women of various races and with bodies, hair, and faces that fall outside the ableist, white, heteronormative confines. These instances are fantastic, yet they leave me spinning at times. I can't help but see much of this as a performative dance and a perpetuation of society's obsession with women's appearance. When I see, for instance, an older woman in an ad, she is still a stunningly gorgeous older woman.

This all suggests to me that, regardless of whether beauty ideals are evolving, the focus remains on how women look, thereby fueling the prevailing narrative that our exterior is the ultimate currency—and that currency is valued more or less depending on where we fall within the oppressive beauty standards.

I asked Cool more about this. Has society made any progress in terms of women gaining true liberation from the way our faces and bodies are perceived? Or has the resistance or aspects of it, such as the body-positivity movement, missed the liberty?

"I do think there is something about the body-positivity movement that has gotten diluted and moved away from its fat-liberation roots," she replied. "It is one thing to say, 'It's okay to have dessert,' but that is very different from the roots of true liberation that say all bodies deserve to have equal access to resources and a life of safety, dignity, and belonging."

As Cool spoke, she referenced the work of Sonya Renee Taylor, the revolutionary poet, activist, and author who speaks and writes about how society has created a ladder of bodily hierarchy. This oppressive and damaging hierarchy is akin to a ladder on which the world places people's physical exteriors based on age, size, race, sexual orientation, ability, and gender, with certain attributes viewed as better and, therefore, higher on the rungs than others.

"The topic of speaking about beauty, body positivity, and true liberation is all very tricky," continued Cool. "Because we all want to feel attractive. And we don't want to make that a not-okay thing to want or to feel. And also, we can't deny the fact that there is body privilege out there in the world."

I hold on to Cool's use of *feel*: The world we live in is saddled with patriarchal and oppressive standards that eclipse true beauty, and beauty is something for all of us to feel. Deep, poetic, soul-stretching beauty is unique to each person and free. It transcends any ideal that falls within predetermined parameters.

But we are gaslighted into thinking otherwise.

Blatant and Cryptic

In her 2024 book *Unshrinking*, philosopher Kate Manne maps the roots of diet culture and anti-fat bias. She illuminates how the world's belittling intrudes on our lives and reveals the ways we can do the life-stretching (albeit challenging) work of dismantling the oppressive forces that control us. I view *Unshrinking* as one of the most impressive books in the library today. Not only because Manne writes with such clarity and wit, but because she helps us see how the narratives about how we look are so dense and historied that they've formed an ideology.

Manne dedicates a chapter to gaslighting and to how this tactic of emotional abuse, which makes us question ourselves, is a favorite of diet culture. She proposes that gaslighting is a systematic process that works to make us feel defective. "We are told we are pudgy and unattractive, and that nobody will ever love us looking like this," she writes. "We are told we are morally lax. We are told it is all our own fault."

Manne's viewpoint can be extended to beauty culture. When the skin around our eyes wrinkles, we're made to think it's because of something we have done wrong—we laxed on sunscreen, delayed using eye serum, or—oh golly!—forgot to book that red-light facial. Gaslighting underscores most of the ads I see. The cryptic tactics, the ninja language, knock us off our center, leaving us to "scramble for a foothold," as Manne writes.

You might know this scramble. I know it well. How many times have I been moving through my day and (actually!) not thinking about my face or body, when an ad for a cream claiming to rid crepey skin pops up in an article I'm reading? Suddenly I'm wondering if I have crepey skin or need a crepey skin cream, whatever the hell crepey skin is. The message is clear: The beauty industry says I need to "fix" myself, and to do this, I need more—more treatments and products.

Of course, women get the brunt of this targeting. We're sold creams, appetite-suppressing drugs, and serums by companies that tell us we need better skin, smaller bodies, and erased crow's-feet. The marketing is violent and perpetuated by social media. The global beauty industry is expected to generate nearly $590 billion by 2028, as brands are using social media influencers at a mind-blowing rate, with influencer beauty marketing valued at more than $30 billion. Blooming research over the last decade has shown social media use exacerbates the pressures girls and women feel about how they look, fueling body-image issues, eating disorders, and fears around aging. The bulk of the research on social media and its effects has, to date, focused on younger women. But this data gap should not overshadow the truth: More women forty and older are on social media, giving reason to see that "social media use is related to body image among midlife women," a 2024 study showed.

When it comes to cosmetic surgery and noninvasive treatments, the numbers have been rising over the last decade. About 45 percent of procedures are performed on patients in their forties to mid-fifties, but more younger women, those in their twenties and thirties, are opting in. One 2022 study linked young women's reasoning to the "importance of appearance to self-worth, concern with social standing and attractiveness, investment in appearance, media influence on body image, and positive attitudes towards celebrities."

Opting for procedures and surgeries is a right. Whether we are succumbing to impossible standards, how we choose to manipulate our body is deeply personal, and I will share with you my personal story about this soon. But first, it's important to reflect on the data. The rise of surgery and treatments and the effects of social media are continuing to impact women across a broad age range. The reality prompts some deeper questions: Are we doing this for ourselves or for the system around us? And how can we know the difference?

Kate Manne showed us that gaslighting attacks a person's mental freedom, and I can't help but see how every facet of beauty culture does this to us as well. The pain we experience around how we look, whether we're forty or twenty, is rarely about us. It's about the agendas and demands of others', which in turn can, at times, make us lose ourselves.

And it can even hurt our connection to others.

"I'm Getting a Thing Done"

A little over a decade ago, I called my close friend Tim and had an odd and brief one-sided conversation.

"I'm getting a thing done," I said, knowing my confidant since seventh grade wouldn't pry. "It's not a big deal. I don't want to talk about it. I just want you to know beforehand. I'll call you in a few days."

I hung up. The next day, I drove myself to have breast surgery. Except for my friend, I'd told no one. I stretched my credit card limit to hire a nurse to look after me the first night. The experience was scary, lonely, and exhilarating.

It wasn't until about a year later that I divulged my secret to my best friend, Maura.

"*What!*" came Maura's retort when I casually said I had implants. "Really? I had no idea you wanted to do that. Wow!"

At the time, it wasn't about keeping a secret from Maura, an endlessly compassionate friend who knows I am hungry before even I do. (For the record, my friend Tim, who's a man, has never asked what I got done, still to this day.) What was driving me to have an intense, major surgery in secret, without the support of my dearest friend, was an unfamiliar feeling of resistance. I always felt like my looks, my body, were for everyone else—every boyfriend, every gawker, every thread of society. The journey of deciding to get the procedure, from interviewing doctors to charging a credit card to pay for it, was lonely and taxing. But there was also an exhilaration to it. Doing this quietly, for solely myself, felt like galloping a horse along a sandy beach. I'll do what I want, I thought. Making a drastic decision with no one weighing in felt revolutionary, as selfish as it was. Thankfully, I healed quickly—a huge privilege, just as paying for it was, even if I had to do it in years' worth of installments.

But as worthwhile as that journey has been, an aspect of it makes me sad. I missed out on having the support of a loving friend, someone who has never judged me. Why did I feel the need to keep my procedure so close? It was shame, I've come to realize. Society has acculturated us women to feel we must look a certain way, but then when we make choices to modify ourselves, we're talked about, ridiculed. How many times have you heard (or maybe said) "She's definitely had work done"? I've said it—and I hate that I have.

A 2021 study examined the psychosocial consequences of aesthetic procedures. It shows that women seeking plastic surgery are subjected to less than positive perceptions by others. So, we're damned if we do . . .

There is another take, however: A different study revealed that women who have undergone elective procedures, ranging from noninvasive treatments to cosmetic surgeries to more, have experienced a deeper sense of self-satisfaction and happiness. In the months following my surgery, I started to hold my head a bit higher. I landed an on-air anchor job and relocated to a new city. There is no way to prove a link between my procedure and landing an anchor gig, but the act of doing something for myself fueled my confidence. Now in my forties, I've come to see that entire experience as an attempt to honor myself in an entanglement in which I wanted to feel safe.

The world of beauty and its ideals is a cacophony of opinions telling us this and shaming us for that, all engineered so we stay obedient and veer from our inner fire and intuition. And often we do stray. We buy products and get procedures in the hope that the results satisfy the other, which is commonly the capitalistic male gaze. We're also seeing that true safety aligns with true beauty, however, which is something we can feel and hold within ourselves. We are seeing how when we listen to ourselves and tune out the noise, we honor our energy and gain power. To fuel this new paradigm, we must cultivate greater compassion for ourselves and one another.

We must aim to make one another feel safe—which is how I felt when I chatted with Sara Wyle. Open and kind, refreshingly irreverent, Wyle talked about motherhood, partnership, and all the weird pressures that come with growing older.

As we sat on the phone, she reflected on turning forty several years ago and how she felt about no longer being "the youngest person in the room," as she put it.

"I'm enjoying this whole process, but I also am very bothered when people say, 'Oh my God, you're forty-three! You look so great.' Because I think, What does forty-three look like?" said Wyle. "I do try hard to take care of myself. I take care of my skin. I try hard to eat healthy to live a healthy, long life with my family. But I'm so bothered by that comment."

The skin on my arms prickled. "I am too," I responded. "I am too!" Then I asked her what she hoped more women our age talked about with one another, especially around our beauty routines, procedures, and even health.

"You know, there's a weird gatekeeping that sometimes happens with women," she replied. "I wish it wasn't like this. I'm kind of the person that if someone is like, 'Oh, wow! Your skin looks good,' I'm like, 'Here's exactly what I do.' I just want to be completely honest about everything. So, I wish we just talked about it more. All of it."

A few weeks later, Lindsey Marie reflected a similar sentiment. The founder of Powerhouse Women, a global community of women aimed at fostering connection, Lindsey Marie has a knack for getting to the emotional point and inspiring women to boldly and loudly act in alignment with who they are. I get fired up when I talk with her.

Lindsey Marie told me that she craves "more open dialogue" from women around procedures, treatments, and other beauty rituals—conversations where we openly share the tricks we choose to use and what we've learned. She sees these conversations anchored in vulnerability and empowerment, where they range from "I feel great about making that decision for myself" to

"Here's what I wish someone would have told me before I was five years into a Botox journey."

"Now, I also honor that that's someone's business if they want to share it or not," she continued. "But I would love more transparency, so we all don't think we're going to age like J.Lo. And even to remove the shame around it."

As I sat on the floor listening to Lindsey Marie, I marveled at how so many women have shared with me a similar desire: We want to feel camaraderie around the decisions we make about our appearances. We want to feel safe. We want to feel free. We want to feel together.

When I spoke about all of this with these women, and when I looked back at when I told Maura about my procedure, their understanding began to melt my angst about my looks in this cruel world. Their shared experiences and fears, some similar to and some different from mine, began to build a life raft that I can see myself climbing atop when the waters of my forties get rocky.

To change our bodies is personal. To partake in procedures and rituals is a right of every woman. In this life, we are all attempting to make our interiors, our wild, sexy, erotic selves, match our exteriors. That is the human experience, and to merge these two parts of ourselves, we must feel safe in one another's company. Unjudged and unfettered. The *you do you* cliché, as platitudinous as it is, is one I stand by if the doing is truly for you and not society's gaze. One barometer to help us decipher our motives can be one another. We can be more open, supportive, and caring when it comes to the pressures we feel around beauty. We can share honest feedback and experiences, which is in our nature. We can give one another grace.

The other barometer is you. Allowing yourself the space to

recognize how codes embedded by the beauty industry are showing up in your life can be a ticket to a new freedom in your forties.

And you and I will explore how to do that.

Beauty Is Personal

For decades, I believed I needed to "keep up" my appearance. Rituals touted as self-care or personal maintenance felt like side hustles—getting manicures, touching up my highlights, making sure my eyebrows were plucked. The simmering heat telling me to, again, "keep up" with these practices seemed to zap their pleasure. Most times, doing these things felt less like taking care of myself and more like taking performative measures to satisfy a judge who was waiting by my door, eyeing me up and down as I went into the world.

Naomi Wolf first got me thinking about the deeper layers underneath my need to satisfy. The feminist author posits that the societal claim over women's appearances is about control and denying us social freedoms. "A cultural fixation on female thinness is not an obsession about female beauty but an obsession about female obedience," she writes in *The Beauty Myth*. Wolf helped me to exact the deeper seed of what I have experienced when I worry about my appearance: a *subservience*.

From this relentless feeling of subordination comes shame, which philosopher Clare Chambers details in her book *Intact*. The world is always telling us our bodies are never good enough, feeding us the narrative that "the body must be constantly modified to remain true to itself," she writes. "Our bodies are always under surveillance, must always be camera-ready—only now, the camera *always* lies. No image is left unfiltered; no photo is left unshopped; the ultimate act of courage is to post without makeup."

Chambers's words are true and heartbreaking, as they illustrate the struggle perpetuated by beauty culture. They're also incendiary and clarifying. She illuminates how "the choices we make about our bodies are inevitably shaped by our social context, and the norms we find there." When so many of us feel shame or feel bad about our bodies, and the ideals we're up against vary depending on gender, race, age, and ability, there is a larger issue at play.

Tucked throughout the lines of Chambers's work is a push for a revolution. When we look at the coercion and the stories, we see how blatant they are. We gain clarity when we interrogate the system feeding us these stories. Those ads making us feel like shit. Those products telling us we're broken. That "antiaging" jargon leading us to feel like turning forty is a fault. They're part of a larger discriminatory system telling us lies.

I feel a similar protest brewing in my body when I read the work of journalist Natalie Angier.

In her book *Woman*, Angier notes how our bodies have been "abominably regarded" for centuries. "[A woman's body] has been made too much or utterly ignored," she writes. "It has been conceived of as the second sex, the first draft, the faulty sex, the default sex, the consolation prize, the succubus, the male interruptus. We are lewd, prima bestial, ethereal. We have borne more illegitimate metaphors than we have unwanted embryos."

But Angier brings us the hope, reminding us that we can see all of this differently.

"But, women, we know how much of this is trash: very pretty, very elaborate, almost flattering in its ferocity, but still, in the end, trash," writes Angier.

What Angier shows us is that we've been taught to perceive our beauty through a lens that tells us what we "should" look like. But this dirty glass is an illusion that has nothing to do with our true beauty and what we want deep down in our bones. As we age, we begin to protest. We challenge stories and stretch our boundaries. I love how Emily King, a money mindset coach, put it when she and I spoke for this book: "Who the fuck gets to dictate what we have to look like?"

I feel a similar protester fire in the countless women I talk with out in the world. I also felt it in every interview I had for this book: At one point, someone brought up the standards of beauty, usually without being prompted. The comments touched on the frustration, heaviness, and sadness. But in nearly all circumstances, they expanded to include sentiments that illustrate the iconoclast in each of us. We all know that no woman, not a single one of us, belongs in some drawn beauty box.

Women's coach Rae Leslie put a clarifying spin on this topic. She reminded me of the force that comes for women in their forties. We become more discerning. "Self-care and beauty in your forties are going to look different because you're going to feel different," she said. When we pay attention to how we are evolving, we move from a place of allowing the beauty messaging to run us to one where we invite our personal beauty desires to inform us. The distinction is between reacting and responding. We can start to lean into the latter by reflecting on what makes us feel beautiful and alive.

A Beauty Ritual Inventory

Let's put this distinction into practice. Take a few minutes to reflect on the beauty rituals and routines you follow. Consider the entire spectrum, from care and grooming practices, like washing your face or shampooing your hair, to more aesthetic-focused practices like painting your nails or having your eyebrows microbladed. Think about things you do daily, weekly, monthly, and yearly.

Now put yourself in the moments of doing these practices. Consider your feelings while doing them, the time they take, and the results they merit. What things do you enjoy? What do you look forward to? How do they make you feel? Healthy and cared for? Beautiful and strong? Sexy and vibrant? Do these practices, routines, or treatments invoke pride in honoring your body?

Next, go deeper. What practices do you not enjoy? What feels like a burden or chore—and why? How do you feel during and after? Do you feel disconnected from yourself? Do they feel like something you must do to "keep up"? Does the time and money spent on them seem worth it or taxing?

The goal is to tap into what leads you to feel beautiful, cared for, and alive. Too often we engage in routines and purchase products because they have been marketed to us, pushed into our minds as something warranting a permanent place on our top shelf or in our schedule. But there is no one-size-fits-all approach to beauty. As you reach for products and engage in routines, let the above questions guide you. Tap into your Autumn Queen to see what makes her feel gorgeous. Deeply, purely gorgeous.

"If you sit with yourself and listen to yourself, you'll see what really works for you," said Leslie, adding that your routine may look wildly different from those around you.

"It's private," she continued. "And it's yours."

Language Matters

If I were to credit one woman for edifying me on the dark alleys of the beauty industry, it would be Jessica DeFino.

"I don't have these rose-colored glasses on about the beauty industry anymore," DeFino, an award-winning journalist and widely respected beauty-industry critic, told me.

Early in her career, DeFino was a beauty editor in the most conventional sense. She tested new products to report on their alleged glow, plump, and gloss. A self-described former "product obsessive," she was deeply entrenched, working at public-facing brands and publications. Then she began to examine how the industry was affecting her—physically, mentally, spiritually, and financially—and made a change.

Today, DeFino authors one of my favorite newsletters, *Flesh World*. Her voice, which reporter Janna Mandell described as giving "the middle finger to the entire beauty industry," is an electrifying compass pointing us all toward the truth. Her essays are thought-provoking, lending a raw vocabulary to the violent lengths that much of the beauty industry takes, from the toxic (and double) standards woven into marketing jargon to the relentless pursuit of monetizing one's self-worth.

Despite being a dissident for years now, DeFino admits she's still shocked by some of the things she sees. "How do brands still feel so comfortable with blatant ageism? We all know this, but something that I don't think is talked about enough is that anti-aging is just the physical manifestation of ageism," she said. "It's a system of discrimination."

DeFino's comment makes me think back to my conversation with Carrie Hammer, when we talked about beauty, autonomy, and de-layering old stories from ourselves. Hammer was the one who first pointed out to me the ludicrous and downright lie behind the term.

"You cannot anti-age," Hammer told me. "This is against truth in advertising. It's not just 'Oh, we're selling things.' It's also sociologically extraordinarily damaging. You're harming the fabric of society."

What Hammer points to is law. The Federal Trade Commission mandates that advertising must be truthful and not mislead us, and this goes for any product—a beauty cream, a serum, a face wash—claiming to stop the natural act of aging. A solution may soften the appearance of wrinkles, but it cannot anti-age anything inside or outside us. In 2014, the Federal Trade Commission called out cosmetics giant L'Oréal for creating advertisements that were deceptive and not backed by scientific proof, ultimately causing the behemoth to settle.

In 2017, *Allure* magazine vowed to its readers to no longer use the term *antiaging* in its publication. "We are making a resolution to stop using the term 'anti-aging,'" then-editor Michelle Lee wrote. "Whether we know it or not, we're subtly reinforcing the message that aging is a condition we need to battle—think antianxiety meds, antivirus software, or antifungal spray."

Lee's later sentences really got me. "Language matters," she wrote. "When talking about a woman over, say, forty, people tend to add qualifiers: 'She looks great . . . for her age' or 'She's beautiful . . . for an older woman.' Catch yourself the next time and consider what would happen if you just said, 'She looks great.' "

For years and years, psychologists have researched the idea that language, the words we use to describe ourselves and others, can be a powerful mechanism for shaping the lives we lead. Subtle shifts in how we approach discussing our appearance as we age can enhance our self-worth, expanding beauty from something prescribed by others to a force we feel within ourselves. As Lee suggested, there's freedom found in dropping the qualifiers and turning the language away from age ("Not bad for forty-five!" or "She looks younger than forty-eight") and toward an eternal sentiment ("You're glowing" or "You're beautiful" or "You look so happy"). The energy goes from reactive to proactive. From vapid to deep.

Let's Go Easier on Ourselves and One Another

Jessica DeFino told me, rather passionately, about the many opportunities women have to be kinder and more giving to one another. "If you just go through the Instagram comments on any famous woman's posts, you can see that so many of the negative comments come from everyday women all over the country and world—and we've internalized these messages, and we're spewing them back at each other," she said. "It's an epidemic. We can ease up on each other."

She quickly added that the larger structural forces that embed these beauty beliefs into society, such as the companies that disseminate the marketing, have a responsibility to do better. But within our reach, we can make a positive difference. "A lot of beauty culture is passed between our immediate spheres of influence. Let's give each other more room."

Carmen Cool believes in the power of creating intentional spaces. So common is our tendency to cut ourselves down when we gather—"Ugh, I hate my thighs" or "I look so fat"— that we forget we're doing it. In instances where there's a history of harmful rhetoric, perhaps with negative beauty comments or shameful body-image talk, she suggests taking a proactive approach and declaring the space a zone of safety and kindness. If it helps, you can use explicit language, such as "We have an agreement that when we get together, we won't put ourselves down or say things that are ageist or fatphobic" or simply "Let's go easy on ourselves here."

These spaces are not meant to muzzle discussion. They are wide open for us to talk about our insecurities, fears, and frustrations, Cool clarified. The emphasis is on reducing the default of negative self-talk and breaking the relentless cycle of harm. It is to move away from criticism—of one another and ourselves—and expand our tendencies toward compassion, acceptance, and joy.

Additionally, we can explore different questions to ask one another. Cool urges us to consider inquiring what is sacred and divine within each of us. We can ask one another: What beautiful thing happened in your life today? What's on your heart this week? What is making you feel free?

When we open ourselves to the deeper aspects of our lives, we see how much more there is to consider than the skin on our faces or the size of our thighs. And the truth is, we might be disappointed in our skin or thighs. "And that's okay," said Cool. "We don't have to love everything all the time. But this is about: What else is happening with me? What are the parts of me that I want to be known?"

Our Beauty Today

Making conscious shifts in how we approach our faces and bodies in our forties—moving away from shameful talk, being discerning in the face of marketing, easing up on one another—can lead to new paths of feeling good and open. Rather than living from the outside in, this is about living from the inside out, free from rules, navigated by an experience of beauty no standard can touch.

I've come to see beauty in my forties as an energetic exchange. There's a giant force trying to rob us of our worth, confidence, and self-esteem, leading us to be reactive and feel small—exactly what the beauty industry wants. But beyond this, there's the grander, wiser spiritual energy of our Autumn Queen. The industry is no match for her. She sees the smoke and mirrors and chooses to align with the practices and products of her choosing.

Jessica DeFino reminded me of the power we hold in the face of the industry. When we examine the beauty-culture conditioning and the marketing messages that say younger is beautiful, we can see just how distorted this messaging is and how it is not a reflection of one's worth. "That makes it even easier to divest," added DeFino.

Much like the beauty-ritual-inventory practice we explored earlier, reevaluating products and practices has been tremendously freeing for DeFino. "There were points in my life when I was wearing a full face of makeup every day, even just to go get toilet paper from CVS," she said. Part of "divesting from the industry" and caring for herself today has meant challenging herself to consider: Where can I let go of a product? And where can I let go of an ideal?

DeFino was quick to clarify that she wasn't suggesting that we all stop participating in the beauty industry altogether. "I'm still a woman in the world," she exclaimed, adding that she wears makeup depending on the circumstances. Participating in certain aspects of beauty culture may make women feel safe, especially if we feel that we'll be judged or marginalized for not adhering to the established beauty standards of a particular situation. Makeup, skin care, and procedures can also be a form of self-expression. "But for me, I've been working on myself in other ways so I can let go of some of those superficial coping mechanisms that don't help me," she added.

There's a freedom found in DeFino's words. I, too, wear makeup. I love natural skin care. And I am open to and curious about tools, tricks, and procedures. But I am done being duped, controlled, or made to feel less worthy if I don't buy into every product, practice, or hype. I no longer want to hustle under the misapprehension that I will not age well or "gracefully," according to the standards of an industry that thrives on my insecurity. I want to live in a world where we are less prone to giving away our precious worth to the outside and more willing to refocus our attention to the reality of our beautiful lives. In my forties, I want to see the impossible-to-clone beauty in every woman and have that reflected to me.

"The most beautiful women I know are so uniquely themselves," Carrie Hammer told me. "And it's hidden in the word!"

"What is?" I asked Hammer.

"Be you," she replied. "Be. You. Ti. Ful. Are you freaking kidding me? It's been hiding in the word the whole time!"

There it is. *Beautiful.* I love this word, even more so now in my forties. I want to be beautiful, in a way that is whole and different and me.

I want to feel beautiful. Experience it and cherish it.

I realized my yearning thanks to Tara Mohr. Mohr explained that within us is a desire to reach for "the sacred and good in our human existence." We all have a thirst for aliveness. What becomes problematic is when we equate having these qualities with looking or being a certain way.

"Underneath our dislike of aging and our desire to look younger, there's a healthy instinct getting distorted and confused—the instinct of wanting to experience beauty in all kinds of ways and to embody vitality," Mohr told me.

The key is to infuse our lives with moments and practices that bring us this aliveness—which, in turn, will embolden our experience of beauty. This can be laughing with dear friends, going dancing, working in the garden, or soaking in the rain. It can mean painting, singing, or meditating. Or it can mean lifting your face to the sun.

These are simple practices, but they can have immense power to help you tap into the transcendent experience of beauty—a truth that always lives inside you, free from the confines of industry ideals. Mohr's insight suggests that rather than something to perform, beauty is innate.

As Mohr and I spoke, my mind wandered to moments I feel beautiful. I think of cracking up on the floor with Maura, having dinner with my friends Tiffany and Arlene, or dancing by myself. In these moments, I don't think of the skin around my eyes or of my changing body. I feel beautiful. I feel alive.

My friend Megan O'Neill exudes aliveness. Being around her, I feel beads of sweat pool on my skin as I watch her glisten. The woman moves with intention and gorgeousness. Take her words she posted on her Instagram:

"Very into 40. Extremely into being a woman. Extremely into being a Black woman. Those have always been 2 particularly difficult things to be, respectively and much more so together. But the perspective I have, what I can so clearly see from this special perch, is a superpower. This continues to be a hard time for women and an even harder time for Black women. But I love existing, I love being here, and at 40 my goals and wants are a little more crystallized."

When I called O'Neill to hear more about what she loves about "being here" in her forties, our conversation naturally went to beauty, not just because she's spent much of her career working as a beauty and culture editor but because her take on the subject transcends boundaries. She didn't talk about makeup or tips; she talked *feeling*.

"You know, I do care about how I look, and I do care about feeling beautiful," she told me. "And I find it in self-expression. That is big for me. I love fashion and style. Getting dressed really matters to me. It helps me move through the day in a more authentic way. Every day is a bit of dress-up."

O'Neill went on to tell me about other things in her life that make her feel strong, sexy, and capable. She loves to move, "to stand on her head while wearing a leotard," and cook nourishing meals for herself, her husband, and her children. I was smiling on my end of the phone. And then O'Neill dropped her last thought on what she's striving for now in her forties: to break free from the industry-fueled, patriarchal male gaze and move toward a deeper self-expression, one where she doesn't feel she has to look left and right for approval.

"To truncate things, I want to wear a thong on the beach and be comfortable with it," she said. "I just want to feel greeeat in my body to such an extent that I'm not conscious of how I look to other people. I want to be self-contained in my confidence, self-actualizing, and not to live off compliments. I mean, compliments are great; it feels good to get a compliment, don't get me wrong, but I want to internally know who I am and not rely on them so much.

"I don't know. . . ." O'Neill continued. "Maybe the thong on the beach is irrelevant, but it's like a metaphor for me. I want to be that comfortable."

Her thong represents freedom. It's a link to living embodied, sweet and salty in our autonomy. In my forties, I am moving toward this feeling, more and more every day.

Reallocating Our Energy

I know, truly I know, all this is easy to write and harder to live. Even with the sunshine of divesting from products and pausing to consider our routines, there will be clouds. Dismal, dark clouds. The messages around us will continue to scream. I hear them often. The comments that pop up in my head are mean and blunt: "You don't look how you did a decade ago" and "Wow! You look tired." But I remember: These are thoughts fueled by a system. They are not truths, and they have no bearing on my essence.

Tara Mohr has a helpful in-the-moment practice for when you feel these self-limiting messages take hold: Notice and name the thought. You can say to yourself, "There it is again, I am being critical about my face" or "I'm having another aging fear—hi, aging fear. I see you. You're allowed to be here, but now I'm going to turn my attention to other things."

Mohr explained that for many of us, that critical inner voice has become our default background to the extent that we don't notice or question it. But when you name it, you shift from identifying with it to observing it. Doing this helps you gain distance from the thought, reminding you that it is not the voice of truth.

There is also immense power in recognizing where you direct your energy. Mohr said we spend a significant portion of our resources—our time, money, and mental energy—satisfying commodified, expectational ideas. "Imagine if we bundled all that energy," she said. Imagine if we as women spent the time and money allocated to procedures and products that we don't truly want and instead put them toward the things that make us feel healthy and secure.

Imagine directing these efforts toward our passions and communities.

Mohr's insight reminds me of the work of Renee Engeln. The psychology professor and body-image researcher writes about the cost of "beauty sickness"—when a woman's emotional energy gets so focused on her looks it become harder for her to see other parts of her life. "Beauty sickness matters in part because it hurts," writes Engeln. "But even more important, it matters because it's hard to change the world when you're so busy trying to change your body, skin, hair, and clothes. It's difficult to engage with the state of the economy, the state of politics, or the state of our education system if you're too busy worrying about the state of your muffin top, the state of your cellulite, or the state of your makeup."

Vanessa Cornell actualized this when we spoke—and she offered a reminder about how we can learn to live differently. She told me how growing up, and through her twenties and thirties, she was aware of the attention she received because of her looks. As she grew older, the shift was palpable. "I remember kind of feeling a loss or a lack," she admitted. "Then I realized: We spend so much of our life searching for that kind of attention because we've been given so much feedback that it's important."

Cornell continued to say how much of our worth and value can be tied up with how the world perceives us. Whether we are considered attractive or not, beautiful or not, these external validations can carry weight. But we hold the power not to let them.

"We get to a place where we get to actively choose to put that aside and say, 'There needs to be room made for other parts of me to be recognized, acknowledged, and valued,' " she said. "I think it's a very powerful thing that can happen with women in their forties. We can start to cross over. We start to say, 'You don't get to have that power anymore. That's old news. I've got so much else going on.' "

Go Toward Her

In the Pulitzer Prize–winning novel *The Goldfinch,* author Donna Tartt writes, "Whatever teaches us to talk to ourselves is important: whatever teaches us to sing ourselves out of despair."

I want you to find ways to sing yourself out of despair and feel the beauty inside you.

For me, reevaluating the world of beauty in my forties has invited me to sing to myself. To check in and slow down. I revel in taking pauses and getting myself to neutral before buying a product or going down a tunnel of negative self-talk. Beauty, according to the standards, has always felt like a destination you eventually arrive at. If you do all the right things—the conforming, the dieting, the obsessing, the creams—you'll get there. I see now there is no there. There is only here, the present moment with our beating hearts.

I want to be in the here with my body and my face. I want to move toward what feels peaceful, nourishing, and beautiful. In doing this, I feel steadier, less prone to bruising. I choose to exist in a world that appreciates my beauty.

So, I release my grip, a bit more every day, and listen to the primal energy of my Autumn Queen. She guides me in the morning and at night. As I wash my face, she tells me to lean into the water with intention. As I press nourishing oils and lotions made of natural shea butter, flower essences, and aloe onto my face, chest, and thighs, she reminds me to thank my muscles, skin, and body. As I dot my cheeks with a rosy balm in the morning, she encourages me to smile and see the crinkles around my eyes as years lived.

My Autumn Queen tells me to carry myself with pride and care for my host with joy.

Now is the time, in your forties, to lean into deep appreciation for your beauty. You've lived so much life; I can see it. You've listened and learned, nurtured and helped. You have all this wisdom. I urge you to let go of any suffering the world has caused you and go toward your beauty.

And when you feel pressure around you, take a minute to see what beauty ideals you might be laboring for. If you're looking to buy a new product, have a procedure, or take a medication, gift yourself a moment to first pause. Take the time to ensure it is for you and only you. And then move toward what makes you feel alive.

If this feels overwhelming, Tara Mohr recommends her Inner Mentor tool. Visualize your older, wiser self, maybe twenty or thirty years into the future. The woman you hope to be one day. Think: How does she care for her body? What does she do for joy? Whom does she surround herself with?

"When you do this, you connect to a vision of the elder spirit in you that's not a culturally conditioned image," said Mohr.

I'd love to practice this tool with you right now. Close your eyes. Think of yourself at eighty years old. Where are you sitting? What are you wearing? How do you care for yourself?

Can you picture her?

I can. She is calm and strong. Her energy is steady. She turns her head to look at you.

"You are of the angelic," she says to you. "Pull yourself from the fire. Go outside. Lift your face to the sun. Feel your beauty."

CONSIDER THIS:

Beauty ideals are fabricated by a system. You have the power to make decisions to satisfy your heart and desires—no one else's.

When you are having a negative beauty or aging thought, name and acknowledge it. This will remind you that the thought is not the voice of truth.

Consider the resources you spend on satisfying others' ideas of beauty. How can you allocate that energy toward things that make you feel beautiful, whole, and alive?

You embody beauty. And you deserve to feel it, always.

What would happen if one woman told the truth about her life?

The world would split open.

—MURIEL RUKEYSER

chapter four

Hitched to Our Truth

A deep look at sex, partnership, friendship, and single life

WHAT SURPRISED ME WAS HOW MY "YES" FELT: AS IF IT WERE a dormant piece of my body jolted awake. My response was physical and giving. The question Will you marry me?, which came from my partner, Christian, that early morning as we pulled off the mountain path we were climbing with four-wheelers, was something I never knew I wanted until that second.

Having been in several long relationships before, I'd had boyfriends broach the subject of marriage. There were no formal proposals but casual mentions: "If we were to get married . . ." or "Maybe when we're married . . ." The few times I heard this, I felt as though I had chicken pox again. The idea of marrying them felt unsafe and stifling.

This time, the thought of marriage came unexpectedly and warmly. I had no inkling Christian would ask. We hadn't discussed getting married. All I knew was I wanted to share secrets with him I'd previously wanted to keep to myself—and I wanted to do that with him forever.

Before that moment in the mountains, I'd been with Christian for three years, yet he was on my mind for more than a decade. Ten years before our first date, our mutual friends began trying to get us together. We lived in different cities, each of us deeply ingrained in our lives, uninterested in anything long-distance. Our mutual friends kept mentioning him to me—until he and I finally collided at said friends' wedding. That night, we stayed up talking, dancing, sharing stories with each other. The following day, we returned to our lives thousands of miles apart. In the years that followed, I would often fall asleep thinking of him, sometimes next to a man I was dating. My skin would burn with a yearning for the peace I felt when he and I were together.

Our partnership began six and a half years after the night at the wedding, when the logistics of our lives synced. He and I were living in the same city and were both single. Months prior, I had left a relationship that shredded my self-esteem and bank account. As Christian and I dated, I realized it was the first time I wanted to lean in with someone and offer more than the caregiver, please-everyone part of me. I wanted to reveal the mess and imperfection that didn't make it through my skin (and a lot of my mess was already evident). I wanted to take care of myself and speak up. Our days dazzled and challenged me and brought me to my knees in self-acceptance.

But through all of this, I never thought we'd get married. I was fresh in my forties. I don't need marriage, I thought. The idea scared me. Initially, I attributed this dissonance to my dismissal of the institution. Why does society always expect a woman to marry, have a wedding, and do all these things? But none of this came to mind when he asked. I just thought of me and him.

An odd sensation came over me, however, in those first few days of being engaged. It was as if I had stumbled upon a realization that provided a metric for understanding. As we called friends and family to share our news, we started talking about when we'd get married and how and where.

"We could have a few small dinners in different cities," Christian said, mentioning Pittsburgh, Boston, San Francisco, and other cities we'd lived in.

"We could have a big barbecue in Montana," I replied.

As we discussed wedding logistics, my stomach churned. I felt dizzy, and my elation deflated. That was when I realized the expectations that were weighing on me. I wanted to be married to this man. I did not want to follow the made-up rules on how to do it.

"I'd get married next week," I said, a day later.

And that's what we did. I had just turned forty-three and was wearing a ninety-dollar dress and cowgirl boots, surrounded by three family members and Montana's Sapphire Mountains. I embodied my Autumn Queen, saying yes to something sacred I had only just realized I wanted. All the while, I was saying no to what had burdened my mind until then: the idea that it all had to look a certain way.

Before we continue, I must admit to you that I wrestled with sharing that story. I wrestled with it because I have wrestled with people's tales of proposals and marriage. I know it's because the world has endless opinions about women and partnership that continue to whip the frothy lie that our worth is contingent on our marital status. Stories about relationships and weddings often reek of achievement and roles that feel stifling and distant. They promote ideals that have never resonated with my heart, although I yearned for love.

In my forties and through conversations with women, however, I have come to realize that the truth of how we partner and not partner today is undefinable, evolving, and wholly our own. We continue to face scripts that prompt us to compare, as we have explored so far in this book. Yet there's so much more truth and light to hold. We all yearn for what we have desired for millennia: the sense of being on the receiving and giving ends of unconditional love, free from the worry of labels, embodied in our truth, and loyal to ourselves.

So, whether you are seeking to stay, enter, or leave a relationship, yearning for love, engaging with multiple partners, grappling with a swell or lack of desire, or simply longing for profound connection in any form, I hope you find solace in this chapter. We'll shed old stories and explore the world of connection—in its intimate, physical, spiritual, and platonic forms—as women in our forties today.

We'll start with what has scared me for four decades.

The Commodification of Marriage

Several years ago, I was scrolling through Instagram when I came across a post that felt as though it had slapped my face.

The post was a picture of a woman I know. She was wearing a

wedding dress and standing in front of a mirror. The caption read: "I did something crazy today . . . I tried on wedding dresses for the first time in my life. I am 32 years old . . ."

The caption continued, "I have waited for him all these years."

I felt as though a Slinky were in my belly. A mix of sadness, confusion, and envy filled my chest. She did something crazy? my then-thirty-nine-year-old mind thought. *All these years?* You're only thirty-two!

What added to my dismay was how I was feeling all this over a post by a woman who is wonderful. (Here's the dark side of social media again!) The sensations flooding me felt odd. I had never salivated at the idea of getting married or having a wedding. Why was I feeling this heat, especially toward a post about a kind person who looked happy?

After ruminating for a few minutes, I continued scrolling. But I never forgot about that post. If that woman felt she had to justify her timing to the world at thirty-two, then what should those of us older than her be feeling? Why is there a clock set, ticking in front of women's faces?

Social media abounds with conflicting superlatives about marriage and the rituals surrounding it. Instagram alone is peppered with hashtags, with many millions of posts stating #JustMarried and #WeddingDress and #HappilyEverAfter. On the other end of what I'll call the wedding-marriage spectrum are millions more for #Divorced and #Separation and #DivorceAdvice. Then there are hundreds of thousands for #SingleForever and #NotGettingMarried.

Countless people have something to shout about their marriages. And in America, the wedding industry seems to be fueling the screams.

The multibillion-dollar behemoth industry is a subset of sectors that capitalize on the fantasy of making one day—or weekend, or even, oh golly, an entire week—the most memorable of a woman's life. (I say "woman's life" because the industry continues to be ever so gender slanted: The idea within a heteronormative couple is that the woman, the bride, is at the helm of all the excitement and planning.)

In 2025, the average cost of a wedding hovered around $33,000. There are the photographer, the floral designer, the wedding planner, the venue and food, the dress, the tuxedo, the invitations, the favors, and the cake—to name a few of the noticeable lump of boxes the industry tries to enforce every engaged woman—and couple—to check. The dizzying array of commodities and ideals eclipses the very act of love it's supposedly championing. "No one wants to find fault with anything so cheering, and so emotionally significant, as a wedding," writes Rebecca Mead in *One Perfect Day*. "But at the same time, weddings often prompt a sense of disquiet—all this, just for one day?—among the guests, and, when they will admit it, the couple at the altar."

People's decision whether to partner and how is one of the most stunningly scrutinized, commodified, and dissected of a human's existence. Marriage is personal and impossible to qualify, but it is still relentlessly . . . qualified. You marry "just in time" or "young" or "later" or "quickly," "quietly," "finally," "happily," or "swiftly," or whatever thought the world wants to adhere to a person's conventional union. Marriage is a magnet to which others' adjectives stick—and for straight women, the expectations and opinions are glue.

"Don't you want to get mayyyy-reed?" an aunt of a man I dated in my thirties once asked me in her thick Boston accent.

"What are you waiting fahhh?" I didn't have the heart to tell her I was trying to get out of the relationship with her nephew. But I steeled myself and replied, "Maybe one day!"

The scrutiny that surrounds a woman who isn't married, whether by her choice or not, is wild. I'd say it's the definition of insanity. Whether I was dating someone or not, I often felt like I was walking through life with a yellow sticky note on my forehead that read, *I'm unmarried, so keep your questions coming!*

"Do you think you will? Do you want to?" were some of the questions I'd field when I was single. Or if I was in a relationship that lasted more than a month, the old "Think you guys will get married?" took the prize.

Society has no interest in understanding that a colossal life change cannot be summed up in a trite, satisfactory answer. Maybe a woman is uninterested or unsure; maybe she's dealing with loss or an abusive situation. Maybe she's financially unstable, searching, lost, found, happy, satisfied, unready, or skeptical; maybe she is not in love, is totally in love, or hates the institution of marriage, or a million other reasons that cannot be reduced to a succinct response. Whatever she is, why must the world demand an answer? As Lyz Lenz aptly writes, "Very few people will look at a couple and ask out loud why they got married. But they will ask every single person why they aren't married yet."

The world tells unmarried women that they're broken. Society assumes and organizes us in uncomfortable, socially constructed categories. One category is deemed "right." The other is for the outliers, which I felt I'd always been. This likely explains why I experienced a pang of envy when I saw that woman's post about her wedding dress. There were countless times in my twenties and thirties when I just wished I could feel different about marriage and the hoopla surrounding it. There were times I wished that I wanted to want what society kept pushing my way. There were times when I wished I wanted to be part of what movies, policymakers, relatives, ad agencies, religious leaders, and romantic comedies touted as the ultimate North Star. There were times when I wanted to want to lean into what was expected of a straight woman like me. It would have been easier to subscribe to the story.

I just never could.

That is, I never could subscribe to the neat, binary, gendered, heteronormative track that Western society has deemed acceptable not only for marriage but for the recognition of love. And not only for the recognition of love but for the recognition of women. Marriage is beautiful. But the pressure to enter marriage in a certain way, by a specific time, is unbearable. And the fact that it has been historically exclusionary to people of color and marginalized communities is horrific.

The question I keep returning to is: Why must unions between people come saddled with stipulations, ideals, and a clock?

The Illusion of Choice

While I have struggled with the parameters placed around marriage, I have always believed in love. Deep, soul-stretching, mind-blowing love. The hard part has been that reigning view of partnership, intimate relationships, and love has been cleaved into two camps for women: married or unmarried. Society aggressively encourages us to think that one is better than the other. Often our families and friends add to this pressure. My mother always applauded my decision "to own my autonomy," as she's put it. Still, for so long I felt left out because of the cultural assumption that women should be married or, at minimum, partnered.

Kristen Genzano, a Portland, Oregon–based women's therapist, told me that however we feel about being partnered, women are continually conditioned to feel they must justify their standing. Our families, cultures, friendships, religious groups, and even current partners teach us so much about who we're "supposed to be," said Genzano. "All of these places and spaces influence and shape us."

Emphasizing this sting are the prevailing attitudes around being single. Society has created an existence where being unpartnered leaves people vulnerable. There are no tax breaks or honorable mentions for being on your own. And if you're a woman, society views being unpartnered with a lingering disdain. Whether or not a woman wants to be single, her intimate relationship status shouldn't warrant approval or mandate her rights and safety.

Journalist Nicola Slawson writes candidly about how the narratives around single women are often steeped in shame and negativity. Additionally, she points out how many of these stories perpetuate the misconception that everyone is in a relationship, perfectly partnered up and happy.

"It's ingrained in everything," Slawson told me when I interviewed her in early 2025 about her book, *Single*. She pointed out that the messaging starts early, as images of parents and family units are woven throughout children's books, just as "Save that for on your wedding day" language gets tossed around so casually. It places blame and makes women feel like they're doing something wrong or are out of sync.

"For ages, I wouldn't talk about how long I'd been single. I was ashamed about it. If anyone asked, I'd be vague," Slawson continued to tell me. "I didn't want to talk about how it felt when, slowly, my friends started partnering off one by one and things were getting serious with their partners. You have this horrible feeling of being abandoned. And there's a feeling where it makes you question yourself."

I felt as if Slawson had pulled those words from my own heart. These messages do make us question ourselves. Even if we're resolute in wanting to be unmarried or unpartnered, there remains a constant reminder of our status. As my friend Katie put it, why is it a default to ask someone if they're married or have children when you're meeting them for the first time?

"I mean, this is all part of our societal norms, but that's literally the first thing people ask: 'So, hey, you married?'" said Katie. "It's like, really? That's it? That's what's interesting?"

I met Katie years ago while we were working at the same company. She has always captivated me with her frankness and warmth. "I feel like it would be more normal to ask 'What kind of stuff gives you energy?'" she continued. "'What do you like to do?' Those things, I think, are more interesting."

To know Katie is to know she bleeds love—for her friends, her family, and her wife, Erin. Before getting married, the two were in a long-term committed and loving relationship. They wanted to keep building a life together, but following any "timelines for heteros," as Katie put it, wasn't all that compelling. When they signed their marriage papers in 2020, their rights were in focus. Justice Ruth Bader Ginsburg had just died, and the two fretted over a retraction of gay marriage—a fear that looms today. "Honestly, we did it for the legality of it and to make sure we had protections," Katie told me.

When I asked her if marriage and kids were pushed on her growing up, she said they were an expectation, given her Catholic upbringing. "It was never overtly said that 'You are going to do A, B, and C' but there was kind of a presumption that I would follow this set pattern and indeed want to get married—and that I would marry a man because, you know, that's who you marry!"

When Katie was fifteen, she told her mother, with whom she's always been close, that she was gay. And while her mother eventually came to realize "that marrying a dude wasn't going to happen," Katie said the question of having kids continued.

"For years and years, she would ask, 'Do you think you want to have kids? Do you think you're gonna have kids?' I was like, 'Wow! When will you stop asking?' And finally, she stopped, but it wasn't until I was in my late thirties," she added. "I think my mom had a life she expected where her kid was going to not be gay, for one, and would marry some guy and then have kids. And that just was never on my agenda."

Katie's clarity inspires me, and her story reflects an energy I felt in my conversation with Lyz Lenz. A journalist and author of several books, including the fiery bestseller *This American Ex-Wife*, Lenz imbues her coverage of issues that impact women with an unapologetic feminist perspective and has notable writings on marriage, motherhood, and women's rights.

I called Lenz to ask more about her perspective on marriage and divorce today. I began our conversation asking her about the idea that women often need to justify their life choices. "Yeah, but you have to wonder if it's actually a choice if we have to constantly defend it," Lenz responded. She told me a story about a recent conversation she'd had with a woman who was considering whether to keep her last name after getting married. The woman's male partner had told her to do whatever she liked. A seemingly supportive and innocuous statement, the man's comment infuriated the woman. "Because he had the choice to be ambivalent!" Lenz told me. "It didn't matter to him because no matter what happened, he wouldn't be the one defending if he was married or not. It wasn't even something he had to think about."

The woman had gone on to tell Lenz that she didn't want to have to constantly justify and defend every aspect of her life. She just wanted to live. Lenz told me it was that very comment that articulated something specific to her about choice.

"You just want to live your life but can't because you have to defend it," she said. "You have to explain why you aren't married. You need to explain why you don't have children, or if you do have children, why you stopped at, say, one or two. It never ends, and it makes sense why people resort to default behaviors that are patriarchal in norm and practice, because it's so exhausting to fight to just live, to work, to afford your rent and groceries, and in the middle of all that, we have to swim against the patriarchal current?

"So that's something I think a lot about—that *illusion* of choice," she continued.

A Changing Culture

When it comes to marriage and partnership, women are constantly negotiating with themselves, trying to close the gap between the connection they covet and the disappointments they experience. Old societal stories perpetuate the notion that when there is imbalance, unhappiness, and dissatisfaction in a partnership, the fault lies within us. And we feel we must fix it. While it's true that every partnership contains a universe of tension points, the attitude that women must grin and bear a bad or unsatisfying union, in any form, is harmful and wrong.

It is evident, though, that women are speaking up in partnerships and marriages, demanding equality, leaving, or opting out of unions. It's gorgeous to see.

The American marriage landscape is changing. Fewer people are getting married. Mindsets around the institution are shifting. In America, people are "more pessimistic than optimistic about the institution of marriage and the family," states a 2023 report. The average age when people are marrying for the first time is increasing. More Americans are choosing to partner without getting married, and an increasing number are opting to remain unpartnered.

The stat that really gets me, though, is about divorces. Women initiate approximately 70 percent of them.

There are numerous reasons why people get married, ranging from religious beliefs, economic security, and companionship to social pressures, the desire for children, or pure attraction, just as there are countless reasons why people get divorced, remain single, choose domestic partnerships, embrace polyamorous lifestyles, or something else. Regardless, women are rowing away from the main current to follow different streams thanks to the forces of feminism and the upsurge of challenges to binary gender roles and expectations.

We are unpacking thousands of years of conditioning that have told us we're only worthy of marriage and motherhood, sex therapist and relationship counselor Cyndi Darnell told me. There is continued pressure to justify our choices when they seem to veer from the conditioned norms. But we're "choosing to not indulge in it," she said, adding that this iconoclastic approach is fiercely evident in those of us in our forties.

"There is certainly something that happens with women forty-plus, where the narrative changes," said Darnell. "In the twenties and thirties, a lot of [the questions], especially for heterosexual women, are around how do I get a good partner, how do I attract the right partner, how do I keep the right partner, what am I supposed to do in a relationship. That shifts dramatically in the forties."

According to Darnell, some questions that begin to rise to the forefront of many women's minds are: Am I content with the decisions I've made? What do I want now, at this time in my life?

I became fascinated with Darnell's work when I read her 2022 book, *Sex When You Don't Feel Like It.* Darnell helps us understand why we have sex, offering a nuanced take on true eroticism and pleasure and the layers of deep intimacy, both with ourselves and others. Ecosystems away from any center-the-man take on sex, her insight shows us that a connection to our erotic energy is the key to deeply understanding what activates us, in and out of a relationship. Her work illustrates how if we want to enrich any aspect of our life that involves *us,* it is essential to first build a rich relationship with *me*. It can be life-shifting to pause and really ask ourselves, What do I want in a relationship? Thanks to our social conditioning of centering everyone else, it's common for us to overlook this question.

In your forties, asking yourself this question is an embodiment of your Autumn Queen. So, I want to invite you to lean into this inquiry, and consider asking yourself the following:

What do I need from partnership?

What do I yearn for in partnership?

How do I want to feel with someone?

Is the partnership I seek sexual? If so, how do I want sex to feel? What do I want to experience?

Taking the time to reflect on these questions after turning forty brought me a great deal of understanding. All the years prior, I had jumped into relationships I thought were right, but they had centered only the man I was with, and I never considered my true desires and needs.

What Do You—Really Truly Honestly—Desire?

Our forties bring a time of reflection and expansion. We evaluate the choices we've made and those we haven't, and as we've been exploring, this questioning often touches on our relationships with others.

When I spoke with women in their forties about partnership and sex, the responses created something resembling a Jackson Pollock painting. Our desires are vast and rich, and our yearnings explosive.

One woman told me she has little children at home and barely any time to be intimate with her spouse, but her sexual fantasies are blooming. Two others are recent empty nesters exploring the opportunity that comes from more room in the house. One woman who recently divorced is jumping in and out of dating, while another is jettisoning dating for occasional casual sex. One woman I spoke with anonymously told me that all she wants is "rough and hard sex" with strangers, though she continues to love her husband. Another who has shared her bed with men most of her life told me she started yearning to be held by a woman.

It took me forty years and countless efforts to realize my main ambitions for intimacy are to feel free, seen, beautiful, and desired. I was always so consumed by pleasing the other person (sound familiar?) that I forgot about my body and needs, sometimes disassociating to get through sex. Yet when I was alone, I yearned for physical connection, using my hands and mind to live out what I wanted to happen in real life. Having faked roughly 90 percent of the "orgasms" I'd had with men (I say "90 percent," but it was likely more), I felt like my fantasy of orgasming authentically and consistently with someone was asking for a first-class trip to Utopia.

Then I got with my husband—and a million things collided. First, and most importantly, I had started to do the work of asking myself what I wanted. And he was the first person who asked me what I liked. What I honestly, wholly liked. Also, when we got together, I had a fuller cup of self-awareness and fewer inhibitions, all of which I chalk up to being older. I walked into a new sexual realm that left me gasping for breath it felt so good. So insanely, unequivocally, vulnerably good. At first, I gave him the credit: "You know my body better than I do!" But he countered, saying my pleasure was because of me.

He was right. I knew my body and what I wanted. And, finally, I was learning how to ask for it. My Autumn Queen was speaking up.

I am not alone in my intimacy and sexual revolution. Droves of women in their forties and older are getting it on in the way they want to get it on. And droves of women are letting go of sex.

As I was working on this book, several new stories came into the zeitgeist that captivated me, two being *All Fours*, Miranda July's impossible-to-put-down novel about a mid-forties married mother who goes on a road trip and has a sexual awakening, and *Want*, in which actor Gillian Anderson invited women to write anonymous letters about their unabashed sexual desires. "We had received enough entries to fill at least eight volumes," Anderson writes in the introduction of *Want*. "Clearly, there was a need."

I interviewed Anderson for an article around the book's publication. She revealed that the topic of women's sexual fantasies gets her emotional because it transcends sex. It's really about liberation.

"How we ended up with the title was innocent," Anderson told me. "It wasn't manipulated. It came innocently, but it is everything. And this is being distilled to encourage women to look at what they want, not just under the covers, but from their lives, and what they want from other people in their lives."

During my conversation with Cyndi Darnell, I mentioned these media examples and asked for her take on women claiming sexual and intimate space in the public sphere more recently.

"We have been seeing this for years" came her reply. She provided additional titles of women in their forties and older who have taken on adventures—sexual and otherwise—over the last several decades, from the 2019 series *Mrs. Fletcher* (based on a book from several years prior) to *Thelma & Louise* in the early nineties and *Shirley Valentine* in the eighties.

"There have been these sort of cult narratives of women getting into middle age and just spiritually saying, 'Fuck it all,'" Darnell said. "And I think we need more of it."

Within this fuck-it-all theme, there is a deeper thread. Darnell brought me into her practice for a minute. She told me she'd been working with a hetero couple who had been married for twenty years, and the woman had recently taken another lover. The marriage wasn't bad, and the couple's story was still evolving. But what was noteworthy was the reason the woman took the lover. The woman wanted more—and she wanted something different.

"I see this happening a lot, whether it's women taking other lovers, or taking other lovers of a gender that they're familiar with, or experimenting with other sexualities," said Darnell. "It always seems to be a surprise when women are like, 'I don't want to do it how we've been doing it,' but women have been saying this, certainly, for over the thirty years I've been doing this work. It's just the degree to which we tune into it and listen to it."

This all brings me to the work of Lisa Diamond. A psychology and gender-studies professor, Diamond has studied how society's long-held assumptions that a person's sexual orientation remains constant over a lifetime fall short. In her groundbreaking book *Sexual Fluidity,* Diamond posits that love, desire, attraction, and sexuality for women can be fluid, not rigidly straight or gay but rather a truth that evolves as women move through life, circumstances, and relationships and come to know themselves more deeply.

Her book, for which she studied more than one hundred women, illuminates how women have reported "shifts in their sexuality over time," including women who identify as heterosexual falling for female friends and those who identify as lesbians dating men. While a long and dated macro view presumed these cases to be few and exceptional, Diamond saw otherwise. She continued her research, and as other research increased, she illuminated how sweeping conventional wisdom about the nature and development of sexual orientation provided an "incomplete picture of women's experiences."

It has been nearly twenty years since Diamond began her research, and she continues to advance her work today, incorporating insights from the evolving landscape of gender, sexuality, and identity. While there is still a lack of formal studies on whether more hetero women are choosing to date or marry women today, what is unequivocally true is how none of us is baked and done in a life. We evolve and change, unearth new desires, and tread new paths. Three women friends of mine, who had historically only dated men, started dating women in their late thirties and forties. They seemed free and happy, safe and excited, and unencumbered by the need to label their choices.

There is self-expansiveness in our culture, and a yearning to break free from qualifiers—even if the world still has other things to say.

Kameko Grant told me she's experienced a backlash when she has switched from being with men and women throughout her life. She had children with a man, then solely dated women for thirteen years, until her late thirties when she fell in love with her now husband, a man.

"People said, 'We knew you weren't a real lesbian because you had kids with a guy before,' " Grant told me. "I'm like, why? Why do we have this need to put everything in a little box, label it, and judge it?"

When women get to talking about labels, our energy tends to lift out of our skin so sharply you can almost hear it crackle. We're too multifaceted to be told we must carry one qualifier at a time, too complex to present as this one thing when inside us is a symphony. Society likes to tell us we're the ranch wife and mother, when, really, we are the cowboy, outlaw, lover, fighter, pioneer, lawbreaker, settler, and wanderer all in one.

"We're taught to be, now you've got on your mom hat, now you've got on your lover hat, now you've got on your daughter hat," Molly Roden Winter told me. "It's as if we're trained for this panoply of roles, and there's not a lot of modeling of the integration that being a whole person requires."

The air felt warmer when I listened to Winter, a talented author. We spoke shortly after the release of her memoir, *More*, in which she details her and her husband's journey opening their marriage to other partners. Droves of women grabbed *More* from the shelves, devouring Winter's stunning words that shatter the fallacy of what makes a fulfilling—and acceptable—marriage. The story she tells is, on one hand, straightforward: It's about polyamory, which she and her husband embarked on consensually as a means of "fun escapism," as she said. But her pages work your soul on a deeper level. They're a passport to a place where a woman is pushing against expectations, claiming her desire, and showing her countless threads.

"One of the beautiful things that happened to me during all this is I started learning to be my full, authentic self all the time," Winter told me about the process of sharing her story so publicly. "I'm feeling closer to a place where all the pieces that used to feel very compartmentalized now feel integrated in me."

Winter didn't know that opening her marriage would lead to her discovering her full, messy, authentic self. She started writing *More* in part out of curiosity, to see if she could map how she evolved from here to there. Friends had commented on how much more expansive and freer she seemed. When she detailed her journey on paper and talked about it openly with others, it became "even more of a living-out-loud kind of situation," she said—something that she wishes for every woman to have.

"Women are all supposed to be serving, and we're not supposed to be physical or even sexual or have anger or needs, to some degree," said Winter. "But this isn't good for anybody. We are all people, and every single one of us needs to have the full range of human experience."

The full range Winter refers to is one that doesn't cement itself in binaries. Our worlds are constellations, and our sexual and relational lives are a universe.

And it is our calling in this life to fully express ourselves, which includes tapping into our desires, revealing what we want, and grabbing it with both hands.

Discovering What Makes You Feel Good

Here you and I are, exploring the terrain of honoring our true selves within the context of sex and partnerships and intimacy. Before we keep going, I want to check in with you. This topic is weighty. It can be both fun and heavy. Whatever you are feeling, be with it and know you are okay.

Now, let's go deeper. Let's discover what makes you feel good. I shared with you how I felt sexually and emotionally free with my husband, but the truth is, I still want to go deeper. I still need to continually work to excavate my desires. Part of this work includes honoring my fluctuating hormones and changing body, embracing the intense waves of wanting to be sexually intimate and of not wanting to—and, wow, do these ebbs and flows come!

I want to delve deeper into myself and explore what I love, both alone and with my partner. I believe this is work we all must do, however we relate to others. Part of our evolution as women in our forties is to stoke our fires and say, "This is what I want."

I reached out to Sinsia for guidance on how to get there and how to start exploring our minds and bodies more deeply. Based in the Netherlands, Sinsia, who prefers the pronouns *they* and *she*, is a somatic sex coach who works with individuals and couples around the globe to help them tap into a sexual life anchored in choice and truth. It was the combination of their title, the Queer Sex Coach, and the gentle words on their website that put me at ease when I contacted them. My sense of comfort doubled when I met with Sinsia over Zoom. They sipped tea and took thoughtful pauses as I asked my questions.

In their practice, Sinsia sees bigger societal messages and patterns interfere with people's true desires. For women, the need to please people and "not take up too much space" is a common barrier. Still, they say the messaging impacts anyone, regardless of gender or sexual identity, and it can cause people to stay "small" and retract into themselves in and out of the bedroom.

Sinsia believes that exploring physical touch alone is a beautiful way to begin discovering how to receive pleasure and take up space in the bedroom. To do this, they suggest the following practice informed by an exercise called Waking Up the Hands, originally developed by bodyworker and somatic sex educator Betty Martin as part of her framework, the Wheel of Consent, created to help people understand the dynamics of receiving and giving.

Leaning into Touch

First, make yourself comfortable in a safe, quiet place, preferably alone. This might be your bed or a cushioned place on the floor. "You want to signal your body that it's okay to relax and just feel," Sinsia gently instructed. "Make a point of seeing if you need to lean back or get another pillow. And ask, Am I warm enough?"

Next, grab an object—it can be anything you can hold—and move it around in your hands. Do this for several minutes. Pay attention to what you feel. Go slowly. Allow the nerve endings in your hands to awaken. Notice what sensations arise in your body and where they are located. What feels really good? What do you want more of?

As you continue this exercise for several more minutes, notice if certain feelings in your hands link to sensations in other places. Maybe you feel a warmth in your vulva. Maybe you become aware of your stomach or thighs.

This exercise is simple but powerful because we feel so much with our hands but rarely pay attention to what we're experiencing, Sinsia told me. "The more you can wake up those nerve endings, the more you can actually *feel*. Then you start to notice what you want." Sinsia said this exercise helps get you out of overthinking and into presence with your body. It unlocks the beauty of noticing. From there, you can explore and change according to what feels good to you.

"If we can do this with our hands, then we can start to do it in interactions with others as well," they added.

While Sinsia's counsel explores the unlocked potential from physical touch, our minds can also be a place to take a journey. And fantasy can be a gorgeous guide.

In *Sex When You Don't Feel Like It*, Cyndi Darnell helps us understand why this is so. She illustrates the Core Erotic Theme, an idea created by psychotherapist and sex therapist Jack Morin that illustrates how the unique blend of who you are, what you believe, and what your sexual experiences are, in combination with your imagination, helps you identify what sparks your erotic thoughts.

To find what ignites you, Darnell expounds on Morin's suggestion to go deep into your body and mind. First, she suggests taking three deep breaths to relax your body.

Next, float imaginatively through time to recall some of your favorite sexual experiences. These can be drawn from real life, movies, or your imagination. Then choose one fantasy that really resonates and reflect on what stands out. Ask yourself:

What makes this so exciting?

What are the conditions that enable this to play out?

What is it about the situation, the people involved (if there are people), and what they're doing that arouses you?

Write your answers in a journal. (I jotted down notes in my phone when I first read Darnell's book.) Don't hold back. Let it rip. There's information here that both touches on and transcends our sexual lives.

"The beautiful thing about fantasies is that they are in the safety of our own head," Cyndi told me. "They show you the parts of yourself that need to be soothed, healed, revealed, known, seen. We don't have to do anything with them. We can if we want to, but they're not necessarily literal translations from life. They're symbols, and so the symbolism of our fantasies can give us insight into what our heart is longing for and what our soul is longing for."

As I listened to Darnell, I was reminded of a line from an anonymous woman's letter in Gillian Anderson's *Want*. It reads, "I guess my number one fantasy is to be made to feel like I am utterly desired. Not because it's just another naked body, but because it's me and my body."

What a truth.

No matter our age, we all want to feel like our interiority matches our exteriority. Since being in my forties, I have felt a deeper urgency for these two parts of myself to match. We owe it to ourselves to go deeper, listen to our erotic self, and take accountability for what we yearn for—because in doing this, we find threads of freedom throughout our entire lives.

The Beauty of Leaving

Our forties mark the beginning of building a richer relationship with ourselves. As Cyndi Darnell told me, it's about asking, What do I want the next twenty or thirty years to look like?

This question will evoke something unique for each of us. It might elicit the desire for more adventure, downtime, intimacy, closeness, learning, laughter, or a million possible other experiences and feelings. As you reflect more deeply, notice the people who come to mind. Who do you want to share these experiences and feelings with? How do these people show up for you? Answering these questions might call for getting closer to your partner, entering or exiting the dating scene, spending more time with yourself, or putting more effort toward friendships.

And it might mean leaving a partnership or marriage.

That last one—leaving—always gets a bad break, especially

when it comes to exiting a marriage. For too long, society has stuck divorce with the words *failure* and *bad*. Divorce is grave, there is no doubt. But the reasons for a marriage ending are as unique and complicated as each of us and therefore belie trite qualifiers and outsiders' opinions. Divorce is the result of a constellation of issues and it affects every woman differently, considering her abilities, socioeconomic status, desires, and health. Sometimes, a divorce can mean heartbreak, other times expansion. It can happen in ways that defeat, puzzle, sadden, embolden, or free a woman. What is important is that we see how the end of a marriage (or partnership) is like the waters in a river, flowing both away from and toward something.

For many women in their forties, divorce coincides with colossal life changes, including an evolution in their bodies.

As we know, our forties mark the arrival of perimenopause for many of us. This time of our lives—which we will talk more about in chapter 6—can be filled with emotional and physical symptoms, such as anxiety, insomnia, and mood swings. If we are in a close relationship with a partner, there is little doubt that these symptoms will impact that dynamic. In 2022, the United Kingdom's Family Law Menopause Project conducted a survey that found 73 percent of women attributed perimenopause and menopause to the breakdown of their marriages. Farhana Shahzady, a family-law specialist and mediator, spearheaded the survey to raise awareness about the changes women undergo and how family law needs to take these into account when dealing with divorce, separation, and related issues. We need to talk about this reality more.

We also must consider how our forties bring with it a host of other massive responsibilities, involving shifting work lives, growing children, and aging parents—all of which can impact a partnership.

But just as an end to one's marriage can mark hardship, it can be a doorway to new joy. Danielle Gates told me that getting divorced opened new worlds. Having grown up in a household where it didn't "matter what you want to do career-wise, your focus will be to get a husband and have a family," she married a man in her early twenties. "So, when I did get married, I had my husband's life, not my own," Gates told me.

The beginning of her marriage "was really fun and great," she continued, but things began to fall apart. She and her husband grew in different directions, no longer sharing the same values, and, ultimately, there was even cruelty near the end.

Gates told me she was initially scared when she first knew her marriage was ending. Her identity was inextricably linked to her relationship. But then she began to widen her scope and refocused her thoughts away from the loss aspect and toward all the potential gain that could come from stepping away. So, at forty-two, she left her marriage.

"I had the opportunity to rethink it all and what kind of example I wanted to be for my daughter," she said. "I felt like a forty-two-year-old twenty-one-year-old. It ended up being great—and I wouldn't change a thing."

As I previously stated, women instigate most divorces today. This truth first came to my attention thanks to Lyz Lenz, one of many women who have publicly revealed the liberating and hopeful sides of ending a marriage. Her divorce proved to be a wide aperture, a path toward equity and joy. "What we wanted was to be free," Lenz writes about the countless women who seek to exit their heteronormative marriages. "I noticed patterns, too—these weren't just stories of women falling out of love, but of a political and cultural and romantic institution that asks too much of wives and mothers and gives too little in return."

Lenz's writing calls for a connection—a deeper, noninstitutionalized connection—to ourselves and a life that centers our souls. Marriage can be beautiful and hopeful. The problem arises when a marriage strips a person of their joy, freedom, dignity, and overall well-being. In those latter cases, divorce isn't just an exit. It's a new portal of safety and dignity.

"Look . . . our lives are extremely precarious," Lenz told me. "We're little spiders on the edge of a windy cliff. We could get blown off any second, and I just think we don't have that kind of time to waste, living in service of anyone else's happiness but our own. It's so easy for women to sacrifice themselves on these pyres, thinking that that's what a good life is. But I have a mother. I never wanted her to sacrifice like that. I always only wanted her to be happy. And I have children, and I know that's what they want for me."

When I hung up my call with Lenz, all I could think of was my mother. I still shiver at the thought of me walking into our home and seeing my father sitting on the couch in shock after she left. It ripped me, and the wound hurts. The pain is not for my mother's leaving, however, but for the years she spent contorting herself to stay (and for the patriarchal expectations that landed on my father as well).

My mother deserved to be free, as every woman does.

These stories tell of gumption and truth. They also tell of physics, because when we move in a direction, we may be heading away from something, but we're also moving toward something else. As Cyndi Darnell points out, our forties are a time we inch in the direction of ourselves. Into focus comes the question What will I value in this time of my life, in terms of my health, joy, work, and relationships?

For the last part of that query, Darnell sees a theme.

"For a lot of women in this mid-trimester of life, they're not focusing on intimate partnerships and they're not focusing on monogamy," she said. "They're focusing on their friends. They're focusing on building community."

Making Friends in Our Forties

As I was writing this book, my husband and I moved from San Francisco to the Pacific Northwest. The change satisfied what we had been seeking: closer proximity to nature, a pace notches below the city, the ability to afford a bit more space. We landed in a quaint home on a quiet street. In the early mornings, my dog and I go out onto the wet grass. I look up at trees cartoonishly big, as though they're from the pages of a Roald Dahl book. I have met a new peace here.

But the first month rocked my core. I sat in the backyard and cried—sobbed, really. Even though I've moved twenty-six times in my life, changing a home is always harder than expected. Still, this move was more intense. This was surprising, because the location offered me the things I'd been wanting, so I couldn't figure out why I kept crying.

Then one day, I looked at my phone log. I had called Maura, Tiffany, Justine, Maura again, Cat, my mother, Maura again, Sarah, and Maura again—all in four hours.

I was lonely.

My husband was going into an office, but with my job being remote, I was at home writing, which was different than when I'd previously moved to new cities and worked in an office or studio. We loosely knew a few people, but no one we had a direct link to. One evening, I saw two women walk by our house. I looked at Christian and let out a hiccup-burp sound and yelped, "Do you think they want to be my friend?" It took physical willpower not to run out my door, thrust my body in front of them, and say, "I'm cool, I swear! Let's hang out!"

We need our friends. Our deep-in-our-soul, life-enhancing friends. Yet society doesn't recognize this as an essential thread in our quilts. Friendship is as important and valid as other intimate-partner relationships.

It was Marisa G. Franco who pointed out to me that we thrive from three types of connection: intimate, which comes from a very close connection with either a partner or a best friend (or both); relational, which links to our wider friendships; and collective, which speaks to our community. Franco, whom I interviewed in 2023 about her book *Platonic*, told me we can feel lonely if any one of these types of connection is missing from our lives. She sees this happening a lot—so much so that she believes our society faces "a friendship famine."

"So, we need friendships to feel whole, to feel good and connected, and to be at homeostasis," Franco added.

Actor and comedian Lane Moore shares this thinking. When I interviewed Moore about her book, *You Will Find Your People*, she spoke passionately about how society has a "flawed system" that is overly focused on partnership, leaving out the importance of friendship. The problem is that whether we're partnered or not, all our connection needs cannot be met by one person.

"So many of us have spent so much of our lives focusing on whether we have the perfect partner because we're told that that matters and nothing else," Moore told me. "But even if you do get into a romantic relationship, you still need friends!"

What I appreciate about Moore's book is how it also emphasizes the hardships often found in making friends, especially as we get older. Similar to my early days in the Pacific Northwest, I have faced deep loneliness other times in my life. Having left my home state of Massachusetts when I was twenty-three, I always lived thousands of miles away from Maura, my closest friend since grade school. I met incredible women and forged new friendships. Some stuck, and some withered. But the more I changed jobs and cities, it became challenging to build a nearby community of women.

"That is a big quality-of-life issue that does not get talked about enough," psychologist Maya Borgueta told me. "A lot of the women I work with have relocated from where they grew up, or they tend to move around a lot, and it can be hard. Loneliness and isolation are huge for women today."

Borgueta specializes in working with women and nonbinary individuals, with the majority of her clientele comprising women of color, queer women, and first- and second-generation immigrants from diverse backgrounds. She said many women she works with feel lonely, even when they do have people in their lives who love them. That is hard in and of itself but what can make it even harder is a sense of shame women feel around this loneliness.

"There's the feeling that if I don't have a solid group of friends, or I don't feel like I have people I can open up to, that it's on me. That's a failure on my part," said Borgueta. "It becomes very hard to talk about."

Borgueta's sentiment landed in my bones. At times, I have felt minuscule when watching a TV show about a group of women who gather for their weekly lunch. It's expected that we all have a baked-in social group, that a sisterhood of women magically forms, and it's easy, perfect, and effortless. But the reality? Having friends, as well as making new ones, takes effort and consistency, the right circumstances, a little luck, and a complementary desire. Sometimes these things line up. Other times they don't.

When I asked Lane Moore if she had any advice for making friends as an adult, I found her response surprising and refreshing.

"I don't like oversimplified advice," she told me, adding that she believes people have grown tired of hearing they must make friendship-making a full-time job. "But it is beneficial to think about what we really *want* in a friend and what fills us up. Too often we tend to think that friendships are about whoever comes along and chooses you. Instead, I remind people that you get to choose."

(She also told me that her best friend is her dog, Lights—a truth I can get behind.)

Let that sit for a second: You have agency in your friendships. You get to decide what you want in your connections with people in your forties, so lean into that.

If you're still curious about how we make friends, especially as grown adults, consider Marisa G. Franco's insight: One step is to engage in things that require "continuous interaction and shared vulnerability," two points she credits to sociologist Rebecca G. Adams. Essentially, the goal is to create a container that allows you to connect with people organically over time. This could happen in a million ways. It could mean joining a weekly or monthly group, becoming part of a coworking collective, attending a regular event, volunteering at an animal shelter—truly, whatever speaks to you. Franco said you want to create the infrastructure that enables you to visit consistently over time while engaging in something you love. When we repeatedly see people, much like we did in school, "we have this unconscious tendency to like them," she said.

Franco's other piece of wisdom really resonated: She advised assuming good intent and thinking positively. Humans have a negativity bias, which leads us to believe that people will reject us. The reality, however, is that we tend to do the rejecting first, which causes people to respond similarly. So, flip the script. When you're open, you naturally encourage others to be open. "People are a lot less likely to reject you than you think they are," she added.

I followed Franco's advice after I moved. Crying in my backyard felt . . . awful, so I decided to open my home to women in my neighborhood and host a casual afternoon tea. Then I thought, How the hell does one do this without any names or phone numbers? I went analog. I wrote a short memo saying, *Hey Neighbor! If you're in the mood for some banana bread and a hot cup, come to my home this Saturday for a women's tea.* I kept the time short, noon to two, and the agenda simple: Swing by, say hi, and kick back for a bit. I printed out fliers and, for three nights in a row, walked my neighborhood to put them in mailboxes. (I felt like I was nine years old selling Girl Scout Cookies.)

"Will anyone come?" I asked my husband in a mild freak-out.

"They'll come," he replied.

A few days later, twelve kind, open, amazing women were sipping tea in my living room. We shook hands and hugged. We laughed. My windows fogged up. At one point, when we were all sitting close in a big circle, one woman who'd been living in the neighborhood for more than a decade leaned toward me and whispered, "This is really wonderful."

It was. But I don't want this story to come across as excruciatingly noble. I hope to continue building relationships with these women, but it's too early to tell. (I also see that putting a note in someone's mailbox isn't an option, even a safe one, for everyone. I would have thought of something else if I'd still been in San Francisco.) But what felt good to me is how I put myself in motion: I assumed good intent, as Franco recommended, and in doing this, I learned more about myself. As much as I yearned for my longtime close friends, I was craving to know more women around me, even just to wave to as they walked by my house. I needed collective connection.

One morning, I chatted with writer Jillian Sanders, who offered some beautiful insight on friendship. She and I talked about our forties and maintaining close relationships during this time. Like me, Sanders lives in a different city from her close friends. The fact that she is so far from her confidants used to bother her, but now she puts energy into planning trips to see them. In between these journeys, she stays connected through regular video calls and texts. And she relishes doing things alone.

As she spoke, Sanders emanated a sense of peace and ease. She seemed connected to herself, and I told her so.

"I have really grown to listen to my body," she said about being in her forties. She went on to tell me that when she was younger, everything was so "fast"—building her career in big cities and making friends. Things happened quickly and hastily. She admitted she often sought approval and wanted to be part of every friendship and circle. It was exhausting.

Now, living in a smaller and quieter city and having gained more wisdom, she has slowed down and tapped into herself. She is more grounded and extends this quality to everything in her life, including her relationships.

"Even now, when I'm at a table with a group of women I've just been introduced to, I will sit back and observe more," said Sanders. "I'll see where a conversation is going, I'll take a sip of water, I'll take a minute, and I'll check in with myself."

Though it has taken me decades to see, I will never be able to unsee this: If there were a proper measuring tool, you'd realize the alchemy of true friendship begins with knowing the gold you have within yourself.

Like Sanders, I see my true friendships and community in my forties as both essential and different than what they used to be—because I have changed. I am more mindful of what I seek and need, steadier in my approach, and more aware of what I want and what I can give.

I hope you can see this in your life in your forties. Friendship is beautiful, yet when it is forced, it can be an energy racket. Listen to your Autumn Queen. Lean into your vulnerability and compassion, take chances when it feels right, and hold tightly to your values. I know connection can be tough; there is nothing shameful in this. We all experience it. I believe every one of us faces loneliness, whatever our relationship or friendship status may be. This feeling can inch toward you like a Midwestern storm, thick with coal-colored clouds.

But you are not under a storm. You are a complicated, gorgeous woman moving through this rumpled thing called life, navigating other people doing the same, and weathering the ebbs and flows of connection.

And you are forever in the company of your most loyal friend: you.

Treat her well.

What Does a Risk Look Like?

The word *risk* holds a lot of weight. It can portend change and growth, freedom and expansion. A risk can transmute something into a new realm. I love this word and what it means—and I love even more how often the greatest of risks, those that stretch us the most, are seemingly the smallest when they happen.

Sometimes they are imperceptible.

Two of the most significant risks I have taken involved leaving relationships. One with a good person whose values differed from mine. The other with a man who would stab the air with his index finger as he stood in front of me and scream into my face. It took me more than a year and three attempts to leave the first relationship. I stayed because I felt there was something wrong with me for wanting to leave. I second-guessed myself when he responded, "What is wrong with you?" after I told him things were not working. Then, one day, I got into my car and drove away, saddled with regret for not doing it sooner.

It took me longer to leave the second relationship. Every time that man yelled at me, I could see his father yelling at him. I could feel his pain, so I carried the abuse he suffered. *I can't abandon him; I can't disappoint him,* I thought. Then, one early morning,

I crept outside our apartment as he slept, clutching my puppy while I waited for my friend Cat to get me. As Cat and I drove away, I looked out the window, lightened by the relief I was safe and burdened—yet again—with regret that I had not left years earlier.

Like so many of us, I stayed in those relationships because I thought it was the noble thing to do. Because I thought leaving would be seen as weak and unkind. Because I did not want to disappoint people. Because I believed that I, a woman of a certain age, unpartnered in this patriarchal world, was the problem.

Never again will I believe these things. Never again will I disappoint myself or the people I love.

I see so many women following this pattern for themselves.

"I think about all of the relationships I've been through, and some have been really good, but many have ended in disappointment," author Katrina McGhee told me. "I am now in my mid-forties, and I am really looking more deeply at commitment and relationships and what that means, and also what will it require of me at this stage of life?"

McGhee, who is upbeat and so fun to talk with, has always "believed in love." She told me that throughout decades of dating she had always grappled with both wanting partnership and worrying how she might have been playing a part in some of the disappointment she experienced, especially as she saw so many of her friends partnered.

"I was always feeling like there was something wrong with me because I couldn't find a relationship that made me feel good," she told me.

McGhee started to realize that there was a deeper, more nuanced reality behind the "happily ever after" she was witnessing.

While lots of people she knew were in good relationships, many were in partnerships that were mismatched and unhealthy or that left them feeling lonely, although they were reticent to leave. And she thought: Why aren't we talking about this more openly?

"I just really wish there were more honest conversations about the sacrifices we make to be partners, especially as women in hetero relationships," she said.

As we spoke, McGhee laughed. "I'm going to be the most depressing interview for your book!" she said. I told her I saw the opposite. I saw a woman taking a risk to look at what we as women continue to face—a structured story that tells us we must be partnered, no matter the cost, and we must endure dissatisfaction (or worse). I witnessed her stepping into her Autumn Queen and taking a discerning look around her. I heard strength in her voice.

"It just feels like at this season of my life, I have so many things. I have my peace, and I have the ability to do things on my own," she said. "So I have to ask myself, Will I still get more out of doing the work to be in a relationship versus being on my own?"

When I spoke with therapist Kristen Genzano, she told me that more and more women are coming to her exclaiming their desires for something different and beyond what has always been expected of them in terms of marriage and partnership.

"They're saying, 'I don't want the thing that my mom had' or 'I don't want the thing that everybody's telling me I'm supposed to want,' " said Genzano. "Because there still aren't a lot of models or examples for things that aren't the traditional or really common experience of marriage."

Genzano told me she's observed a trend of fewer women "grappling with others' expectations of them" but rather seeking the guidance and space to figure out what they truly want.

This is when I asked her how we can find that space for ourselves.

"We have to learn how to disappoint others," she said. "We have to learn how to hold and express anger, how to get okay with being uncomfortable, how to recoup the parts of us that—for one reason or another—were not allowed to be expressed throughout our development."

She qualified this by saying that learning to disappoint people and expressing anger "can be painful and hard" at times, but they are actions we must take.

What was wild about hearing Genzano was how her words reminded me of what Cyndi Darnell had told me. It was as if the three of us were in the same room, having a conversation about all the ways we push against the norms and step toward ourselves.

"We have to get used to being uncomfortable," said Darnell. "We must start taking risks—and that means imagining your life in a way that is different than what you're living now, then considering how you can spend your time working towards one piece of having that come true."

That "one piece" can be anything. It can be as simple as opening a savings account for yourself, taking a language class, or saying no more often. It may mean disappointing someone, and that is okay. It may mean you start looking at partnership with a more discerning eye, like McGhee is.

"This is how we start to change culture," added Darnell. "It is by making these tiny little decisions to not participate in a cultural script that is not built for us. I recognize that not everybody has that freedom and privilege. But for those of us who have the option, we must leverage it and flex it."

So, here we are. I want to ask you: What does taking a risk look like right now?

Take a moment to settle into this. Close your eyes. Listen to your breath.

What does taking a risk look like?

Does it look like leaving or entering a partnership? Does it look like taking a lover, asking a woman to get coffee, texting an old friend, moving to a new city, opening your relationship, speaking up to your partner, saying "I love you," saying "I like you," booking a solo trip, exploring a fantasy, showing your partner where it feels good, staying home by yourself, having a threesome, crying in front of him, breaking down next to her, leaning on their shoulder, saying "I'm sorry," saying "Never again," or saying "Yes!"?

Only you know what it looks like. Just remember, these risks, big and small, quiet and loud, will open you to experience more of the fullness of you.

"It's about constructing an entirely new way of relating to yourself, your emotions, and to the people around you that has not been done before," added Darnell. "This is about creating something brand-new from the ground up."

It is about continuing to move toward what feels free—which brings me to the story of Chianti Lomax.

I connected with Lomax, an author, positive-psychology practitioner, and women's coach, just after she had released her book, *Evolving While Black*. Our time together was brief, but we covered endless ground. She spoke about finding the courage to write her story in the face of an oppressive system. Having grown up in

Southern Black culture, "where you don't talk about things; you sweep it under the rug and move on," she experienced a massive change in her life when she started taking positive-psychology classes. Decades of influence and scripts floated away.

"We don't recognize how much of our decisions are influenced by our belief system," Lomax told me. "When we recognize this and how some of these systems don't even belong to us, we start to think, Am I really living my life the way I want to? Am I making these decisions because I truly believe it or because someone told me to believe it?"

Many of Lomax's clients are married and have children, a fact she finds interesting given that she is unmarried and does not have children. But it also makes sense to her. She believes these women are drawn to her coaching work because "so many of them had never given themselves permission to be anything other than mom or wife," she said.

Suddenly, Lomax got excited. She wanted to tell me a story about the previous night. She had gone to a dinner gathering in recognition of Juneteenth. One of the discussion topics was What does freedom mean to you?

"This was a room of Black and brown folks, so we get to talking about the things built to keep us from succeeding," she said. "And we ask each other, 'Is freedom even real for people who look like us?' "

When it was Lomax's turn to speak at the dinner, she thought of her grandmother and how proud she would be to know her granddaughter had written a book and was living her life on her own terms and not according to what others expected of her. "I sat up and said, 'All these things are very real—systemic racism and patriarchy—and, collectively, we have a long way to go. But we can continue to fight for our collective freedom, and we can also fight for our personal freedom.' "

As she continued, her voice grew louder and her breaths deeper.

"I said, 'Freedom to me is creating a day that is good for my nervous system. Freedom to me looks like unsubscribing from the idea that I cannot be considered whole or complete unless I am married to a man. Freedom to me looks like the idea that I am already worthy. Freedom to me means knowing that I am in my fully expressed version of my womanhood without being a mother—and I love my nieces and nephews! Freedom to me is knowing that I'm already a full, complete woman, and I don't need these beliefs that you must do these things or fulfill these roles or identities in your life.' "

Lomax said she paused and looked around the table. All the women, married and unmarried, were nodding vigorously and clapping.

CONSIDER THIS:

No matter your relationship status, you are whole.

You can revel in being alone. You can enter or leave a relationship anytime. You can say and have what you desire.

You can always discover new pleasure in your body.

You can ask yourself: What is a risk I can take—right now, this moment, in my forties, for myself?

You are born to one mother, but if you are lucky, you will have more than one. And among them all you will find most of what you need.

—CLARISSA PINKOLA ESTÉS

chapter five

Our Maternal Unfolding

On having and not having children, seeing our wholeness, and mothering ourselves and one another

A FEW YEARS AGO, A WOMAN I'VE KNOWN MY ENTIRE LIFE called me. The urgency in her voice was thick and choking. She wanted to tell me about the woman she had just met.

"A lovely woman," she described to me. "So beautiful and strong. But . . ."

"But what?" I asked.

"It was so sad what she said."

She went on to tell me how she and the woman got to talking about children. The woman never had any, for reasons unspoken. "But my life still has purpose," she had said.

"Isn't that heartbreaking? That she even needed to say that?" said the woman who called me. "That she felt she had to prove it out loud?"

"What did you say to her?" I asked.

"I said, 'Of course your life has purpose. Of course it does. Of course it does.' "

The Bittersweetness

In the introduction, I told you how in writing this book, I wanted to interrogate the old stories surrounding our forties and shed light on all the wonder, challenge, change, and beauty we face in this decade. In my quest to both better understand this time of our lives and reveal its nuances, I have repeatedly come to the topic of having and not having children. Regardless of where women fall on the parenthood spectrum, this massive topic has a significant impact on our lives. We talk about it to one another, swapping stories of raising children—with the heartache, labor, and joy it brings—and of not having children, and the myriad emotions accompanying that truth. And when in our forties, the additional need to care for aging parents comes into the fold for some of us. In this chapter, we will journey through all of this, including how motherhood and non-motherhood are evolving today. And we will touch on what I believe to be the even larger question we all face: How can we tap into the energy of mothering that is inherent in all of us?

In truth, it feels as though I have been writing this chapter for my entire life. As I type these words, I am sitting at my desk, and my face is about to mirror the liquid that falls from the clouds outside my window. My chest feels warm, and I can feel my heart—*thump, thump*—yet my throat is constricted. My sensations are similar to those I feel when I listen to Ravel's *Boléro*. A bittersweetness swells inside me.

As a woman without children, in my forties, I am moved by the topic of having and not having children unlike anything else. The mere idea of motherhood waters my every emotion. Nearly every morning, I text or talk with my best friend, Maura, who is raising her young daughters with her husband, Matthew. Most days, Maura is upbeat and happy (and hilarious, as she is), leaving me in awe as she juggles school drop-offs, dance, and insatiable bellies, all while she works full time and navigates the well-being of her aging parents nearby. Other days are fraught with an endless onslaught of worries and things to do. "I just feel like I can't keep up," she said to me recently. "I can't focus. This is just . . . It's so much. And I can't get sick! I can never not feel well. It's not an option for me."

My heart feels heavy when Maura tells me these things. I want to be there for her, mother her. We live thousands of miles apart; it's been this way for years. While I know we're each meant to be where we are, I wish I could pop over and help her with the girls. There's a duality to my yearning: On one side is a desire to build a semblance of a village where we help to carry the weight of this life, where we watch each other's kids and dogs, bring wrenches to fix toilets, and share meals regularly. And on the other side is my own personal journey. I want to know what it is like, firsthand, to nurture little bodies and minds. I feel resolute that motherhood was not my path. And still, I yearn.

I mentioned my feelings to spiritual teacher Mitra Rahbar. I told Rahbar how although the fact that I do not have children is because of my choice, I often feel as though I am floating on a pond of grief, joy, relief, and confusion—and the edges have expanded since being in my forties.

"Of course," Rahbar replied kindly. "For women, the forties bring an awareness of time, our biological clocks, and our bodies are changing. It marks when we start going into a different kind of womanhood."

Rahbar told me in her work as a healer and guide, she sees women in their forties looking at motherhood through a new lens. Questions often arise: Do I want children? Do I want more children? Do I miss my children? Do I face not being able to have them? Am I relieved, confused, grateful, tired, overwhelmed?

"These are questions many women ask in their forties," she said. "It's in the background of your head."

Before we move forward, let's first ground ourselves in this topic. Take a moment to tap into how you feel around the topics of children and motherhood. What comes up for you? Whether you have children or not, yearn for them or not, or are confused or not, I hope you feel safe and seen in this chapter.

Who Am I Without Children?

Safe and seen is how I felt when I talked with Angela L. Harris. Over Zoom one afternoon, we shared our thoughts and feelings about this charged topic. For Harris there was never a question about whether she would be a mother. Rather, a statement, clear and true, lived in her body: That's not something I'm interested in.

This sentence started floating through Harris's mind two decades ago, when she began seeing friends and family members her age having kids. She saw the babies and bottles and felt a conviction that she did not want to turn down that road.

"I was more focused on my education and securing my security," said Harris, who is a dean at a liberal arts college.

So, she kept her truth to herself, never officially stating it to her family. She put her head down and worked feverishly, checking off bachelor's, master's, and doctorate degrees. Thankfully, there was no family battle to fight. "I think my parents probably always knew," she said of her choice, adding that they never pressured her to give them grandkids. "I think, if anything, they saw me as this driven child, a driven woman who wanted to make her mark."

Around her late thirties, there was a shift. Harris began to yearn for camaraderie in her life as a woman without children. More so, she felt guilt and shame around never having a desire to have kids. "I thought, If I'm feeling this, I wonder if other sisters are feeling this. And more so, if other Black women are feeling this," she told me.

At the time, she couldn't find literature that touched on the emotions of women who do not have children. She decided to create a survey focused on Black women who, like her, chose not to have children. The queries touched on their reasons and feelings about it. Harris sent the survey to her friends, asking them to share it with their communities. She was struck by all "the rich information" she received about people's lives without children, and, especially, by the readiness of women wanting to talk about it.

Informed by the results of her survey, she compiled these stories of women. She started writing a book and formed a community,

No Bibs, Burps, Bottles, that honors African American women on their journey living without children by choice and by circumstance. They gather and talk about their experiences, sharing emotions and challenges, as well as joys and excitement.

As Harris spoke, I could feel her fever for the topic. An entire community has sparked from her asking other women how they felt about living without children.

"It was clear," she said. "I was not alone in this."

Like Harris, I always knew. Whether or not it was intuition or foresight, for as long as I can remember, I felt strongly that I would not be a mother to my own children. Yet the feelings that surround my answer can be described only as a stunning marriage of conviction, confusion, relief, and loss. My not having children has caused me more grief, angst, clarity, elation, pride, and longing than any other choice in my life—and as I said, these feelings have taken on an electric charge in my forties.

I have been active in my choice. Still, my existence without children has been the marker by which I've felt society has judged me most. Who am I if I am not a mother? Who am I without bearing children? Who am I without birthing or adopting and raising a baby? Who am I without camp, school, and playdate scheduling? Am I whole, complete, and worthy?

"It's as though the world has made this the most defining element of a woman's life," my friend Shrankhla told me several years ago. I closed my eyes when she said it. There's a level of emotional labor for women without children that often goes unnoticed by the world at large.

Whenever I've been asked, "Do you want kids?" I experience agita—every damn time. My physiology changes. A wash of what feels like hot acid scorches my chest. Because there is no neat response. Expressing my feelings about the topic proves to be as challenging, limited, and impossible as language itself. It's like trying to mold a handful of lotion into a ball. I can scoop the fact from my mind and state it, but everything jiggles and oozes before I can form a perfect anecdote. My emotions around not having kids are too damn vast and contradicting. On any day, I can feel both clear and confused, relieved and empty, joyful and sad.

I've anchored my life in my conscious choice. I've used birth control and been clear with my partners. Avoiding pregnancy became obvious to me when I became sexually active in my teens. But as I grew older, an occasional late period would feel as if I were standing on the edge of a cliff. I had become accustomed to the angst of not wanting to get pregnant, but I could never harvest its root. As Sheila Heti writes in *Motherhood*, "Whether I want kids is a secret I keep from myself—it is the greatest secret I keep from myself."

I've spoken my truth, my deep secret, quietly to close friends and family. I've known—but I've always worried. Was I making a mistake? Was I missing out? Did I fully and truly know? Does any woman?

"You would be such a good mother," a therapist told me.

"Don't rob yourself of happiness," a distant family member mentioned.

There were years in my thirties when I felt fixed in an outlook. I was stuck in the feeling that I was not only letting myself down but disappointing the world and "the kid that is waiting for you to be its mom," as a woman said to me. But nothing ejects a woman from feeling fixed in society's script like an unexpected pregnancy—and that happened during my late thirties.

It was early spring. I was dating a man from whom emanated

such pain that his presence felt like a dark web. As I was driving along the I-10 freeway in Los Angeles, on my way to see my dear friend Teal, a jolt of awareness pierced my mind. Where was my period? I was always on time. No way. There's absolutely no way.

I called Teal and asked if she would buy me a pregnancy test. When I arrived, she had two. (That's the friend she is.) We stood in the bathroom, looking at the line that begs you to hold your breath.

"Oh, Stace." She looked at me for a second. "You're pregnant."

"No. No. No. No."

That night, I told the man I was dating two things: I was pregnant, and I was not going to have the baby.

Several days later, I went to the gynecologist. I lay there and glanced at the ultrasound screen, looking at what the doctor was pointing to—the confirmation that I was pregnant. It was minuscule—a grain of sand. I felt heavy, sad, and resolute.

The doctor disrupted my second-long spell. She asked me to take a minute and look her in the eyes. We were closely acquainted at that point, as she'd just looked inside my body.

"This is your life," she said to me. "Your body."

She paused for a second before she continued. "You do what is right for you. No one else."

I have thought of that doctor countless times since. I remember the way she delivered the facts without any side of judgment, the way she looked into my eyes as a woman and person, a whole being. She acknowledged the pressure I was experiencing, and she confirmed, subtly and strongly, that to have or not have that baby was my journey—solely mine.

The weeks that followed my abortion were a hormone-dipping

haze. I was treading waters of so many feelings—anger, frustration, loneliness, fear, exhaustion, relief. Through it all, I did not have one second of regret. Or guilt. My decision to end my pregnancy was the right one for me. I would display this on a billboard: Having an abortion was one of the most intimate, profound, and true decisions of my life.

It is a decision every woman has the right to make for herself, and we cannot give up the horrifying fight for this right as abusive administrations strip it from us. Ever. I am grateful for my decision, and ever more grateful I had a doctor who cared for my body and was able to help me—two truths too hard to find for so many of us.

Yet even years later, after I made this critical decision, I still sometimes swim with the question Am I enough?

The Pressure to Explain

Of all the conversations I've had with women who do not have children, one theme consistently emerges: We feel we're letting people down. It may be family, a partner, or the grander aspect of society, but there's always an other in this personal equation.

Women's therapist Kristen Genzano shared with me that a life without children was clear for her, but she still wavered. "Even though I knew, there were some phases where I thought, Am I sure I know? Do I know I know?" she told me.

Where she felt the most contention, though, was in how she felt others would respond to her choice. She grew up in a religious community, which she is no longer a part of, where the universal expectation for women was to marry and bear children. "And if you don't, then what are you doing?" she said. "Disappointing others is something I've personally really grappled with."

Our culture tends to think about women having or not having children in binary terms—you are a mother or not—and rarely considers the constellation of reasons, emotions, and obstacles every woman faces around this subject, as well as the maternal energy we may feel despite our motherhood standing. The spectrum of why women have children is vast and eclectic, the same as the spectrum of why women do not have children. The factors of ability, desire, choice, and fear all collide, making this an excruciatingly personal and impossible-to-define truth in every one of our lives.

Yet we still feel compelled to defend our position. As Genzano said, "There is a lot of 'How do I explain this to others?' "

The need to justify the ways in which maternity does and does not show up in our lives is part of our work as women to release ourselves from patriarchal expectations. But despite the judgment we face, the truths of women's lives, with and without children, are evolving rapidly today.

For one, women are waiting longer to have children. The average age of a first-time mom in 1970 was twenty-one. That age has risen to over twenty-seven. Data from the CDC also shows that women in their twenties have fewer kids than in prior decades, but the number of women in their forties who have given birth for the first time has risen over the last forty years—so much so that between 2021 and 2022, births to women aged forty to forty-four rose by 6 percent, and for women forty-five and older by 12 percent.

While more women are waiting longer to have kids, there are also more women having fewer or none. There's been a steady decline in birth rates (the number of live births to every woman) over the past decade. Fertility rates, which show how many children a woman has, have also steadily declined since the early 1970s. In the mid-1960s, a woman had on average five kids. Today, the average is just over two.

It feels cold to talk about something as life altering and personal with statistics. These numbers show noteworthy trends but still do not capture the nuances of parenthood and nonparenthood. There's no way to honor every emotion and reason behind a woman having or not having a child. For women who choose not to, research points to reasons touching on broad societal trends, including desires to focus more on careers, as in Angela L. Harris's case, to political uncertainty, shifting norms in gender roles, concerns around ableist judgment, financial worries and limitations, lack of social safety nets and familial support, and stressful all-encompassing jobs—to name only a few of the uncountable reasons. There is the grave reality of maternal mortality: Among all high-income nations, the US has the highest rates of maternal mortality—and racial and ethnic inequities prevail, disproportionately impacting women of color.

There is also the massive concern about climate change. Researchers from the University of Bath surveyed ten thousand people aged sixteen to twenty-five across ten countries, including the United States. Nearly 40 percent said they were hesitant to have children because of climate change. While we are all vulnerable to anxiety over long-term temperature shifts and weather patterns, these issues do not impact everyone equally. Race, socioeconomic status, and place of residence all play substantial roles in how one is affected by and responds to climate change.

In her book *Climate Anxiety and the Kid Question*, Jade S. Sasser offers a study of the burdens that come from the long-term shifts in weather patterns and temperatures spanning the world and how these costs impact people's lives, including their decisions around having families. She looks deeply at how communities of color are more vulnerable to environmental threats, including disproportionate exposure to air pollution worsened by climate change. Sasser writes: "Understanding climate anxiety and its relationship to reproductive anxiety and the kid question adds a dimension to the multifaceted fight for justice by revealing the ways the unjust systems causing climate change have pervaded not only our environments and communities but also our minds, hearts, and deepest desires around children and family."

Sasser's words illuminate one critical aspect of why the conversation about women having and not having children requires compassion. It is an existential choice.

And for many women, it is not a choice.

Wanting and Not Having

Approximately 11 percent of women of reproductive age have experienced fertility issues in the US, and treatments such as in vitro fertilization are wildly expensive and physically and emotionally taxing. The same can be said for other paths toward parenthood, including adoption and surrogacy. (It's impossible to state how many women are attempting or wanting to adopt, as national statistics on this issue are lacking.)

Add to all of this that we are in a period where women's fundamental rights to have or not have a child are being increasingly challenged by the day. In 2022, the Supreme Court ruled to revoke the federal right to abortion, a grim decision that continues to threaten women's health, lives, and freedoms.

The emotions, challenges, and unanswered questions surrounding maternal health and desires form a galaxy of their own. For more than four years, my friend Annie Daly, a journalist with a smile that outshines the sun, embarked on a journey to conceive with her husband, which opened a new portal of both hope and pain. Since the age of thirty-six, Daly has gone through countless rounds of intrauterine insemination (IUI), eight taxing rounds of in vitro fertilization (IVF), and numerous surgeries. It has been a physical and spiritual waterfall. Doctors have pointed to medical reasons, including Daly's endometriosis, low ovarian reserve, and high autoimmune response to pregnancy for why she hasn't been able to carry a pregnancy to term. But more so, my friend has been met with more shrugged shoulders than she can count.

"They just say, 'We don't know why,' " she told me of her experience. " 'You still could get pregnant. You probably won't, but you could.' And so then I'm like, Okay, did I do enough? Should I do one more round? Maybe I didn't do this right."

The self-blame has scorched my friend over the years. She couldn't believe she did one round of IVF, let alone eight. And after every round, there was always that critical voice in her head blaming her and her choices—the foods she ate, the workouts she did. It was all my fault, she thought.

Daly has found catharsis in writing about her journey, producing soul-stretching essays and meticulously reported stories. "I think it's almost my social responsibility to share where I am in the moment," she told me, shedding light on the shame, self-blame, and sadness often surrounding pregnancy loss and infertility. "There are a lot of women who just don't want to talk about it."

Daly's sentiments touch on the colossal nature of this chapter's topic. The sum of the reasons a woman does or does not have children is greater than the parts. Giant questions of desire, ability, and safety intersect. There are no binaries here. The truth of living with or without children transcends neat answers. Between the definable truths of fear, uninterest, a lack of support, and physiological inability exist the liminal yet just-as-valid reasons of apathy, self-worth, anxiety, and confusion.

Whenever someone asks me, "Do you want kids?" my chest constricts. I usually answer "No," or "I don't think so," before using my journalistic tactic of turning the spotlight on them. But I want to say, "Yes, I want kids. And no, I don't want kids. And yes, I want to be a mother. And no, I don't want to be a mother." I want to say, "I am confused. I am scared. I worry that I do not have a substantial well of time, self-worth, ability, belief, money, intellect, support, and courage."

I want to answer with the truth: My reasoning is too vast and contradictory to explain.

"When you drill down to the individual level and speak to people about their reproductive identity and feelings about parenthood, you will find incredibly nuanced and varied experiences," author Ruby Warrington told me.

I spoke with Warrington several years ago, shortly after the release of her book *Women Without Kids*. An insightful journalist, Warrington merges her journey of living child-free by choice with the stories and perspectives of other women without kids, weaving in deep historical research. Warrington developed what she calls the Motherhood Spectrum, a concept to acknowledge the nuance of any person, regardless of gender and biological sex, and how a person's experiences of having or not having kids are influenced by a multitude of factors that may shift throughout one's lifetime.

"I see this as a kinder, more compassionate, and more humane way of thinking about experiences of parenthood and non-parenthood," said Warrington.

Essayist and journalist Meghan Daum sheds light on a facet of the kaleidoscope of reasons of why people do not have children in the introduction to *Selfish, Shallow, and Self-Absorbed*, in which she edited and compiled essays from men and women on why they chose not to have kids. Daum writes that to read the perspectives "is to notice that, in many ways, the common theme is that there is no common theme." Of the sixteen people featured in the book, "no two reached the decision [not to have children] in quite the same way."

What I appreciate about Daum's reflection is the nuance it contains, and also, her inclusion of men, whom mainstream media often leaves out. When I conducted a simple online search for "celebrities with no kids," the four top articles that appeared, each from a popular national magazine, nearly all listed—an average of 93 percent—women. This proves the deeper cut. Society links the topic of having and not having children only to women rather than acknowledge that it's a reality for any human. The reasons are personal and private. Simple and complex. Painful and joyful.

But women are the ones judged for not having children. We are the ones to which the adjectives and questions stick.

We Deserve More Generosity

Language can fall short in offering humanity the breadth of what we experience. Mainstream rhetoric around the topic of people without children tends to use two words: *child-free*, more often used to describe a person who does not have children because of choice, and *childless*, more often used to describe a person who cannot have children because of circumstance, which can be for countless reasons, from infertility to socioeconomic challenges. (These words are sometimes used interchangeably.) There are also the phrases *women without children* or *women without kids*.

"You can read a whole book just on this," Katie Maynard, a Seattle-based therapist and social worker, told me when I asked about her preferred terminology.

In her neurodiversity-affirming practice, Maynard focuses much of her work on supporting people who do not have children, an interest that stems from her own life. When casually talking to people about her personal experience of non-parenthood, she sometimes says, "I don't have kids" and "It wasn't in the cards," but the term she most often uses is *childless*.

"And I want to take the word back, because I think it gets a bad reputation," she told me. "People think, Oh, it's pitiful. You're not *less*. And I'm like, *Less* isn't always a bad thing!"

Explaining why you may not or don't have children can be a challenge. "It's not a sound bite," said Maynard, emphasizing how complex and varied non-parenthood is. "And I think people don't tell their stories because of that."

Adding to this is the negative connotation. Most stories anchor women without kids in inferiority. Old narratives, steeped in patriarchy, feverishly encourage the belief that having children is a necessary ingredient for a full life and is the ultimate role for a woman. Therefore, if we are not mothers, we are seen as disruptive and odd, different and less than.

Further judgment lands on the why. Does a woman not have kids because of choice? Well, then, she's considered selfish and weird. Is it by circumstance? Oh, how sad and barren.

Ruby Warrington points to these views in her work. She coined the term *the mommy binary* to illustrate the falsified albeit harmful divide that exists between mothers and non-mothers. Society likes to pit us against one another, claiming one way of living is more worthy of praise while the other elicits pity or contempt. One step further, the non-mothers who made the conscious choice not to have kids "tend to come out painted with the least flattering brush," as Warrington told me. Such division is one of the many reasons why she believes it's essential to move past these limiting tropes and instead focus on what unites us as women.

I agree with Warrington. This falsity of a binary hurts us. Each of our truths behind parenthood and non-parenthood is vast and may or may not mirror that of another. Whatever *with* or *without* or *less* or *free* describes exists uniquely in each of our souls. But what is universal and shared is the pressures we all face as women—mothers and non-mothers alike. Our lives in our forties are too rich and complex to succumb to binaries. We owe it to ourselves to concentrate on what unites us.

We also deserve more generosity, and that must start with how we feel about ourselves. Rarely have I felt judged by other women for not having kids. And in the few cases when I have detected a hint of a limiting opinion, I've always seen that it was my own feelings that were muddying the waters. I was projecting my sense of inferiority onto the conversation.

When I spoke to Sara Wyle about her experience of having her daughter and the weight of motherhood, she was honest and inclusive. She told me she always wanted to be a mother, knew in her bones it was her destiny, but she has immense compassion for her friends who feel ambivalent or lost around the decision. Parenthood is not for every woman.

"I'll say to my friends, 'Would it be so devastating if you didn't have a child?'" said Wyle. "If that's the feeling you have, then do it. If not, don't. That's okay. I love my daughter; I'm so happy that I had her. But I'm the first person to say motherhood is unbelievably life-changing."

And it goes without saying: hard. Beyond-words hard.

Caring for Others in Our Forties

About a year ago, I sat in Maura's kitchen eating a burger. I had just flown across the county to visit her and her family, something I try to do at least twice a year. I was going in for a big juicy bite when I heard it: projectile vomit splattering into a bucket.

"Oh, noooo!" Maura yelped, and ran across the room to Eva, her little girl. Eva was sick. The vomit kept . . . coming. All the while, Eleanor, her older daughter, was in her room nursing a belly that the spit-up gods had emptied an hour earlier.

"I cannot believe this," Maura said as she ran to get more towels.

As I sat there, waiting for a command to help that never came, I thought about what I was witnessing: My lifelong friend, a girl with whom I used to ride bikes at age eight until the summer sky turned into a navy blanket, was now in her forties and carrying the colossal role of mom.

I knew that the Marine-level urgent response Maura was giving her girls was one of countless similar efforts of motherhood happening throughout the world that very second.

Caring for children is a mosh pit of action. It encompasses every emotional aspect of life and weaves it into a complex web of rewards, complications, triumphs, and obstacles. As Maura described it for me one day, motherhood is "an invisible, never-ending emotional and cognitive strain on our physical being." And as she described it to me another time, it is "hilarious," "so fun," and "the best thing ever."

Given the significant intersection that is motherhood, it is shameful that there is no social safety net to support it. As we explored in chapter 2, the acts of mothering and caregiving are tragically undervalued in the United States. Our nation lacks in maternal and caregiving rights, offering no federally protected family leave or any comprehensive care programs. We are in a particularly charged climate, as the administration's efforts are slashing funding around maternal and women's health.

While it has never been an easy time to be a mother, the present moment is particularly challenging—and with this, the decade of our forties brings with it all its obstacles and brilliance, adding yet another layer to the multifaceted role.

Today, motherhood offers a plane of existence unlike any before it. In America, the age of first-time mothers has been increasing. More women over forty are giving birth, with data showing a notable rise in women between ages forty and forty-four. Just as the reasons for not having children are numerous, those for having kids post-forty are also endless and cover a vast spectrum that includes desire for motherhood, advances in fertility treatments, financial standing, and the presence or absence of a partner. Whatever the reason, one thing is for sure: Mothers in their forties today are caring for kids of all ages—and it's gorgeous to see.

Maura told me that one of the biggest hurdles she faces day-to-day is managing the mental load—that invisible category of caring for a family, which includes keeping life going, handling daily chores, and planning for tomorrow.

Adding to this is the endless concern. "It's terrifying in many ways," Maura told me about motherhood in her forties. "We are constantly worried and anxious for our children's well-being and safety. Our brains toggle back and forth between thoughts and worries about our kids, and now our own parents. It's such a complicated time."

In that moment, Maura touched on yet another thread: aging parents. The forties naturally bring the fact that our parents, if they are still alive, are older and may be approaching or already at a point where they need help. (The same goes for other older guardians and relatives, such as aunts and uncles.) Elders growing older can impact any of us, regardless of whether we are mothers and irrespective of our age. But the forties have a way of really underscoring the *adult* in being an *adult child*. And for some mothers, the need to care for aging parents and growing kids puts them in a "caregiving sandwich," as demographers refer to it.

The unknown—the evolving changes and caregiving needs—scares Maura at times, but she finds solace in seeing other women face similar obstacles. "I can honestly say I have never felt more understood than when I read about it," she told me. "And hear it from other women. It's just nice to know we're not alone. We are all going through so much."

"Yeah, but I don't know how you do it," I responded. "You have two little ones. I can barely keep up."

"No, no, no," came Maura's reply. "You have a ton going on. You have a stressful job and a dog and friends and an aging mom and stepdad and a full life. You have a ton going on too. We all do."

Whether we identify as mothers or not, we must articulate our struggles to one another more. We must see one another, talk to one another, and help one another. The messy weight of life anchors all our lives, and it can become heavier in our forties. What gets us through is our instinct to care.

Nothing is more tenacious than our ability to honor the noun *mother* and enact the power of its verb.

The Energy of Mothering

Merriam-Webster first defines *mother* as a noun. *Mother,* it states, is "a female parent," "a woman in authority," or "an old or elderly woman." My eyes scroll down. Then I see the verb. Paired with the preposition *to, mother* becomes a verb. It morphs from a noun to an energy, a universe. *To mother* is "to give birth to," "to give rise to," or "to care for or protect like a mother."

Possibility flows through me as I read this. I experienced a similar feeling when I talked with Peggy Fitzsimmons. Fitzsimmons has worked in counseling and healing for nearly three decades. Through her work and her book, *Release,* she helps people free themselves from spiritual, emotional, and physical clutter.

When we spoke, Fitzsimmons took me back to when she was

thirty-six and working as a wilderness therapist. She started missing her period. She took pregnancy tests, but they always showed up negative. While she and her then-husband were not trying for children, they were always thinking "maybe later," she said. But then something odd started to happen: She began having hot flashes and panic attacks, and was just feeling . . . off. She sought medical counsel. The first doctor she saw waved her off and said she was fine, adding that she was "too young" to have anything related to hormonal decline. Her mother scoffed at this, telling Fitzsimmons, "Of course it's hormones, what does he know!" But then another doctor told her something she never expected: She was experiencing premature ovarian failure.

The word *failure* lodged into Fitzsimmons's mind. "I asked the doctor, 'Do I have a few months if maybe I wanted to try to get pregnant?' " Fitzsimmons told me. "And she said no. It was over."

Fitzsimmons said she hung up the phone, walked over to her husband, who was lying on the couch, lay on him, said "I'm a failure," and wept. Even though she wasn't yearning to have a child, the experience "kicked off a whole bunch of stuff" inside her. The decision—the mere possibility—"felt all of a sudden taken from me," she said. Plus, there were the expectations. Growing up, everyone in her world had the mindset of "get a partner, get married, have a kid, get the dog, get the house, and live out your days kind of that way."

So where did being in premature menopause leave her?

Fitzsimmons didn't know it just then, but her diagnosis opened something incredible. She realized that although she would not have biological kids, she still yearned to create and nurture. There was a fire inside her. She began leaning into the divine when she was out in nature, asking the trees and sky for answers.

She put the question How am I supposed to give birth in this world? out into the universe.

Fitzsimmons said the answer came quickly: "Give birth to yourself first."

"And that's what started everything," Fitzsimmons continued. She left her marriage. She moved across the country. She went to work at the Omega Institute, where she explored various healing modalities and trained in holistic mind-body approaches. She began working with people to help them live in harmony with their inner selves. Through all her adventures in the spiritual and material realms, she leaned into her maternal energy.

"I have realized over time that the number of people I have mothered, either as clients or friends or through helping people declutter . . . I mean, it's quite staggering!" she said. "So, I didn't know the love of being a parent intimately, but I have felt that energy come through me in my different roles in life."

As Fitzsimmons told me this, I was joyful. And I was hopeful. *Mother* may be a beautiful noun that I am not, but *mothering* is a verb I live. It's a verb all women—and people—can do if they choose.

"That's what people must understand," said Fitzsimmons. "Mothering is the divine feminine energy. It's an energy of nurturing, and an understanding of the other realms that we're part of. The divine feminine, that's what's being called for now."

Months after Fitzsimmons and I spoke, I got on the phone with Mitra Rahbar, whom we heard from at the start of this chapter. A poet and spiritual guide who has authored two books on tapping into the divine, Rahbar has helped me use my heart to see the light I often overlook.

Generous with her wisdom, Rahbar shared with me the

tension she faced in her Persian culture when she decided not to have children.

"It was a huge thing for many people, including my relatives, to stomach," she admitted. "But I always say, 'I have a lot of children, but they're not my biological children, and I'm comfortable with that.'"

What is essential to see, Rahbar continued, is that there are many different types of mothers, and we can choose how we want to embody this energy. Some of us are born to mother one child, while others are born to mother many. Some of us are meant to be aunts, mentors, teachers, or healers. Rahbar pointed to the gravity of aging parents and elders and how that requires us to further mother. How we choose to honor our maternal inner fire is up to us.

It is up to you.

Then Rahbar told me something I had never considered.

"Stacey, one day, you may decide you want to have a child. No one can foretell that. This is an important thing to also know: None of this is made in stone, and it may change as we come to new places within ourselves," she said. "We all get to choose how we want to channel this energy. But what is so important is that we learn to also mother ourselves."

How to Mother Yourself

I argue that every age is a good time to mother yourself—but I carry a fierce argument for doubling down on this in your forties. As we have been exploring, this is the decade of a major intersection of awakening, of physical and emotional changes, and of facing and letting go of old stories and considering new paths. The pressures from society and life are intense. You may be mothering people—whether little ones, teenagers, or grown adults. You may be mothering work dreams or hobbies. Whatever your life holds right now, I know it is full—and that is why you must lean into this beautiful energy for yourself.

Rahbar believes one way to do this is to speak kindly to yourself—much like we learned from Kristin Neff at the beginning of this book. Show yourself fierce yet unflappable compassion. Practice changing your inner dialogue from one of admonishment ("Ugh, I failed again") to one of encouragement ("I am trying hard and I will keep going").

"Think of it as how a nurturing mother would say, 'Don't worry, you can get back up!' after a child falls," said Rahbar.

You can also mother yourself through habits, or "sacred practices," as Rahbar calls them. Give yourself moments to "allow the sacredness of you to be there, fully." Spend at least several minutes a day in silence, ideally in a quiet, beautiful place, like at a park or near a window. Allow yourself this so you can find an ease within. Take in the air around you. "Try to empty your mind and just be," added Rahbar. "Slowly, you will come to a place that is pure love and acceptance."

As I have learned to mother myself, what I have found most amazing is how my care begets more care. With every bit of healing energy I give to myself, I feel more inclined to take better care, whether it means getting enough sleep, turning away from email, eating well, or resting. I want to mother myself more and more as I grow into my forties. And I want to mother the women around me.

Because when we take the time to do this, we see maternal

energy not as exclusive but as essential and free for every one of us to give and receive.

It is the light that ignites our forties.

It is the energy that brings you home.

The Paths We Do and Do Not Take

Now that I'm in my forties, my feelings about not having children are so colossal I cannot find their edges most days. Joy blurs into sadness; gratitude seeps into longing. I'm moving closer to the day when the consideration of even having a biological baby will no longer exist. It is a haunting reality even as I live consciously in my child-free choice. And as Rahbar told me, maybe one day my mind will change. But what has surprised me over these decades is how I have never wanted to reverse my decision, even as parts of the heartbreak have intensified.

"I appreciate you bringing this up," Kristen Genzano told me when I shared my feelings. "Because when I turned forty, I started to feel more . . ." Genzano paused for a few seconds. "Grief. And I hesitated there because it's not regret. It's grief."

The question I then asked Genzano was one I had repeatedly asked myself: "Why the grief?"

"It's the grief of something, an experience, that I didn't get to have, and I won't get to have," she said. Genzano then told me that, years ago, she had a conversation with a woman twenty years her senior who also did not have children. The woman reminded Genzano that it is impossible to go down both paths, and no matter which one we venture down, there will always be grief.

"So, I sit here, and I grieve what it would have been like to have a child. And I also have plenty of friends who have kids who are open enough to say to me, 'I wonder what it would be like not to have kids,'" she said. "I think it's really important to recognize and honor that we get one life, and you get this choice—if we're lucky enough, because some of us don't get the choice. But there's grief in either way."

It is human to wonder about the paths we do not take. How would our lives feel if we'd had that child, married that person, or finished college? Where would our hearts be if we lived in Paris rather than Detroit? Or Vancouver over Missoula? Thinking about this haunts me, but I find solace in author Cheryl Strayed's words. The paths we do not take are what she calls our "sister lives."

"I'll never know and neither will you of the life you don't choose," Strayed wrote years ago in response to a reader conflicted over whether to have children. "We'll only know that whatever that sister life was, it was important and beautiful and not ours. It was the ghost ship that didn't carry us. There's nothing to do but salute it from the shore."

Reading Strayed's words and talking with Kristen Genzano and Katie Maynard pointed me toward something so critical to acknowledge in our forties: Within this life exists an endless world of experiences. The vastness of this truth becomes crystalized when we look at the universe of parenthood and nonparenthood. And just as there are endless truths, there is also room to feel it all, honoring the quilt of emotions that make us human.

"It's okay if a person is feeling quite content in not having kids one day, and then they show up at brunch feeling sad about it," said Maynard. "It can flux and flow throughout the various things we do in our life experiences."

When we are sold false binaries around living with and without children, hearts will break, and people's truths will always get overlooked. Motherhood—parenthood—is one of the most gorgeous things in this life. There is no right way to do it, just as there is no right way to come into it. The stories and reasons are as infinite as the stars.

And a life of non-parenthood is just as gorgeous and essential. It may still take time for the world to catch on to this, but it lives within the worlds of women. Mothers and non-mothers, we are all, in our own ways, juggling days filled with grief and loss and joy and laughter and pain and longing and wonder. To be a parent—or not to be—are both truths that make us who we are.

All Our Callings

Earlier in this chapter, we visited with my friend Annie Daly, who has endured an intense journey trying to conceive a baby through IVF. She and her husband have now chosen to explore surrogacy. At the time of writing this, the couple has matched with a woman who may carry their child. I asked Daly, who had recently celebrated her fortieth birthday, how she felt about her continued journey.

"Mentally, I feel so much stronger, and I am just more self-aware and confident in my ability to handle what comes my way," she said. "I feel like I have more of a voice because I've had to develop it in a much deeper way over the past couple of years."

But there is a struggle, Daly admitted. She still faces the unknown. Surrogacy is, of course, not guaranteed; nothing is. And she still may have to undergo another round of IVF to get an embryo. The decision feels right, in many ways, and also intense.

"There's been this discrepancy between the extreme move of surrogacy versus the fact that, in my head, I associated surrogacy with having to be the type of person who views motherhood as their *one* calling," she admitted.

The truth is, Daly sees motherhood as one of her *many* callings. "Journalism is a calling of mine. Being a good friend is a calling of mine. And a good partner. A good daughter. I have so many callings," she added. "So it took me a little while to come to peace with the idea that I deserved to pursue surrogacy—that even though I viewed motherhood as one part of an already full life, I still deserved to do everything I could to hopefully make that dream happen. That it was not greedy or unjustified. And that just because I did not pin all my hopes and dreams onto motherhood did not mean I was less deserving of it than other women who were able to become mothers more easily."

I thanked Daly for her admission—because, too easily, we can reduce the universes we contain.

"I will say this, though: I haven't lost hope, and hope can be a dangerous thing during IVF, because your hope is crushed, and it's hard to get it back," she said. "But I continue to keep getting it back. Sometimes I don't even know what I'm hoping for, but I've accepted that I'm already in a place where I was not expecting to be. So now, I have hope as I watch things unfold."

Daly's story emphasizes just how much we need to hold hope and be kind. And how much we all need the energy of mothering. Having and not having children brings us to our knees.

We are the ones who will help one another up.

Often, I find myself wanting to reach out to the doctor who helped me end my pregnancy. I have thought of her countless times, marveling at how steady she was in her belief in me. I was then a woman nearing forty, able in numerous ways to have and raise a baby but resolute in knowing that was not my path. That doctor saw me for who I am: a whole woman, complete in her sovereignty. I didn't realize it then, but she recognized the burden I felt about how society merges motherhood with full womanhood, and she guided me beyond that.

That doctor mothered me and, in doing so, gave me the gift of seeing that my life is my own to cherish.

I want you to celebrate your life. I want you to see it as your own. I want you to mother in all the ways you're called to. I want you to let your Autumn Queen come forward, giving you strength as you watch your life unfold.

Now in my forties, I let this force run through me like a river's waters. I mother in small and large ways, in my work, friendships, and family. I mother Maura's girls when I visit, helping to put little wild arms into pajamas (and hold buckets when the throw-up gods come back). I mother my work and my friends, my passions and dreams. I mother my own mother as she moves into her later years.

And I mother myself. As Mitra Rahbar told me, when we each learn to be the source of nurturing and love for ourselves, we can navigate this life with greater acceptance. When we say to ourselves, "You are okay and you are loved," we give ourselves the strength to make healthier choices, to be more mindful parents, and to mother our society in all the ways it needs.

Because we need one another.

When I close my eyes, I see all of us. I see a woman who has given up her child for adoption. I see a woman holding her newborn. I see a woman who is struggling to conceive. I see a woman who is anxious over a pregnancy she does not want. I see a woman who lost her son. I see a woman who lost her daughter. I see a woman juggling the joys and hardships of raising a toddler on her own. I see a woman who is caring for her aging father. I see a woman who is caring for her mother who has early dementia. I see a woman who is ambivalent about if she wants a baby. I see a woman who is resolute in her decision. I see a woman raising five children while working full-time. I see a woman caring for her best friend's children.

I picture all of us moving through this world, separate in our realities but united in our truth, all part of an infinite dialogue that spans a lifetime.

CONSIDER THIS:

You can feel joy and sadness, grief and fulfillment, knowing and longing, and every other emotion around having or not having children.

You can wonder about your "sister lives" and honor them.

Contrary to societal messaging, you can see that there is no tidy answer to how and why children may or may not be in your life. This truth is wholly yours.

Ask yourself: How do I want to mother myself? How do I want to mother others? How do I want to mother my creativity, work, passions, and fire?

You must take full charge of your health, and your healthcare.

—SHARON MALONE, MD

chapter six

Our Health

Facing changes, speaking up, and doubling down on true care in our forties

THE CENTRAL GOAL OF THIS BOOK IS TO HELP YOU UNEARTH your truth, express the wildness within you that society attempts to muzzle, and live your life compassionately and loudly. It is to help you wake up every day with your inner Autumn Queen afire in her power and know yourself in an impossibly chaotic world. It is about having your gorgeous interior match your exterior as you continue to carve a path that may share similarities with other women but that is still uniquely yours. It is about encouraging you to have a free, generous relationship with your work and creativity, your beauty, your partnered or unpartnered life, and your mothering energy.

To have all of this in your forties—and beyond—you must prioritize your most significant coconspirator: your health. You must care for your body with a newfound urgency and tend to the waters of your mind as if it were your most essential job.

Because it is.

In this chapter, we will explore how to take care of yourself in your forties. We'll examine the changes we encounter as we enter perimenopause, the shifts our bodies and minds may undergo, and some foods and habits to consider to optimally nourish and bolster ourselves.

We will also examine the darker aspects of the system that surrounds us. Like the old structures we interrogated earlier, our health care system has overlooked and suppressed women for ages. Understanding its shortcomings is critical for advocating for ourselves and one another.

This leads me to say something before we move ahead: Health is a tough topic to parse. Deeply personal, it means different things to each of us. Our health can be daunting to even think about, considering how the United States lacks an inclusive structure of care. Receiving the medical attention we need can be costly, often beyond our accessible means. I have read too many health-focused stories that assume everyone has adequate health insurance and a doctor on speed dial. That is not reality. As someone who has struggled with inadequate health coverage and, at times, had none, I know how challenging it can be to navigate this maze.

I hope that these pages offer you pockets of knowledge. I hope they inspire you to double down on your health and listen to your physical, emotional, and mental needs. Because, undoubtedly, they are speaking.

What in the World Is Happening?

A few years ago, squished amid a crush of women at a holiday market, I was talking with my friend Megan. She was exasperated.

"Where are the women who look like me? Where are the ads and stories of women going through what I'm going through?" she said.

Megan, who was in her mid-forties, had just gone through a bout of shingles. Eerily, I had just recovered from my second bout the month prior, the oozing blisters sprouting in the same spot (as shingles does) on my nose.

"It was horrible," Megan said as she continued to tell me about her flare-ups, which had led to a brief bout of Bell's palsy. "And there's been so much other stuff."

I related to the "other stuff." Shortly before I turned forty, my body started to feel as though it were fighting a new challenge every month. Cold sores exploding on my lip. Pain in my vagina and vulva. Deep exhaustion. Multiple urinary tract infections. Wild fits of anxiety. Dry skin. And random moments when I felt like I was wearing toddler clothes.

What in the world? I kept thinking.

Conventional doctors told me I was okay. Armed with skeletal health insurance, I got blood tests and sat in front of multiple practitioners, most of them kind, some of them dismissive. They told me similar things: to watch my stress levels and take prescription antivirals when I suspected another cold sore or shingles outbreak coming on. Their acknowledgment in those moments seemed well-intentioned, but I garnered little insight into something bigger: My hormones were starting to fluctuate, stress was taking a harder toll, and my physiology was changing.

Everything in my rational mind knew things were shifting, but I didn't expect to feel so lost. I thought that this time would come with people waiting to guide me, or that my gynecologist would at least send me a postcard telling me to pack accordingly for the adventure ahead. Instead, I felt like I was walking across the Bonneville Salt Flats alone.

I laughed as I told Megan I used to think shingles was a ghastly rash that landed on the backs of older men, giving them an excuse to walk around without their shirts. She smiled for a second, then her face muscles dropped. She told me she was tired of how women are little informed about this time of their lives.

"There really needs to be more out there for us," she said. "There has to be."

Megan is right. It makes sense she and I compared battle stories about when we were ill-equipped: Women have been kept in the dark when it comes to their health. We've been underresearched, underreported, and cast aside in the medical world—the impacts of which we will look at later in this chapter.

Right now, you and I will dig into our bodies and minds in our forties. What exactly is happening?

Our Changing Bodies in Our Forties

At some point in this decade, most women will experience physical changes and symptoms that reflect an evolution happening within their bodies. Exactly what and when is unique for each of us. As I mentioned, I started feeling shifts right before I turned forty. For many women I've spoken with, the mid-forties marked a significant turning point. My colleague Meghan Rabbitt told me that things were "pretty much rocking and rolling" when she entered her forties—but along came forty-five, and the music shifted.

"I was like, whoa—things are changing," Rabbitt told me. "Things are looking a little different. They're feeling a little different. I don't bounce back as quickly after illness or a week of unhealthy eating. It's been . . . interesting."

It was fascinating to hear this from Rabbitt. Synthesizing information about women's health is her passion and career. As a widely respected health journalist and the author of *The New Rules of Women's Health* (an incredible and comprehensive resource), she has been covering women's wellness since the early 2000s, holding editor and reporter positions at national publications.

Rabbitt told me that what continues to surprise her most in her reporting, particularly lately, is how many women in their forties (and fifties) are unaware of the specific care they should seek. We may know we should schedule an annual gynecology appointment. And if we're "really on it," we may book an annual physical. But we often overlook other critical appointments and health screenings we need at this stage of our lives—often because we lack proper guidance. And because life is busy.

"Women are just so focused on the health of their families and others that we fall by the wayside," continued Rabbitt. "The dog gets more checkups than we do."

Dena Geiger shared a similar concern. A family nurse practitioner and functional-medicine provider, Geiger focuses on perimenopause and menopause care at her women's health clinic in northwest Montana. She told me that too many women don't know how to best care for themselves in their forties (I'm raising my hand here!)—and it's not their fault.

Consider Geiger's point: When women get pregnant, there is anticipatory guidance on what to expect. There are the doctor's appointments that increase in frequency, and classes and support. But as we head into our forties when things may start to change? It's the opposite story. "And so many women go into it blindly and think they're losing their mind," added Geiger.

What's also critical to consider is the evolving context of our lives and how that can impact our health and how we feel. Things can get more stressful in our forties. The volume gets turned up. Kids are growing or leaving the house. Parents are getting older and possibly needing care. Relationships are evolving or ending. We're entering or leaving marriages. Our libido may fluctuate. Work is challenging or changing. Our hearts are desiring new things. This can all start to compound.

"Now you have all of those stressors, and your hormones are starting to decline, so you're not compensating as well and you may lose your ability to cope; you're waking up irritable, and maybe you're starting to gain weight," added Geiger. "That's why in your forties, it's essential to take stock."

The Perimenopause Journey

For many women, our forties mark the start of perimenopause—the gradual transition to menopause, which is the permanent end to having a period and reproductive abilities.

During perimenopause, our ovaries' production of the hormones estrogen, progesterone, and testosterone begins to decline. This change in hormones causes our fertility to drop and impacts our periods. Every woman experiences perimenopause differently. Research has shown the mid-forties are the average start of perimenopause, but for some women, it can begin in their thirties, and for others in their fifties. The length varies as well, ranging from several years to a decade or even longer.

Geiger told me to think of perimenopause as puberty in reverse. Puberty is the long transition when a girl's body begins releasing hormones that trigger the ovaries to start producing and releasing eggs. During puberty, hormonal fluctuations can lead to a roller coaster of emotions. If you think back to it, you likely experienced changes that differed from your friends. We all go through it, but to varying degrees and lengths. Perimenopause is just as unique, said Geiger. As our body's production of hormones slows and our egg supply decreases, we may notice a myriad of changes, from our skin texture to our moods to our mental clarity.

"It's all a process that leads to menopause—and menopause is day three hundred sixty-six without a period until our last living day," she added.

Geiger's analogy helped me better understand how perimenopause can be difficult to decipher. No light goes off signaling our body's decline in hormone production. No email comes in telling us a shift is beginning. The start of the process can be nebulous and hard to detect, even indecipherable. We can confuse it with other health changes or vice versa. And because education and conversations around perimenopause and menopause have only recently started to claim space in the zeitgeist, we may go into the journey "blindly," as Geiger put it, with little knowledge about what is happening to us.

But we know something is happening. Changes in our hormones can ignite a bevy of symptoms and physiological issues. These can include hot flashes, night sweats, shifts in sexual desire, trouble concentrating, vaginal and vulva discomfort, sleep issues, joint and muscle aches, heavy sweating, PMS-like symptoms, urinary tract infections, greater susceptibility to illness and disease, and dozens more.

We may also experience mental and emotional changes. Women going through perimenopause have an increased risk of suffering from fluctuating moods, anxiety, and depression. We may feel off, erratic, rageful, or simply not like ourselves. Perimenopause is a universe in which there are infinite stars of symptoms composing varying constellations of how we may feel.

"When women are presenting with symptoms for the first time in this phase of life, they are often surprised," Dr. Uma Naidoo told me. "They think, What is happening to me? I was okay all my life."

Dr. Naidoo, widely known as Dr. Uma, is a global pioneer in nutritional psychiatry, a field that examines the impact of food and nutrients on cognitive function, mental health, and emotional well-being. A trained professional chef and nutritional biologist, Dr. Naidoo founded the Nutritional, Lifestyle and Metabolic Psychiatry Service at Massachusetts General Hospital, the first hospital-based clinic of its kind. Her bestselling books, *This Is Your Brain on Food* and *Calm Your Mind with Food*, offer insight into how our dietary and lifestyle choices can have a direct impact on our cognitive abilities, as well as our mental and emotional health.

Dr. Naidoo told me that our forties are when we really must understand that there is a correlation between the hormonal changes and physiological changes we're experiencing. Mood swings, irritability, depression, or anxiety may become part of our days. "For some women, this may be new, and for some women, they may have experienced this before, but it becomes heightened during perimenopause," she added. "All these things are very real."

Explaining how hormonal changes can impact women mentally and emotionally, Dr. Naidoo noted that declining estrogen levels can disrupt the brain's neurotransmitters—chemical messengers responsible for facilitating communication between nerve cells and other cells—specifically dopamine and serotonin, which are involved in modulating inflammation, regulating mood, maintaining focus, promoting pleasure, and influencing sleep. These disruptions can lead to mood swings, panic attacks, irritability, brain fog, and even greater sensitivity. Additionally, a decline in progesterone can lead to decreased GABA, the neurotransmitter that promotes relaxation and reduces stress, which can result in new or heightened anxiety and depression.

This is all rather intense. I feel it. You may too. Here's what to know: We can bolster ourselves in the face of these changes. Natural tools, including nutrient-rich foods and practices that care for the body and brain, can offer empowerment and healing—and that is what Dr. Naidoo wants every woman to understand. Too many of us tend to think we "are stuck with this and just have to endure this very uncomfortable time," she said. Quite the contrary. This is a time to lean into radical agency and self-care.

It starts with the simplest shifts and practices.

How to Naturally Support Your Body and Mind

I wish for you to treat your physical, mental, emotional, and spiritual self in your forties with absolute reverence. (I want every woman of every age to do this.) I wish for you to fill your plate with fresh vegetables grown in the sun and gulp cool water. I wish for you to sit and enjoy your meals, let your head fall to the pillow earlier, and pay attention to the habits that deplete you. Even if you have been doing so already, this is the decade to lean into your care with a newfound urgency. Because, as I wrote earlier, caring for your health is your most essential job.

I'm in no position to proselytize here. For most of my life, I have seesawed in the face of true care. Getting ample sleep, moving consistently, and choosing a green vegetable over some artificially colored, processed snack were all choices that often crumbled in the shadow of stress, relationships, and deadlines. But no longer. As I have grown into my forties, I have felt the impact of putting my body, mind, and spirit first. True care is the most vital factor in feeling strong and embodied in this decade. It is *the* ingredient that gives us the power to shed old stories and lean into our Autumn Queen.

What is hopeful is knowing that taking good care does not have to be difficult or cost prohibitive. What you and I are going to focus on now are simple foods and practices that every one of us can consider weaving into our routines. But first, one important note: What I include are suggestions for some natural lifestyle tools. By no means does this offer an extensive look at all the ways you can support your well-being in your forties. Health is personal and unique. As you experience changes and symptoms related to perimenopause, you may seek support in the way of prescription medication, as well as other interventions such as hormone therapy, which we will get to soon. That is your right and journey.

The Powerful Impact of Nourishing Foods

An optimal starting point for taking better care of ourselves in our forties is our diet. Eating fresh, whole foods can have a direct impact on our physiological, mental, and emotional well-being. As Dr. Naidoo told me, "Food is such a powerful tool for any woman."

One reason why food can be so powerful is that it has an impact on our gut microbiome. Within our gut resides a community of trillions of microbe cells that contribute to various aspects of our health, including immunity, digestion, circadian rhythm, mood balance, mental health, and hormone balance. "The gut microbiome is one location that produces, modulates, and interacts with hormones," said Dr. Naidoo.

Also critical to know is the connection between our gut and brain. As Dr. Naidoo explains, these two organs are in different parts of the body, but they originate from the same cells during embryonic development. After the gut and brain become two separate organs, they remain connected in our body through the vagus nerve (also known as the tenth cranial nerve). The vagus nerve acts like "a two-way messenger between the brain and the gut," said Dr. Naidoo. It is also worth noting that most of our serotonin receptors are located in the gut. Often referred to as "the happiness hormone," serotonin is a neurotransmitter associated with boosting mood. Low levels of serotonin have been linked to symptoms of depression and anxiety.

I highlight all this to emphasize the direct connection between your gut and brain, and your gut and emotional and mental well-being. Therefore, it's beneficial to eat nutrient-dense foods that optimally nourish these aspects of your health, especially as you enter the time where you may face symptoms related to hormonal changes.

So, in your forties, Naidoo suggests reaching for these beneficial foods:

Berries and colorful vegetables. "These all bring fiber, fiber nutrients, antioxidants, and anti-inflammatory properties to your gut," said Dr. Naidoo. Plus, they're rich in vitamins and minerals. Naidoo emphasizes leaning into leafy greens, as they contain folate, also known as vitamin B_9, an essential nutrient that helps ward off low mood.

Fatty fish, such as salmon and sardines. The essential omega-3 fatty acids may help reduce inflammation and support brain health and mood.

Chia seeds, flaxseeds, and pumpkin seeds. These provide plant-based omega-3 fatty acids, fiber, and magnesium, which promotes relaxation. They also contain zinc, which Dr. Naidoo says can help regulate levels of the GABA neurotransmitter.

Herbs and spices. While these add flavor to food, they also pack a punch in terms of antioxidants and vitamins. The golden spice turmeric, derived from the root of the *Curcuma longa* plant, may reduce inflammation and anxiety. To make this more bioactive for your body, Dr. Naidoo recommends adding a pinch of black pepper. She also loves fresh rosemary, which research shows may support cognitive function.

Extra-dark chocolate. "Extra-dark natural chocolate is rich in polyphenols and also magnesium, which may help to reduce stress and support neurotransmitter balance," said Dr. Naidoo, who emphasized avoiding chocolate filled with sugar. "I'm talking about the natural, extra-dark chocolate."

Green tea. My personal favorite, this tea is rich in antioxidants, and also theanine, an amino acid that is associated with stress reduction and the promotion of relaxation.

Good Health Habits in Our Forties

I mentioned at the start of this chapter that I entered my forties feeling physically low. Of course, I was spinning over this decade, but I was also facing health obstacles I'd never had before. It all was overwhelming, and I felt like it was happening to me. But after deep personal excavation, research, and many conversations with women—all of which led to this book—I realized how nothing was happening *to* me. Things were changing in my body and life, and it was up to me to adapt and evolve. The stressed-soaked, put-myself-second, sort-of-caring-for-myself way I was living was not going to help me overcome the health issues I was facing, and it certainly was not going to allow me to thrive in my forties.

I realized: I was getting in my way. I was the obstacle between feeling how I was feeling and feeling the best that I could. I was the one allowing emails to creep into my nights, letting myself go to bed too late, and forgetting to drink enough water, all of which amplified the health issues I faced. I was guilty for allowing my old habits to remain, which meant I was responsible for changing them—which I did. I began to see caring for myself not as a chore but as an act of utter creativity and boldness. A privilege and an honor.

I chatted about my conviction with Dr. Mariana Calleja Ross, a physician trained in palliative care who focuses on holistic living and writes an insightful newsletter, "The Feel Good Life," about preventive medicine, emotional care, and nutrition. Over Zoom, we talked about taking care of ourselves and growing older. Dr. Calleja Ross told me that before she turned forty several years ago, she started thinking of her well-being in this decade in a more creative sense. She asked herself, How do I want to feel?

"I looked at it as an experiment," she told me. "I had always cared for myself, but I remember thinking, I want to feel happier and healthier." So Dr. Calleja Ross began to amplify her care. She started trying exercises she hadn't done before, paying even more attention to her nutrition, and weaving in more time for fun.

"So now it has become about consistency and wanting to take that feeling well into my forties for however long I can. And it's made me think about all the other things I want to do in my life, even professionally, of how I want to feel and where I want to see myself."

These days, when Dr. Calleja Ross works with her patients, she asks them to consider how they want to feel—mentally, emotionally, and physically—today and in the future. She encourages them to view their health as an empowering opportunity to take conscious actions.

"That's what I tell people all the time, in my consultations or when I write: Look deeper. Look inside of you. Look at your feelings. Think about how you want to feel," she added. "And as women, we're only just now starting to learn that we can do that."

As both Dr. Calleja Ross and Dr. Uma Naidoo stated, health is personal and unique. Every woman must listen to her body, seek counsel from a doctor, and incorporate what works for her. But like Dr. Naidoo's nutrient-rich foods, there are some changes and rituals all of us in our forties can further lean into or adopt:

Prioritize sleep. Getting good-quality, uninterrupted sleep is essential for helping to improve your mood, lowering anxiety, and allowing your body to rest and regenerate.

Move your body (however you are able). Research shows that women in perimenopause are prone to exercise less. But this is when we must move our bodies. Exercise is crucial for boosting our self-esteem and self-worth, supporting our cardiovascular health, releasing endorphins, which make us feel good, and enhancing our overall quality of life. Regular moderate exercise also may improve quality of sleep and reduce symptoms of anxiety and depression. Further research suggests that consistent moderate exercise, including both resistance and cardiovascular exercise, may reduce hot flashes.

Consider strength training. More and more research shows that requiring your muscles to work against some form of weight is incredibly beneficial for women. It can help offset muscle-mass decline in women—another potential symptom of hormonal changes—build bone density, and improve cognitive health. For me, lifting weights a few times a week has made an immense impact on how I feel in my forties.

Stay hydrated. "When you are dehydrated, you can feel more anxious," said Dr. Naidoo. That is why she suggests carrying a sustainable water bottle with you and refilling it on the go. Sipping water can also help to curb hunger pangs, which she said sometimes happen when you haven't had enough to drink. "My big tip is if you go into the supermarket and you have cravings or hunger pangs, drink a bottle of water, because it actually could be that you are thirsty from the day and haven't had enough to drink," added Dr. Naidoo.

Pay attention to stress. This is easy to say and harder to implement, especially given how life in your forties can intensify. But simple, accessible practices that pull you away from the daily grind, such as going for a walk and getting into nature can have tremendously positive effects on mood, mental clarity, anxiety, depression, and overall quality of life.

Be mindful about alcohol. As I researched this book, I repeatedly heard from women about how alcohol impacts them differently now that they're in their forties—and by differently, they meant negatively. Every woman metabolizes her drinks differently, no matter their age. Still, some experts suggest that alcohol may exacerbate symptoms related to perimenopause, including hot flashes. So if you drink, pay attention to how your body feels.

Supporting your health in your forties is a highly individualized journey. It can be overwhelming at times. But rather than aiming to do everything perfectly, perhaps the goal should be deepening your relationship to how you feel and exercising your right to put your body, mind, and spirit first. That is why Naidoo said it is important to continue to educate yourself and communicate openly with your doctor.

And I will add to this: Tap into your intuition. Call in the power of your Autumn Queen. Much like we examined the impact of divesting from cruel beauty ideals on our sense of beauty, adopting a healthy diet and proactive habits can serve as a portal to feeling great and appreciating your body, face, and mind. Doing this is as essential as anything because, as we will look at now, we are not just navigating a new health frontier.

We are finding our way in a world that has led us astray.

Menopause Misinformation, Hormone Therapy, and Seeking the Truth

I don't remember the first time I heard the word *menopause*. But I remember the first time I had a conversation about it. I was in my early twenties and my mother was telling me how for both her and her mother, my grandmother Tai-Tai, menopause came without a whisper. "It was poof!" my mother told me about her period. "One day, it was just . . . gone."

I was confused. Was there not more? My mom and I never talked much about health or sex, but this story seemed particularly vague.

As I've grown older, I've come to learn this evasive dance has been the show for so many women my age.

"My mother didn't talk to my three sisters and me about menopause at all," Sara Wyle told me. "Not a word. Not *one* word!"

Eighty percent of women under forty receive inadequate information about menopause. Many perimenopausal and postmenopausal women feel shame around the topic. This makes sense, as women have been socialized to be uncomfortable talking about having their periods, let alone losing them. For so long, social narratives were dominated by stories of women shriveling, laced with a contempt for the aging female body. The narratives were dismal and condescending.

When I turned forty, I started to read more about perimenopause and menopause. Around this time, a swell of books had been published on the topic, and since then, more have continued to be released. Thankfully, we're having a revolution, with a robust cohort edifying the world about the transitions we go through, from doctors to celebrities and influencers speaking up and out about this time in our lives.

The first report that really put the pieces together for me was a 2023 article in *The New York Times Magazine*. The piece, written by journalist Susan Dominus, was titled "Women Have Been Misled About Menopause." My coffee grew cold as I read Dominus's reporting. The article illustrates how perimenopause and menopause are worlds more than what conventional, patriarchal language has led us to believe. It details how personal and unique the transition is, and how underreported and misrepresented it has been. And any true, meaningful conversation about them requires the acknowledgment of multitudes: of change and loss, newness and possibility, confusion and enlightenment.

What was so compelling about this article was the language of its writer. Dominus's words were so electric that I recognized them as the wave of conviction a reporter rides when they are personally fueled to say what needs to be said.

Dominus wrote how conversations about menopause lack a clear vocabulary, causing it to be hard for women to express what they're going through and make decisions about their health. She gave the example that we have the terms *postpartum depression* and *premenstrual dysphoric disorder*, but nothing about menopause. "Menopause—that baggy term—is too big, too overdetermined, generating a confusion that makes it especially hard to talk about," Dominus reported.

Relief and rage washed over me as I read this. One reason why this topic is so convoluted for women is because we literally do not have the words for it.

Another area in which we have been misled, one that Dominus aptly reported on in her article, is hormone therapy.

Menopausal hormone therapy is a treatment that incorporates the use of hormones, including estrogen, progesterone, and testosterone (alone or in combination), to treat the symptoms associated with perimenopause and menopause. The therapy dates back to the early twentieth century. By the mid-twentieth century, the therapy was building steam, and by the 1990s, approximately 15 million women a year were receiving a prescription for hormone therapy.

Then came a giant hiccup. The Women's Health Initiative (WHI), the longest-running, most extensive health study on women conducted in the US, published findings between 2002 and 2006 that linked one combination of hormone therapy to increased risks of health issues. A frenzy ensued. Droves of women across the country stopped their hormone prescriptions.

But there was a major flaw: This study showed only a certain combination of hormones for a select group of women. The information was hard to parse and therefore was misreported. The stories that came out missed key information and a wider look, but they were grim and understandably invoked fear.

In the time since, further studies and analyses have looked more closely at the matter and underscored the benefits of hormone therapy. There are also risks, as there are with any supplementation or prescription, but the information is nuanced, just like menopause itself. And it varies for every woman.

Monica Molenaar told me that the WHI study created "a culture of fear" around hormones for so many women. "But I'm heartened by the information that's getting out there, thanks in part to us and all the other people in the space right now talking about it," she said.

The "us" Molenaar referred to is Alloy, the women's digital health company she cofounded with Anne Fulenwider, which offers science-based treatments and information for perimenopause and menopause relief through its anchor service in menopausal hormone therapy.

When she was thirty-nine, Molenaar had her ovaries removed after she received a positive test for the BRCA gene, which studies have shown may present an increased risk in certain cancers, including ovarian and breast. She said the surgery was worth it, but it catapulted her into an early menopause.

"Literally nobody talked to me about the fact that I was going to go into menopause the next day," she told me. "They didn't offer any hormones, which I asked the surgeon about. He told me, 'Yeah, you can get a prescription when you need it.' But what did *that* mean?"

Molenaar's question mirrored so many other women's confusion. For years, clear guidelines informing women about what to know about perimenopause and menopause and their changing bodies were lacking. Women were in the dark about what to ask, look out for, and seek. But as Molenaar said, more information is getting out there. She told me she is gobsmacked by the women who come to Alloy every day who are thankful not only for access to hormones (customers meet with a certified hormone expert online to obtain a prescription, which is then mailed to them) but also for the nonjudgmental, straightforward information and education.

Thanks to women like Molenaar, Fulenwider, Dr. Uma Naidoo, Dena Geiger, and countless other pioneers in the field of women's research, conversations around perimenopause, menopause, and hormones are rapidly advancing. There is a palpable shift. Women are getting louder. We are swapping stories, sharing reassuring anecdotes, and exchanging resources.

It all makes Dr. Amy Consson happy.

Dr. Consson is a board-certified internist and certified menopause provider who founded a clinic in central Montana focusing on menopausal care. She previously worked as an internal medicine doctor and found herself limited, especially when it came to caring for women in their forties and older. She wanted to get more granular and really help women as they needed it.

I asked Dr. Consson, who offers menopausal hormone therapy in her practice, if this is the right choice for women in their forties. She said it is case by case. Menopausal hormone therapy requires care that is highly focused and personalized.

"Is there value in hormone therapy in the perimenopause or menopause transition? Absolutely. But it's not something that every person is a candidate for," she said. "It comes with risks, and it comes with benefits."

So, what do women do? I squeezed the phone, wanting Dr. Consson to point me to a miracle. But then I realized there is no such thing. Not in health, not in life. It's all a personal journey. She responded kindly and enthusiastically: "It's about having a deep conversation with your doctors."

Leaning into specifics, Dr. Consson suggested the following:

Seek out the counsel of a doctor who specializes in perimenopausal and menopausal care—ideally a practitioner who is certified by the Menopause Society. (Dr. Consson said they should have this certification listed on their websites.) Trust yourself as you build this relationship: You want to work with a practitioner who is empathetic and listens.

Consider all the options. There is not a one-size-fits-all approach. Hormone therapy comes in various forms and can be administered in different ways, including creams, patches, pills, sprays, and gels. Inquire about it all with your provider.

Inquire about the benefits and the risks. And ensure the doctor you work with "is willing to modify your plan as needed," added Dr. Consson.

And always do your research. Look at science-based data from reputable sources, including the American College of Obstetricians and Gynecologists and the North American Menopause Society.

Dr. Consson said another critical part of seeking any perimenopausal and menopausal care is to ensure you and your doctor are looking at your overall health. Some symptoms women experience in their forties may or may not be directly linked to perimenopause, she added. Life can get more stressful in our forties, as Dena Geiger illuminated earlier in the chapter. Or we may not be giving ourselves the care we need. What we are experiencing could be associated with a range of possibilities related to the contexts of our lives, including children, relationships, diet, work, aging parents, or loneliness. "It's so important to look at the entire picture," said Dr. Consson.

For too long, we haven't looked at the entire picture because we've been led astray. We didn't hear about all the nuances and intricacies of not only the physical, mental, and emotional journeys we undertake in our forties but also the possibilities and hope—and there is so much possibility and hope. The stories focused on the loss and hardship. Or the quick "Poof!" my mother and grandmother went through (although I wonder if they were gritting their teeth and bearing it, as so many of us do).

Thankfully, the scope is widening. We are starting to see our options both inside and outside the doctor's office. As I write this, it's hard to scroll without seeing menopause in a headline. A growing community of doctors is focusing on it, companies are providing symptom-relief care, lawmakers are pushing for more research, and some workplaces are even offering menopause-related benefits. This is all needed.

What is giving me the most hope, though, is how the story around perimenopause is evolving to mirror the truth: This is a wild time for our health. It may be marked with intense ebbs and flows.

It is, by nature, a time of change, which is so beautifully symptomatic of our forties.

Feeling Safe in the Doctor's Office

So far in this chapter, we've talked with experts who make it their mission to ensure women feel safe, seen, and valued in the company of their work. But this hasn't been the norm when considering the history of women's health. Our health care system has overlooked and suppressed women's bodies and needs.

In the following pages, you and I will explore the darker

aspects of the medical world to gain a deeper understanding of what we truly face in our forties. We will look at how health nomenclature, breakthroughs, studies, and general information have decentered women. This is hard, but it is an essential part of our work in learning to care for ourselves in our forties. When we see how the systems around us are mired in abusive patriarchal roots, we equip ourselves with the tools to thrive beyond them.

A little history to start: Before 1993, clinical trials were not required to include women. Until that point, extensive research on medications had focused primarily on male biology. But even with this change, gaps in research and knowledge persist. Information on everything from heart health to brain function has been skewed toward the needs and functions of male physiology—a horrifying disservice considering the biology of women and men have colossal differences.

Dr. Ashita Gehlot first noticed a gap in the attention paid to women's bodies during her time in medical school. She said men were studied and considered the "norm," whereas women were studied primarily for their reproductive qualities—viewed, as she put it, as "biological vessels."

"There just wasn't any addressing and care about what our bodies go through," Dr. Gehlot told me. "Is it the same as a male body? Are the physical characteristics, psychological characteristics, and social things that are happening to us the same as the male counterpart?"

This male-centric emphasis bleeds into other areas, from research to legislation around the care of women and people who do not fall into the gender binary.

"I don't care where you stand on the political spectrum," Dr.

Gehlot continued. "Think about it: Who's making those policies? There's been a lack of representation of women's health, and, subsequently, a lack of representation in medical care."

A board-certified obstetrician and gynecologist, Dr. Gehlot has been practicing medicine for over fourteen years. In her practice in Fort Worth, Texas, she sees a range of women patients from early adolescence to postmenopause. Throughout our conversation, she spoke rapidly and passionately.

I asked Dr. Gehlot what prompted her to branch out and open her own practice after starting her career in conventional medical-office settings.

"After sitting in offices for over thirteen years, I've seen that people in medicine don't look like me," she said. "And I didn't want to go to another office where all I hear is a one-sided conversation. I turned forty, and I was like, fuck it. I can do this."

But there was more.

"I really wanted to create a safe space for women. There was just such a *need*."

As I have been writing this book, we have witnessed both immense highs and lows in women's health. In 2024, President Biden signed an executive order to expand research on women's health—the largest and most comprehensive in American history. To no one's surprise, strong, steadfast women were at the helm of this decision. First Lady Dr. Jill Biden and Maria Shriver teamed up to advocate for the bill's passage, mobilizing President Biden, the federal government, experts, the private sector, and others to change the course for women.

The news was stunning and exhilarating, as was Shriver's speech at the White House. She spoke about how women face illnesses and "no one knows why." We make up two thirds of

Alzheimer's cases, "and no one knows why." We make up 80 percent of diagnosed autoimmune diseases, and Black and brown women are more likely to develop endometriosis and face pregnancy-related complications. "And we don't have the research to tell them what to do about it," continued Shriver. (Black women are up to four times more likely to die from pregnancy and birth-related causes than white women.)

To say that our world is in dire need of more funding, research, and rights for women's health would be a drastic understatement. It's our right to have this, and we need it. A 2024 study from Deloitte found that women use more services in the health care system than men, including mental health care, radiology, emergency room services, office visits, and labs. The greater propensity to seek care comes at a price: It's estimated that working women spend over $15 billion more annually in health care costs than men (including deductibles and out-of-pocket maximums). Even with the provisions against gender discrimination written into the Affordable Care Act, women are showing more eagerness for care but getting less health insurance value.

About a year after President Biden signed the executive order, a new US administration came into the fold and began cutting funding, gravely impacting the health care, reproductive rights, and safety of women and trans people.

When I spoke with Dr. Gehlot, she reminded me that even in the darkness there is a light: women. We can equip ourselves with the knowledge of how our bodies function, of what we need, and of the obstacles we face so we can best care for ourselves.

One tool to do this is our intuition.

The Patient Always Knows: A Look at Medical Gaslighting

Like the bedroom, a doctor's office is a space where we are called to be physically, mentally, and emotionally vulnerable. Our doctors and medical-care teams are meant to be fiduciaries for our well-being. We expect them to listen and care, as we put our bits and parts on the line with the gripping hope we will receive what we need.

We expect to be safe—but that is not always the case.

Medical gaslighting, when a patient feels a medical expert has dismissed or overlooked their health condition, is serious—and it's especially pervasive for women. Growing research underscores gender bias in the medical world, and how more women feel dismissed, overlooked, and unheard when it comes to their care than men. A 2024 systematic review found women's experiences within the health care system to be "overwhelmingly negative and encompassed in medical gaslighting, leading to the worsening of health conditions."

In her groundbreaking book, *All in Her Head,* Dr. Elizabeth Comen, an oncologist, reveals the lies about women's bodies that originated centuries ago yet persist today. These narratives have led women to justify and apologize for their bodies.

"This past is a presence in every doctor's office and every research institution; in medical exam rooms, anatomy cadaver labs, hospital hallways, and operating rooms," writes Dr. Comen. "It haunts our footsteps as we navigate the medical maze of women's health that was built by men whose ideas about women, while sometimes well-intentioned, were limited at best, paranoid, misogynist, and abusive at worst."

Dr. Comen's writing reminds me of my conversations with Dr. Ashita Gehlot and Dr. Amy Consson, who both emphasized *safe* and *safe spaces* and *find a doctor who will listen* when we spoke.

These words were on my mind when I reached out to Brandi Sellerz-Jackson, a life doula and advocate for Black women's maternal health. I called Sellerz-Jackson to ask her how women can advocate for themselves in and out of the doctor's office. As my questions left my mouth, I realized how privileged, even trite, they were. It's one thing to want to advocate. It's another thing to be able to.

"Many women don't feel safe enough to even do that," Sellerz-Jackson told me.

Medical gaslighting is especially egregious for Black women and women of color, coupled with the barbarism of medical racism. Since 1995, Boston University has conducted the Black Women's Health Study, the longest and largest of its kind, to reveal the disparities and inequities that Black women face and the consequences they suffer. The study has revealed how Black women over age fifty-five are twice as likely as white women of the same age to die from diabetes, more likely than other racial and ethnic groups to die from cardiovascular disease, hypertension, stroke, lupus, and several cancers, and face greater challenges traveling to hospitals and accessing quality health care.

Medical schools have perpetuated fallacies about Black women feeling less pain than white women, leading students to believe these erroneous claims.

"It's infiltrated the health care system," Sellerz-Jackson told me. "It's saturated the space—and it is killing Black women."

Sellerz-Jackson continued to talk frankly and kindly. Sharing information is her way. Ten years ago, after suffering from a miscarriage, she started publishing articles on the shame and stigma that surround women. She opened conversations around pregnancy and pregnancy loss, motherhood, and the overlooked care of women. As her writing grew, so did her community. Now a mother of three, she is the founder of Moms in Color, a collective that celebrates diversity within the motherhood space, and the author of *On Thriving*. Sellerz-Jackson has taken her activism to Capitol Hill, where she spoke in support of the Black Maternal Health Momnibus Act, a movement dedicated to expanding and improving the investments and attention paid to the health of women of color.

As we talked, one thing kept bubbling to the surface: women's rights. She told me that during her work in the birth and postpartum space, she saw too many women unaware of their rights or scared to lean into them.

"I saw so many parents that didn't even know their rights," she said. "I would see their inner child come up and go 'I'm scared to ask for what I need.'"

Sellerz-Jackson wants every woman—and every person—who feels unsafe, unheard, or not listened to in a medical setting to know that she can speak up. You can ask for another nurse, make an appointment with a different doctor, or leave the room.

"A lot of us, as women in this body, have been taught to be quiet and not to trust our bodies," she added. "We've been taught that someone else knows more about our bodies than we do. But we know our bodies. We know our voice—and we can use it."

Months after talking with Sellerz-Jackson, I spoke with Efrat LaMandre, who spoke passionately about the subject of speaking up and listening to ourselves.

"The patient *always knows*," LaMandre told me.

I heard conviction in LaMandre's voice—and when I learned her story, I understood why. For years, she worked as a family nurse practitioner in conventional medicine. She loved her work, but her mindset changed when her wife, Gina, fell gravely ill with several autoimmune conditions. One symptom was psoriasis so severe that Gina couldn't wear shoes. The couple sought the counsel of several doctors. In most appointments, they felt unheard as the doctors sent them home with prescriptions for heavy doses of medications. Nothing was working. And something was missing, LaMandre told me. She and her wife felt there had to be a better path. They eventually sought the counsel of an integrative medicine provider who listened and put Gina on a protocol that considered her holistic well-being, from her sleep patterns to her diet. Gina started eating differently and caring for her body in new ways—and, eventually, she healed.

LaMandre's experience with her wife's journey prompted her to earn a PhD in integrative medicine, an emerging field of medical care that incorporates alternative approaches—including diet and lifestyle changes—to consider a person's social, biological, psychological, and spiritual well-being. Today, she is widely known as both Dr. E and the Medical Disruptor by her patients and droves of followers on social media, where she offers insights to help people revolutionize their medical and self-care journeys. One of the most significant aspects of her work is educating people to listen deeply to themselves when they feel they're being dismissed or condescended to.

"Because, again, people know," LaMandre told me. "Patients know their bodies."

It can be so easy to second-guess ourselves. To fall into the trap of thinking it's all in our heads and we should just keep quiet. And as LaMandre and Sellerz-Jackson show us, it can be hard to find the space and counsel that listen and make us feel safe. But we cannot give up on this. We must talk to one another and fight for it.

We start by listening to ourselves and knowing that the quest for more—more safety, more answers, more listening ears—is a right every woman deserves.

Our General Health: More Things to Know in Your Forties

Early in this chapter, Meghan Rabbitt made a comment that resonated with me. She said when it comes to women caring for themselves, too often "the dog gets more checkups than we do."

Think about that for a second: How many times have you put aside an appointment because you were too busy? Or your child, spouse, elderly parent, or pet needed attention first? Or you were scared or tired? Or if you are like me, you did not realize you were due to have an exam?

There is no shame. I have pushed out more appointments than I can count over different reasons—fear, exhaustion, time, others' needs, an I'll-get-to-it mentality, and shoddy health insurance. But I am writing this to you in full accountability: I will never do that again. I will show up, do the work to find the doctor, make the appointment, and get the care I need.

I want you to do the same.

I know that finding care can be a challenge, especially in today's system, but make it your mission to never give up on your health. I see your inner Autumn Queen speaking up and out, calling doctors, asking questions, and demanding a safe space. And if she must get creative to make this all happen, she will.

Now, let's take stock. We have explored ways to care for ourselves through nutrition, movement, and rest. We have also explored more specific medical options for perimenopausal care. Here, we will take a macro look at the general tests and counsel to seek in our forties—beginning with these tests:

Mammograms. Unless you have been directed to do so at a younger age, forty marks the start of when to get your annual mammography. In 2023, the US Preventive Services Task Force (USPSTF) lowered the recommended age for women to get yearly mammograms from fifty to forty—a change instigated by a rise in cases of breast cancer in women, including an increase in younger women. Approximately 11 percent of all breast cancers occur in women younger than 45. And Black women are 41 percent more likely to die from the disease. Be sure to schedule an annual mammogram starting at forty—and be consistent every year.

Cervical screenings. Medical guidelines recommend that women between the ages of thirty and sixty-five should be screened with a Pap smear every three years and an HPV test every five years. It is always recommended to check with your doctor for their specific recommendations, however.

Colonoscopies. Plan to get one at forty-five, as recommended by the USPSTF, which moved the recommended age down from fifty. Dr. Ashita Gehlot underscored this importance, as colon cancer is a leading cause of cancer death in women and men.

These three tests serve as a starting point, but every one of our needs is unique. I asked Dr. Gehlot if there is a checklist of health questions that women in their forties should be asking their doctors.

"Before you ask that, the question needs to be: *Who* should you ask?" she replied.

Gehlot said that every woman in her forties should have a "trifecta" including a primary care physician, a gynecologist, and a dermatologist.

Primary care physicians, she explained, "are a gateway to good health, and they align you with any needed specialists." Think of them as the base camp for everything regarding your health. It is critical to note here that it can be hard to score an appointment with a primary care doctor these days. Gehlot recognizes that many are "inundated" with patients, a fact that can also limit the doctor's time spent with a patient. Do not let this deter you. Ask friends, family, and community members for recommendations of doctors. If you have insurance, search your provider's directory for the nearest location. Let your Autumn Queen take the reins and consistently call and email offices. The wait period can be long, so investigate this for yourself sooner rather than later. When I moved during the writing of this book, I had to make several rounds of calls to primary care doctors, many of them cold calls, before securing an appointment.

Next, a gynecologist is essential for annual women's exams, sexual health care, and recommendations for breast and colon cancer screenings. A gynecologist is also a critical starting point for seeking care around perimenopause.

And third, according to Gehlot, women must seriously consider a yearly skin-cancer screening exam with a dermatologist. "I've found so many patients to have had non-sun-related skin cancers," she told me.

With that trifecta in place, Gehlot suggests women then arm themselves with the basic questions. In your appointment, start by asking, What should I be doing right now, at my age, where I'm at?

From there, get specific. Ask about relevant cancer screenings. Look into if you have a family genetic history that leaves you predisposed to certain illnesses. Inquire about proper nutrition, as it varies depending on a woman's lifestyle and location. Ask about your bone and cardiovascular health. "Heart health is critical for women in our age group," Gehlot said. "More women are living longer with more chronic health conditions—and our cardiac biology is not the same as male's."

Gehlot recognizes that this is a bounty of information. If it's too much, she urges women to simplify. Start with asking your doctor one question: What are some parameters I should look at now and in my future?

This, she said, will open the doors to deeper care.

It feels good to have these questions, to add them to your growing arsenal of knowledge about how to best take care of yourself in your forties. As Meghan Rabbitt told me, "This really is a time where you have to take the reins."

When I spoke with family nurse practitioner and functional-medicine provider Dena Geiger, she reminded me of the power of taking inventory, just as my conversation with Dr. Mariana Calleja Ross did. Set aside time to reflect on your health. Think about how you currently feel and how you want to feel. Consider where you can better show up for yourself. Ask yourself: What am I doing to really take care of myself? How well have I been eating? Am I just dumping calories in or am I nourishing myself with whole foods? How is my sleep? How do I feel when I wake up? Can I go to bed earlier? What is my alcohol intake? Am I exercising? What is bringing me joy?

Consider the information these questions are providing. Be curious. Get creative. Think about how you can start to honor your body, mind, and soul in new ways.

Taking care of yourself in your forties can be an opportunity to grow, to get to know yourself more deeply, to reach new places. This is a calling to lean into this time of creative fire and passion, to see that the exhaustion and obstacles of some days can give way to lightness and healing the next.

Because you are always an evolving work in progress.

Let's Keep Talking

The decisions we make for our health—what we do, whom we ask, how we care—are messy, complicated, imperfect ones. The best we can do is continue to educate ourselves and make informed choices.

And to know that we are not alone.

"I want people to talk about it more—the hormones, the changes, all of it—because it doesn't mean the end of your life," Sara Wyle told me. "We're all going through it. We might as well talk about it."

Wyle then said something that made me smile. She told me how excited she is about this chapter of her life. So far, the forties have shown her that there is so much to look forward to, and she wants to honor every second of this chapter by taking care of herself now. "I'm forty-three. I'm fantastic now, and I still will be when I'm fifty-three and sixty-three and seventy-three!"

Like Wyle, I, too, am looking ahead with excitement, and I'm doing that by taking stock of the present and paying attention to my mental, physical, and emotional needs—attention I craved when I entered this decade.

Sometimes, when I cannot fall asleep, I'll do a scan of my body. I close my eyes and think of my ovaries and the fewer eggs they're holding. I think of my heart pumping oxygen-rich blood through my arteries and my ribs keeping it safe. A tenderness washes over me when I do this. I feel protective of my organs, like I want to fight for them—for mine, for yours, and for every woman's. And never do I want to take any part of my changing body for granted.

When I spoke to Stephanie Long, she reminded me how quickly things can change. She received a breast-cancer diagnosis several years ago when she was thirty-six, and with that came an arresting realization.

"I don't want to come across as bragging, but my body always worked," she said. "My periods were regular. It all worked the way it was supposed to. And then, all of a sudden, things aren't working. I was living my life. I went to bed. And the next day, I woke up with blood coming out of my nipple, and I had stage-two breast cancer. I wasn't expecting any of this."

Even as Long told me this grave story, she sounded joyful and strong, and I told her so.

"I am," she replied. "It's like, okay, now I'm starting a new chapter. I'm recovering from chemotherapy and this cancer journey. I'm going to be rebuilding; I'm going to be getting myself back."

As I listened to Long, I thought of how we're all potentially one diagnosis or health story away from one another. When we share what we're going through, we open doors, gift one another our stories of hardship and healing, and offer solace in similarities and awareness of differences. We also exchange names of physicians we feel safe around.

"It's super important that women talk about how they're doing and what they're doing," said Dr. Amy Consson. "What are we doing to fill our souls? What are we doing to nurture our relationships?"

A 2024 report revealed that women have a significant appetite for more open communication about health and health challenges. Of the more than 2,300 women surveyed, 64 percent agreed with the statement "I wish women talked about their health issues more."

I can relate to this. When I talked to my friend Megan, whom we heard from at the start of this chapter, and to other friends about growing older and various health issues, I felt connected with something bigger than me: a growing collective force. We're all facing the unknown of tomorrow—beautifully, separately, and together.

As Dr. Ashita Gehlot reminded me, another compelling reason for us women to keep sharing stories about our health is that it's a way to fight the system. Swapping knowledge and support is how we make room for the truth of who we are and what we demand.

"When we see that we are more than what medically, psychologically, and socially has been anticipated of us, we can have such a more robust life," said Gehlot.

A robust life—one that is rich and healthy and solely yours—is what I see for you in your forties.

Take care of yourself and go grab it.

CONSIDER THIS:

Now is the time to be creative and bullish about your health. Make your physical, mental, emotional, and spiritual well-being your most essential job.

You can speak up and out and demand the care you need.

You can reevaluate how you approach your nutrition, peace, and practices that deeply support you in this chapter of life.

You can ask yourself: How do I feel? How do I want to feel? How am I truly caring for myself now?

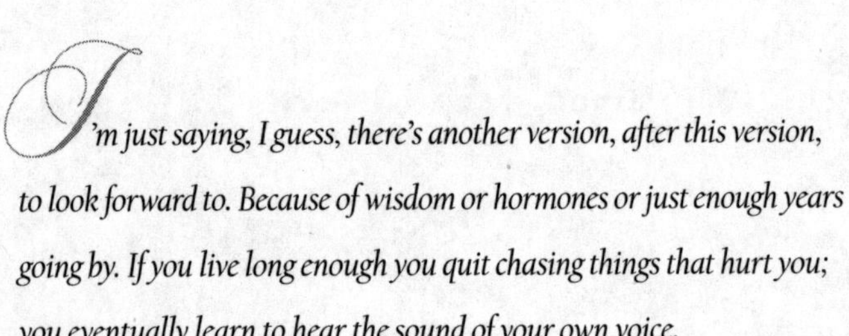

I'm just saying, I guess, there's another version, after this version, to look forward to. Because of wisdom or hormones or just enough years going by. If you live long enough you quit chasing things that hurt you; you eventually learn to hear the sound of your own voice.

—PAM HOUSTON

chapter seven

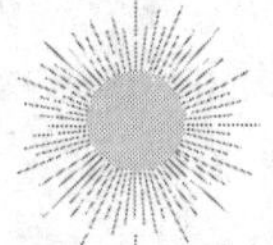

Being 40

Embracing this time, these days, and this life

I KEEP A COPY OF *WOMEN WHO RUN WITH THE WOLVES* ON my desk. Its pages are warped from years of taking it into bathtubs and onto buses, planes, and trains. I often open the book to a random page when I need a sense of grounding or a swell of energy.

Jungian psychoanalyst and author Clarissa Pinkola Estés writes that every woman has a natural essence inside her, steeped in innate integrity, creativeness, and agelessness. She believes we must accept and express our wild individuality, our authentic beauty, and the shape of our soul. "These words, *wild* and *woman*, cause women to remember who they are and what they are about," writes Estés. "They create a metaphor to describe the force which funds all females. They personify a force that women cannot live without."

I guzzle these sentences. Estés's work gives language to a truth that gets suffocated in society's weeds. She shows us that every one of us is unique, beyond the measure of any all-encompassing definition. We are lush. We are whole. We are wild. And we need more literature and modalities to remind ourselves of this.

It was my internal wild woman, my Autumn Queen, who screamed for me to reach out to Caitlin Rose Marvaso. For weeks, as I was deep in working on this book, rage's inky black eels were waking me in the middle of the night. I felt hot and swollen. Fiercely mad and frustrated. Whatever it was—perimenopause, life, stress—I yearned for the counsel of someone who could break me free.

Marvaso is a somatic therapist who combines psychotherapy with embodied movement, often in the form of sensual dance. Versed in attachment-based and trauma-focused therapies, she explores how our histories impact the connection we have with our bodies. She listens in a traditional talk therapy way, but more so, she guides, anchoring her practice in movement and music.

When she greeted me in her Bay Area studio, holding both arms out like a *T* until I walked into them, I knew I was supposed to be right there with her.

I told Marvaso that I had been feeling disconnected from myself and yearned to feel grounded in my body again. I couldn't break out of this disassociated haze I had been in for weeks. Movement and dance have always been forms of therapy for me, but often I get lost in the details, sheepish in the face of worrying about how I look. Dancing at home, by myself (usually to Robyn), with my hair slicing the air, is my preferred method. But I hadn't even been feeling like doing that.

"I have a song for you," she said after we'd been talking for twenty or so minutes. "Will you join me?"

I walked out onto the floor, just me and her, the sun jutting through the studio windows. The song she put on was moody and fierce. She and I mirrored each other on our mats. Marvaso led the way, and I followed.

"You hold a lot in your hips," she told me. I didn't understand at first, but then she continued to move, her own hips flirting like butterflies, and I felt the tension down there. She told me to breathe, to touch myself, to listen to what my body wanted. Song followed song. One bright and springy, the next dark and thick. I moved. I breathed. I let go.

It all felt like a mix of coolness and heat. Like the inside of my body was a tie-dye tapestry of emotion. I was safe, turned on toward myself, and loose. After the last song, Marvaso lowered the volume and invited me to get still on the mat. I touched my wet face and tasted a saltiness in my mouth.

Then I exhaled what felt like the longest breath I had ever released from my body.

We Need Movement

I've danced with Marvaso several times since then. Our time together showed me two transcendent truths:

We need to move our bodies. Not performatively, but to release our inner wildness.

And we need other women to help us see ourselves.

First, I would like to explore with you the movement aspect.

Our nervous systems are beyond taxed these days. Headlines, cell phones, deadlines, expectations. This cacophony depletes the messaging system of the brain and spinal cord, causing us to be in a loop of tension and anxiety, spiking our cortisol, and pulling us away from our bodies. And for reasons we explored earlier in this book, we may face amplified stress in our forties, adding to the noise in our modern lives.

An essential practice we can do to counter this stress is move our bodies in ways that feel good, as I learned from Nahid de Belgeonne.

"Movement is very regulatory, and it's how our brains evolved," de Belgeonne, a somatic movement therapist, told me. "When our ancestors, who were hunter-gatherers, were being chased, they would have run away from something, and that dissipated the cortisol. Then they would get back to their community and rest."

I had reached out to de Belgeonne because her book, *Soothe*, claimed permanent space on my shelf. Known as the Nervous System Whisperer, de Belgeonne is present and warm, and her work is accessible and immediate. She teaches us to listen to our body's bio-intelligence and to know, deep within us, that we can choose how we respond to stress, stagnancy, and emotional trauma. We can slow down, tap into our breath, and move.

Our movements needn't be grand or choreographed. We can do what our bodies are capable of. Perhaps that means gently shifting our hips, taking a slow walk, dancing in any form our bodies can manage, or simply reaching our arms to the sky.

The wisdom I have gained from de Belgeonne's work complements what I learned from Marvaso, whom I called several months after our first session. I wanted to explore why she believed movement can be so transformative for women. Marvaso told me that dance, in any form, is a way for us to tap into our divine feminine and unlock our emotions, two channels we do not access enough. It is a way for us to be free.

"Our pelvis is like a bowl that is always collecting emotion, it's collecting years of trauma, it's collecting offenses, and this can make us stiff," she said. "It's up to us to move our body to release all that and to tap into our desire and femininity."

Spending time with Marvaso brought me to start dancing with myself again. Alone, in my home, I'll put on music. I'll shift my bones and muscles in ways that feel erotic and good. Sometimes I sit and rock my hips to the music, feeling the ground underneath me.

I tell you about Marvaso because I want to invite you to do the same when you're feeling stuck or scared, overwhelmed or rageful. Or maybe tired or stagnant. Consider this: Find ten minutes to be with yourself, ideally alone. Put on a song that makes you feel and move.

"If you're willing to do just *that*," Marvaso added, "you showed courage for yourself."

Too often we convince ourselves we're not worthy. We feel we're too old, clumsy, big, small, uncoordinated, the list goes on. "But remember, all of that chatter is coming from the mind, and we do not move or dance from that place—and that is why dance can be so addictive," continued Marvaso. "You feel the shift. You feel it cascading down into your body. And your body is saying to you, 'Yes. I need this. Please, please, please be here with me.' "

A Woman Is a Mirror of Another Woman

Marvaso's wisdom is another reminder of how much women need one another. When we are embodied, full in our Autumn Queen, we act as mirrors for one another, gently reminding one another to breathe, listen, move, and feel. We help one another stay present as we face all that we've covered in this book—the stressors of life, the demands of the world, the changes in our bodies.

"There's something in our conditioning where we think we're supposed to be able to do it all alone," Vanessa Cornell told me. "We have this perception, and we look across at the images others are projecting, and we think everyone's got it figured out."

The opposite is true. You know this. I know this. Still, we need to hear it more often. That is why Cornell holds groups for women, to offer a place of permission. A space to gather in safety and to talk about what is going on in our lives. No Instagram filter. No dinner party small talk. Just the truth.

Women have been gathering in circles, around fires, and across lands and cultures and villages for our entire human existence. We've held one another close to share stories of hardship, healing, loss, and joy with our sisters, daughters, and friends, and with strangers. To be witnessed and to witness is in our blood. Hearing your feelings in another woman's story can shift your life. One admission leads to another's nod, which results in long, shared exhalations.

"It's amazing what happens to women when they hear from other people that they're struggling with the same things," Cornell told me. "It's such a source of connection."

I experienced this time and time again speaking with women

for this book. Moments of sharing have sometimes been unexpected and in random settings—in a corner at a party, in line at the grocery store, while crossing paths in an office. One woman will offer an anecdote, something scary, something intimate, something fun. Hearing it feels as though she has unlocked the gate of my fretting. "I do tooooo," I'll say. "I feel that exactly."

I know you and I are far from each other, but I have felt connected with you during this journey. You have been in my heart as I have put together these pages, weaving together one giant conversation with all of us women. As I write, I wonder how you are feeling, what you are thinking, who you are becoming in your forties. I have thought about your Autumn Queen and the clothes she wears and the scent she carries. I have felt your power, nodded with you in doubt, and shared in your sadness and joy.

I have been in awe of you, so honored by your openness to be here, in these pages, on this journey, moving toward hope.

Because that is what this life is about: finding hope in one another as we get closer to ourselves.

One piece of advice I hold close was given to me by April Snow, a psychotherapist who specializes in working with highly sensitive individuals. She told me that one of the kindest things we can do for ourselves and one another is to move toward genuine vulnerability, to be honest with our feelings and lean into our exchanges.

For instance, when someone asks you how you're doing, instead of automatically saying, "I'm fine," Snow suggested going deeper: Consider saying, "I'm feeling a little tired today, thanks for asking. How are you?" or "I've had a rough week, but I'm okay right now." Extend what is real. As Snow added, when we model emotional intelligence and vulnerability, "we create a safe space for others to express their emotions and offer validation, curiosity, and encouragement."

So I encourage you to do just that. Open your precious heart to another woman. Send a text to a friend you haven't talked to in a while. Invite a neighbor over for tea. Ask a woman you cross paths with to meet at a park bench to chat. Stop attending events that make you feel less than and instead sign up for a local gathering that surrounds you with women who are like-minded and kind.

Be open. Be honest. Be free. And lean into the warmth of one another. At times, our forties can all feel like too much. Life can take us down in moments. We all experience it; it's like we're falling. But when we express our real selves to one another, we see the truth: We are not falling. We are rising.

We are living.

Across Time and Space

I opened this book with the statement *This all feels different.*

I now know why. This all feels so different because I am different. This time is different. Our forties are so beyond-words powerful and filled with change and possibility. As Mitra Rahbar told me, our forties are when "we see the diamond inside ourselves."

"Women are dream supporters," said Rahbar. "We support other people to soar. But our forties becomes the time when we start asking ourselves, How do I support myself to soar?"

I now see that this is all different because I am finally letting myself soar. I am still the incredibly sensitive, in-my-head woman I was at the beginning of writing these pages. I still have questions. I still worry about what people think, albeit much, much, much less. And perhaps, like you, I'm still seeking answers. But I am now open and eager. I am calmer and stronger. I see how I am capable.

Writing this book revealed a new opening for me. It moved me beyond the societal-built maze that kept me taking lefts in a square of second-guessing, and it sent me out into a verdant field.

I hope something on these pages pointed you toward your verdant field—because it is there for you, waiting with your Autumn Queen to tackle this one gorgeous, precious, complicated chapter that is your forties.

Speaking of hard: Several years ago, Kara Lawson illuminated a truth that I've held on to like a talisman.

I interviewed the star athlete and coach of the Duke Blue Devils women's basketball team after one of her pep talks to her players went viral. She was telling her team that too often people wait for life to get easier. We think, I just need to get through this, and I'll be good. I just need to move through the holidays, get through the season, move past this hurdle, and things will get easier.

"It will never get easier," said Lawson. "What happens is you handle hard better."

You handle hard better.

That's what our forties hold for us: a sparkling well of strength to handle hard better.

Life will always bring mountains. Society will continue to judge us. Ageist and sexist comments will abound. Beauty ideals will continue to center thinness, youth, and fabricated perfection. People's opinions about our relationship status and if we do or do not have children will persist. Work will challenge us. Our health will demand greater attention amid a tough medical system. As long as we're alive, we're not exonerated from the tough stuff.

But we can handle hard better.

You can handle hard better.

You can let your Autumn Queen lead.

You can see how the patriarchy has fueled stories that don't belong to you.

You can find your power inside and outside your work, reevaluate your ambition, and pull at the threads of what makes a "good" career to weave something new, peaceful, passionate, and true.

You can embody and feel your deep-in-your-soul beauty, divest from hurtful ideals, and make decisions solely for you.

You can marry, divorce, marry again, divorce again, open a relationship, be single by choice or not, yearn for partnership, want something different, fantasize, and beyond. And you can be vulnerable and lean into connecting with other women—those you've known for ages, those you've just met, and those just around the corner.

You can know that your life is brimming whether you do or do not have children, and you can mother yourself and the people, projects, and animals you love.

You can be bullish about your health, reach for nutrient-dense foods, and care for your body in new and creative ways.

You can ask for help, befriend yourself, be vulnerable, move your body, and lift your head to the sky when your days are hard.

You can look inside to your younger self—to your inner twelve-year-old and twenty-two-year-old and thirty-five-year-old—and be there for her. She's made mistakes. The world has hurt her. And now she looks up to you, watching as you honor your heart and aim to live your fullest, strongest, most beautiful days possible.

May your forties teach you that you can hold yourself across time and space. That you can always expand your story. That you can reach down and pull yourself from the fire, every day, and choose to move through this moment, this hour, this time in lockstep with beauty, hand-in-hand with yourself.

One More Story to Share . . .

I call my mother one afternoon. She answers, and I say that I'd love to interview her.

"You can record this, sweetie, for your book," she tells me.

I ask my mother about leaving all those years ago, when she was in her forties. She seems to have built a life of joy since, but I want to know if she found peace.

"I guess it took me down a different path," she says. "But I will never forgive myself. The pain I caused."

"But I forgive you," I say to her. "You had to do it, I know you did. And I want *you* to know that."

My mother starts to cry. We sit on the phone, silent for a few seconds. I can picture her chin quivering.

"What do you want for me now, Mama? Now that I'm in my forties, what do you hope for me?"

The energy whirls between us, thousands of miles apart.

"I want you to be ambling across the prairie, in peace and knowing yourself," she says. "That's what I want for you. I want you to be free."

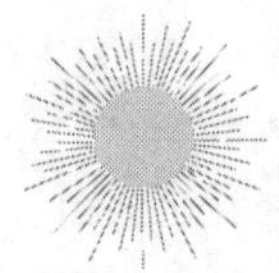

Acknowledgments

Every thread of this book came from the graciousness of others. A quilt of stories, these pages are a marriage of vulnerability, truth, and love gifted by immense people.

My greatest confidante and companion in facing the exhilarating journey of compiling all this was Cassidy Graham, the editor of my literary dreams. Cassidy, you brought to this endeavor a giant heart, keen sense, and matchless clarity. Your name should be on this cover. Thank you.

My most profound sense of awe goes to Meg Thompson, the literary agent with an endless well of integrity and transcendent light. Meg, you embody an unparalleled grace, intuition, and power for good. Thank you for championing me and so many. And thanks to Tess Brown.

The encouragement of Maria Shriver is the foremost reason my fingers first touched the keyboard to write this book. Maria, it's been an honor to learn from you and to witness how you encourage people to live with an open spirit, mind, and heart. You evolve this world. Thank you for showing me the treasures worth working for in this life.

I am indebted to the team at The Open Field and Viking/Penguin at large who offered me support and lent their incredible skills to these pages: Brian Tart, Meg Leder, Nina Rodríguez-Marty, Carolyn Coleburn, Rachel Wainz, Nick Michal, Gabriel Levinson, Sabrina Bowers, Nayon Cho, and Hanna Richards.

The time and insight so many women gifted me will remain tucked in my heart. Thank you to Steph Jagger for introducing me to the powerful Autumn Queen, and to Alyssa Nobriga, Karin Brummell, Camille Styles, Kara Loewentheil, Vanessa Cornell, Chianti Lomax, Deepa Purushotaman, Kameko Grant, Anna Malaika Tubbs, Dené Logan, Valerie Rein, Kristin Neff, Jen Gottlieb, Brigit Ritchie, Carrie Hammer, Sister Monica Clare, Rae Leslie, Meredith Baird, Natalie Silverstein, Satya Doyle Byock, Kathy Caprino, Amina AlTai, Lesley Jane Seymour, Tara Mohr, Erin Ryan, Patty Bechtold, Anne Campbell, Rashel Hariri, Carmen Cool, Sara Wyle, Lindsey Marie, Emily King, Jessica DeFino, Meghan Rabbitt, Kristen Genzano, Cyndi Darnell, Nicola Slawson, Gillian Anderson, Megan O'Neill, Molly Roden Winter, Sinsia, Jane McClain, Danielle Gates, Marisa G. Franco, Lane Moore, Maya Borgueta, Jillian Sanders, Katrina McGhee, Mitra Rahbar, Angela L. Harris, Ruby Warrington, Annie Daly, Katie Maynard, Peggy Fitzsimmons, Barbara Stamis, Dena Geiger, Dr. Uma Naidoo, Dr. Mariana Calleja Ross, Monica Molenaar, Anne Fulenwider, Randi Friedman, Dr. Amy Consson, Dr. Ashita Gehlot, Brandi Sellerz-Jackson, Efrat LaMandre, Stephanie Long, Caitlin Rose Marvaso, Lisa Diamond, Nahid de Belgeonne, April Snow, Kara Lawson, Christine Morrison, Lisa McCarty, Deganit Nuur, Mitzi Starkweather, Ana Tajder, Barbara Huson, Robin Finn, Joy Sullivan, Menah Adeola Eyaside Pratt, Stephanie Sarazin, Wendy Strgar, Elizabeth Lorenz, Oliva Weadock, Angela Saini, Jennifer Craig Gilbert, Tammy Dash, Wynne Wong, Justine Higgins, Kerri Steen, Lauren Shea, and Tiffany Williams.

My gratitude goes to the following souls who have enriched my creative life: Elise Loehnen, Kiki Koroshetz, Christina Schwarzenegger, Jaspre Guest, Shrankhla Holecek, Meghan Rabbitt, Kate Wolfson, Cydney Weiner, Mara Freedman, Jaclyn Levin, Lauren Westphal, Madison Bridges, George Mumford, Gwyneth Paltrow, Carson Meyer, Lan Jaenicke, Megan Papay, Sharyn Alfonsi, the late Sietze Vanderheide, Mike Olmstead, Teal Cannaday, Lisa Olliges, Ted Donaldson, Christine Hanway, Brittany Snow, Sarah Lonsdale, Julie Carlson, Josh Groves, Kim-Minh Huberwald-Leong, Rebecca Dove, Linda Caan, Kat Rudu, Buffy Maguire, Emily Frankoski, Sandra Fish, Marcy Cole, Hayley Dickson, Martie Cook, Lindzi Scharf, Phil Stutz, Jing Gao, Erin Collins, Lori Marble, Alex Gordon, Quinn Ezralow, Eamonn Bowles, Nichole Perkins, Eva Yazhari, Mark Allison, Ann Scott McGilchrist, Nada Jones,

Jan Whitt, Jenn Schraven, Jayne Williams, Jessie Douglass-Smith McGraw, Donna Aldrich, Lisa Ligon, Sarah Cassidy, Cathleen DaCosta, Laleh Shahideh, Adrienne Levy, Lindsay Regan, and Jeannie Danelo.

I am indebted to the King County, San Francisco, Norwell, Missoula, and Darby public libraries.

Thank you to my soul friends and family: the Gomezes, Timothy Hajjar, Stephanie Hajjar, Tiffany Hutter, Noa Franco, Arlene Deredoorian, Amanda Cooey, Justine Higgins, Shane Higgins, Sarah Swanson, Teal Cannaday, Baker Machado, Catherine Barr, James Barr, Ina Damm Muri, Elaine Lauterbach-Hampsten, Rachael McKeon, Brittany Aikey, Kerri Steen, Lauren Shea, Katie and Erin, Barbara Stamis, Eric Meltesen, Kevin Larson, Eric Scott Moore, Megan Posner, Dave Posner, Doug Brega, Barry Blaisdell, Sheila Finn, the Inzanas, the Gracelys, Sasha Hnatkovich, Danielle Bober, Ava Lindsay, Elizabeth and Ryan Lindsay, Bee Gracely, Regan Cordier, and Patricia Edge.

My heart and future will always be full thanks to Gary and Jan Liddell. And my mind and outlook will forever be stretched thanks to the late James Caan.

Thank heavens for Andi MacHowl (and Lucy, Charlie, and Cinnamon).

To my beautiful mother, Lynn Lindsay: What a gorgeous adventure being your daughter has been. Thank you for your love. And thank you to my bonus dad, Wayne Lugaila.

To my giant soul of a father, Ray Lindsay: Your short time here left a mega-example of kindness and joy for all of us to follow. I carry you with me.

To my dearest forever friend, Maura Gomez-Kwedor: My life has safety, warmth, and belly laughs all because of you. I cherish our friendship. And thank you to Matthew Kwedor, Eleanor, and Eva.

Last—and first and forever—of all, to my husband, Christian Edge: Thank you for sharing your colossal capacity for adventure, connection, fun, hard work, and hope with me. I now understand the reason for this life: It's to immerse ourselves in these days, as dark, light, cruel, or joyful they may be. You showed me this, and you opened my heart to see that I want to dive in side-by-side with you.

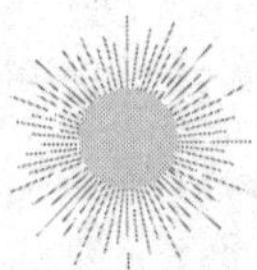

Notes

ix *"I want to believe":* Mary Oliver, "The Ponds," *House of Light* (Penguin Press, 1990), 63.

INTRODUCTION: WHY DOES THIS ALL FEEL SO DIFFERENT

9 ***As author Sharon Blackie writes:*** Sharon Blackie, *Hagitude: Reimagining the Second Half of Life* (New World Library, 2022), 4.

14 ***A growing number of us:*** Sarah House, Shannon Seery, Nicole Cervi, and Jeremiah Kohl, *Party of One: How Single Women Stack Up in the U.S. Economy* (Wells Fargo Economics Special Commentary, 2023), externalcontent.blob.core.windows.net/pdfs/7a16f5a8-b531-403c-bb1e-ed14d5cbd8b2.pdf.

14 ***Those of us getting married:*** Richard Fry, "A Record-High Share of 40-Year-Olds in the U.S. Have Never Been Married," Pew Research Center, June 28, 2023, pewresearch.org/short-reads/2023/06/28/a-record-high-share-of-40-year-olds-in-the-us-have-never-been-married.

14 ***There are more households headed:*** Jake Hays and Rachel Minkin, "Rising Number of U.S. Households Are Headed by Married Same-Sex Couples," Pew Research Center, June 12, 2025, pewresearch.org/social-trends/2025/06/12/rising-number-of-u-s-households-are-headed-by-married-same-sex-couples.

15 ***delaying having kids:*** Brady Hamilton, Joyce Martin, and Michelle Osterman (National Vital Statistics System Rapid Release Quarterly

Provisional Estimates data series, report no. 38, 2025), cdc.gov/nchs/data/vsrr/vsrr038.pdf.

15 ***and more are doing so unpartnered:*** Gretchen Livingston, "They're Waiting Longer, but U.S. Women Today More Likely to Have Children Than a Decade Ago," Pew Research Center, January 18, 2018, pewresearch.org/social-trends/2018/01/18/theyre-waiting-longer-but-u-s-women-today-more-likely-to-have-children-than-a-decade-ago.

15 ***A cloud of financial insecurity:*** Matt Bruenig, "How Many People Live Paycheck to Paycheck?" People's Policy Project, March 19, 2025, peoplespolicyproject.org/2025/03/19/how-many-people-live-paycheck-to-paycheck.

15 ***Wealth gaps cast:*** Federal Reserve Bank of St. Louis, *Shares of Wealth by Wealth Percentile Groups*, accessed on October 22, 2025, fred.stlouisfed.org/release/tables?eid=813804&rid=453.

CHAPTER ONE: LOSING AND FINDING OURSELVES

20 ***"Until we can understand":*** Adrienne Rich, "When We Dead Awaken: Writing as Re-Vision," *College English* 34, no. 1 (1972): 18–30, doi.org/10.2307/375215.

23 ***We absorb messages:*** Kara Loewentheil, *Take Back Your Brain: How a Sexist Society Gets in Your Head—and How to Get It Out* (Penguin Life, 2024), xxvii.

26 ***As Stauffer writes:*** Rainesford Stauffer, *All the Gold Stars: Reimagining Ambition and the Ways We Strive* (Balance, 2023), 10.

34 ***Science journalist Angela Saini:*** Angela Saini, *The Patriarchs: The Origins of Inequality* (Beacon Press, 2023), 198.

34 ***"It's about people":*** Saini, *The Patriarchs*, 198.

34 ***Anthropologists have also:*** Angela Saini, "How Did Patriarchy Actually Begin?" BBC News, May 29, 2023, bbc.com/future/article/20230525-how-did-patriarchy-actually-begin.

35 ***Women came to be seen as property:*** Saini, "How Did Patriarchy Actually Begin?"

35 ***As author and scholar:*** Anna Malaika Tubbs, *Erased: What American Patriarchy Has Hidden from Us* (Flatiron Books, 2025), 11.

35 ***"While patriarchy is present":*** Tubbs, *Erased*, 11.

36 ***"For any woman, it is":*** Isabel Allende, *The Soul of a Woman* (Ballantine Books, 2021), 38.

37 ***In the thirtieth edition:*** Maureen Murdock, *The Heroine's Journey: Woman's Quest for Wholeness* (Shambala Publications, 2020), xvii.

38 ***Researchers from NYU and Princeton:*** Lin Bian, Sarah-Jane Leslie, and Andrei Cimpian, "Gender Stereotypes About Intellectual Ability Emerge Early and Influence Children's Interests," *Science* 355, no. 6323 (2017): 389–91, doi.org/10.1126/science.aah6524.

39 ***To support this, Rein:*** Brian G. Dias and Kerry J. Ressler, "Parental Olfactory Experience Influences Behavior and Neural Structure in Subsequent Generations," *Nature Neuroscience* 17, no. 1 (2014): 89–96, doi.org/10.1038/nn.3594.

41 ***"We fight ourselves":*** Stacey Lindsay, "A Better World Begins with Self-Compassion: Dr. Kristin Neff Shares How Loving Ourselves Can Lead to More Resilience," *Maria Shriver's Sunday Paper*, July 23, 2022, mariashriversundaypaper.com/kristin-neff-on-having-more-self-compassion.

41 ***She believes there are two:*** Kristin Neff, *Fierce Self-Compassion: How Women Can Harness Kindness to Speak Up, Claim Their Power, and Thrive* (Harper Wave, 2021), 5.

41 ***"It might mean":*** Lindsay, "A Better World Begins with Self-Compassion."

43 ***While most of the research:*** Rachel F. Rodgers, Ruthann C. Hewett, and Genevieve P. Nowicki, "A Sociocultural Model of the Relationships Between Social Media Use and Body Image in Midlife Women," *Eating Behaviors* 53, no. 101867 (2024), doi.org/10.1016/j.eatbeh.2024.101867.

47 ***As Griffin writes:*** Amy Griffin, *The Tell* (Dial Press, 2025), 67.

CHAPTER TWO: THE WORK OF OUR LIVES

60 ***"At some point":*** Joy Harjo, *Poet Warrior* (W. W. Norton, 2022), 20.

61 ***She felt like:*** Sister Monica Clare, *A Change of Habit: Leaving Behind My Husband, Career, and Everything I Owned to Become a Nun* (Crown, 2025), xii.

62 ***"As I got older":*** Clare, *A Change of Habit*, 43.

73 ***"As much as my peers":*** Satya Doyle Byock, *Quarterlife: The Search for Self in Early Adulthood* (Random House, 2022), xiv–xv.

74 ***"Quarterlife is not a":*** Byock, *Quarterlife*, xv.

78 ***Three out of four adults:*** Luisa Garcia, "Americans Grapple with Affordability Crisis: 'Hard for Me Just to Survive,'" CBS News, June 12, 2025, cbsnews.com/news/americans-grapple-with-affordability-crisis-hard-for-me-just-to-survive.

79 ***A 2024 analysis by:*** Isabela Salas-Betsch, "The Economic Status of Single Mothers," Center for American Progress, August 7,

2024, americanprogress.org/article/the-economic-status-of-single-mothers.

79 ***We still face a:*** Richard Fry and Carolina Aragão, "Gender Pay Gap in U.S. Has Narrowed Slightly Over Two Decades," Pew Research Center, March 4, 2025, pewresearch.org/short-reads/2025/03/04/gender-pay-gap-in-us-has-narrowed-slightly-over-2-decades.

79 ***In 2021, Mayo Clinic:*** Stephanie Faubion et al., "Impact of Menopause Symptoms on Women in the Workplace," *Mayo Clinic Proceedings* 98, no. 6 (2023): 833–35, doi.org/10.1016/j.mayocp.2023.02.025.

80 ***Two years later, research:*** Chartered Institute of Personnel and Development, *Menopause in the Workplace: Employee Experiences in 2023* (October 4, 2023), cipd.org/uk/knowledge/reports/menopause-workplace-experiences.

80 ***There is also a growing:*** Darby E. Attoe and Emma A. Climie, "Miss. Diagnosis: A Systematic Review of ADHD in Adult Women," *Journal of Attention Disorders* 27, no. 7 (2023): 645–57, doi.org/10.1177/10870547231161533.

88 ***As the world plummeted:*** Ariane Hegewisch et al., *Women at Work Five Years Since the Start of the COVID-19 Pandemic: Any Progress?* (Institute for Women's Policy Research-C531, 2025), iwpr.org/wp-content/uploads/2025/03/Women-at-Work-Five-Years-Since-the-Start-of-the-COVID-19-Pandemic-fact-sheet_March-2025.pdf.

88 ***Additionally, schools closed:*** Jenesse Miller, "COVID-19 Has Hit Women Hard, Especially Working Mothers," *USC Today*, June 18, 2020, today.usc.edu/covid-19-women-job-losses-childcare-mental-health-usc-study.

88 ***The closure of:*** Brooke Lepage, "The Child Care and Early Learning Workforce Is Underpaid and Women Are Paying the Price," *National Women's Law Center*, May 2023, nwlc.org/wp-content/uploads/2023/05/child-care-workers-5.25.23v3.pdf.

88 ***In a 2020 article:*** Claire Lampen, "The Pandemic Is Squeezing Women Out of the Workforce," *The Cut*, November 17, 2020, thecut.com/2020/11/coronavirus-pandemic-forcing-mothers-out-of-the-workforce.html.

89 ***And while some research:*** Erin George, "Mothers' Employment Has Surpassed Pre-Pandemic Levels, But the Child Care Crisis Persists," *US Department of Labor Blog*, May 6, 2024, blog.dol.gov/2024/05/06/mothers-employment-has-surpassed-pre-pandemic-levels-but-the-child-care-crisis-persists.

89 ***Bhattarai noted that:*** Abha Bhattarai, "Mothers Are Leaving the

Workforce, Erasing Pandemic Gains," *The Washington Post*, August 11, 2025, washingtonpost.com/business/2025/08/11/mothers-leaving-workforce-large-numbers/.

89 ***Additionally, approximately 300,000:*** "Employment Status of the US Population by Race, Sex, and Age," US Bureau of Labor Statistics, August 2, 2025, bls.gov/news.release/empsit.t02.htm.

89 ***"This isn't a coincidence":*** Katica Roy, "300,000 Black Women Have Left the Labor Force in 3 Months," MSNBC, July 17, 2025, msnbc.com/know-your-value/business-culture/300000-black-women-left-labor-force-3-months-s-not-coincidence-rcna219355.

90 ***Garbes, a writer and:*** Angela Garbes, *Essential Labor: Mothering as Social Change* (Harper Wave, 2022), 12.

90 ***"If we were to":*** Garbes, *Essential Labor,* 10.

91 ***In* The Trouble with Passion*:*** Erin A. Cech, *The Trouble with Passion: How Searching for Fulfillment at Work Fosters Inequality* (University of California Press, 2021), 12.

91 ***"I felt like my work":*** Amina AlTai, *The Ambition Trap: How to Stop Chasing and Start Living* (Open Field, 2025), xxv.

100 ***The funding goes:*** Shiri Chilazi, *Advancing Gender Equity in Venture Capital,* Harvard Kennedy School Women in Public Policy Program (October 2019), hks.harvard.edu/centers/wappp/publications/advancing-gender-equality-venture-capital.

100 ***A growing body of science:*** Jeanne F. Duffy et al., "Sex Difference in the Near-24-Hour Intrinsic Period of the Human Circadian Timing System," *Proceedings of the National Academy of Sciences of the United States of America* 108, no. S3 (2011): S15602–S608, doi.org/10.1073/pnas.1010666108.

100 ***Our testosterone levels:*** Sonia Ponzo et al., "Menstrual Cycle-Associated Symptoms and Workplace Productivity in US Employees: A Cross-Sectional Survey of Users of the Flo Mobile Phone App," *Digital Health* 8 (December 2022), osf.io/preprints/psyarxiv/as2eb_v1.

CHAPTER THREE: ON BEAUTY IN OUR FORTIES

106 ***"Beauty seemed to mean":*** Sister Monica Clare, *A Change of Habit: Leaving Behind My Husband, Career, and Everything I Owned to Become a Nun* (Crown, 2025), 53.

109 ***Yet when we worry:*** Renee Engeln, *Beauty Sick: How the Cultural Obsession with Appearance Hurts Girls and Women—and Its Impact on Health and Happiness* (Harper, 2017), 8.

110 ***"Maintaining our physical desirability":*** Elise Loehnen, *On Our*

Best Behavior: The Seven Deadly Sins and the Price Women Pay to Be Good (Dial Press, 2023), 118–19.

112 ***As Cool spoke, she:*** Sonya Renee Taylor, *The Body Is Not an Apology: The Power of Radical Self-Love* (Berrett-Koehler, 2021).

113 ***She proposes that gaslighting:*** Kate Manne, *Unshrinking: How to Face Fatphobia* (Crown, 2024), 151.

113 ***The cryptic tactics:*** Manne, *Unshrinking*, 153.

114 ***The global beauty industry:*** "The Beauty Boom and Beyond: Can the Industry Maintain Its Growth?" McKinsey, September 11, 2024, mckinsey.com/industries/consumer-packaged-goods/our-insights/the-beauty-boom-and-beyond-can-the-industry-maintain-its-growth.

114 ***Blooming research over:*** Fatima Mougharbel et al., "Heavy Social Media Use and Psychological Distress Among Adolescents: The Moderating Role of Sex, Age, and Parental Support," *Frontiers in Public Health* 11 (June 2023), doi.org/10.3389/fpubh.2023.1190390.

114 ***But this data gap:*** Rachel F. Rodgers, Ruthann C. Hewett, and Genevieve P. Nowicki, "A Sociocultural Model of the Relationships Between Social Media Use and Body Image in Midlife Women," *Eating Behaviors* 53, no. 101867 (2024), doi.org/10.1016/j.eatbeh.2024.101867.

114 ***When it comes to cosmetic:*** Lina Triana et al., "Trends in Surgical and Nonsurgical Aesthetic Procedures: A 14-Year Analysis of the International Society of Aesthetic Plastic Surgery," *Aesthetic Plastic Surgery* 48, no. 20 (2024): 4217–27, doi.org/10.1007/s00266-024-04260-2.

114 ***About 45 percent of procedures:*** American Society of Plastic Surgeons, "American Society of Plastic Surgeons Breaks Down 2022 Plastic Surgery Trends Among Different Demographics" news release, December 7, 2023, plasticsurgery.org/news/press-releases/american-society-of-plastic-surgeons-breaks-down-2022-plastic-surgery-trends-among-different-demographics.

114 ***One 2022 study linked:*** Ross L. Pearlman et al., "Factors Associated with Likelihood to Undergo Cosmetic Surgical Procedures Among Young Adults in the United States: A Narrative Review," *Clinical, Cosmetic and Investigational Dermatology* 15 (May 2022): 859–77, doi.org/10.2147/CCID.S358573.

116 ***It shows that women:*** Sarah Bonell, Sean C. Murphy, and Scott Griffiths, "Under the Knife: Unfavorable Perceptions of Women Who Seek Plastic Surgery," *PLOS One* 16, no. 9 (2021): e0257145, doi.org/10.1371/journal.pone.0257145.

117 ***A different study revealed:*** Jürgen Margraf, Andrea H. Meyer, and Kristen L. Lavallee, "Well-Being from the Knife? Psychological Effects of Aesthetic Surgery," *Clinical Psychological Science* 1, no. 3 (2013): 239–52, doi.org/10.1177/2167702612471660.

120 ***"A cultural fixation on":*** Naomi Wolf, *The Beauty Myth: How Images of Beauty Are Used Against Women* (Chatto & Windus, 1990), 187.

120 ***The world is always telling:*** Clare Chambers, *Intact: In Defense of the Unmodified Body* (Allen Lane, 2022), 4.

120 ***"Our bodies are always under":*** Chambers, *Intact*, 2.

121 ***She illuminates how "the choices":*** Chambers, *Intact*, 6.

121 ***In her book* Woman**: Natalie Angier, *Woman: An Intimate Geography* (Mariner Books, 2014), x.

121 ***"But women, we know":*** Angier, *Woman*, x.

124 ***Her voice, which:*** Janna Mandell, "Meet the Beauty Industry Watchdogs Calling Bullsh*t on Brands and Retailers," *HuffPost*, June 25, 2020, huffpost.com/entry/beauty-industry-watchdogs-estee-laundry-jessica-defino_l_5eea6a09c5b6d4397ade4f1a.

125 ***The Federal Trade Commission mandates:*** Federal Trade Commission, "L'Oréal Settles FTC Charges Alleging Deceptive Advertising for Anti-Aging Cosmetics," news release, June 30, 2014, ftc.gov/news-events/news/press-releases/2014/06/loreal-settles-ftc-charges-alleging-deceptive-advertising-anti-aging-cosmetics.

125 ***In 2017,* Allure *magazine:*** Michelle Lee, "*Allure* Magazine Will No Longer Use the Term 'Anti-Aging,'" *Allure*, August 14, 2017, allure.com/story/allure-magazine-phasing-out-the-word-anti-aging.

131 ***"Very into 40":*** Megan O'Neill (@megagirl), "Among the Goings-On Last Week," November 12, 2024, instagram.com/p/DCR2JvuuNNI/.

133 ***"Beauty sickness matters":*** Renee Engeln, *Beauty Sick: How the Cultural Obsession with Appearance Hurts Girls and Women—and Its Impact on Health and Happiness* (Harper, 2017), 7.

134 ***In the Pulitzer Prize–winning novel:*** Donna Tartt, *The Goldfinch* (Little, Brown, 2013), 771.

CHAPTER FOUR: HITCHED TO OUR TRUTH

138 ***"What would happen if":*** Muriel Rukeyser, "Käthe Kollwitz," *The Collected Poems of Muriel Rukeyser* (University of Pittsburgh Press, 2006), poetryfoundation.org/poems/90874/kathe-kollwitz.

144 ***In 2025, the average cost:*** Kirsten Francis et al., "The Knot 2025

Real Weddings Study," The Knot, updated February 26, 2025, theknot.com/content/wedding-data-insights/real-weddings-study.

144 *"No one wants to find":* Rebecca Mead, *One Perfect Day: The Selling of the American Wedding* (Penguin Books, 2008), 3.

145 *As Lyz Lenz aptly writes:* Lyz Lenz, *This American Ex-Wife: How I Ended My Marriage and Started My Life* (Crown, 2024), 48.

151 *Fewer people are getting:* Carolina Aragão et al., "The Modern American Family: Key Trends in Marriage and Family Life," Pew Research Center, September 14, 2023, pewresearch.org/social-trends/2023/09/14/the-modern-american-family.

151 *In America, people are:* Kim Parker and Rachel Minkin, "The Future of the Family," Pew Research Center, September 14, 2023, pewresearch.org/social-trends/2023/09/14/the-future-of-the-family.

151 *The average age when:* US Census Bureau, "Median Age at First Marriage," *American Community Survey* (2023), data.census.gov/table/ACSDT1Y2023.B12007.

151 *More Americans are choosing to partner:* Richard Fry and Kim Parker, "Rising Share of U.S. Adults Are Living Without a Spouse or Partner," Pew Research Center, October 5, 2021, pewresearch.org/social-trends/2021/10/05/rising-share-of-u-s-adults-are-living-without-a-spouse-or-partner.

151 *Women initiate approximately 70:* Michael J. Rosenfeld and Katharina Roesler, "Stability and Change in Predictors of Marital Dissolution in the US 1950–2017," *Journal of Marriage and Family* 86, no. 1 (2023): 154–75, doi.org/10.1111/jomf.12932.

155 *"We had received enough":* Gillian Anderson, ed., *Want: Sexual Fantasies by Anonymous* (Abrams Press, 2024), ix.

155 *"How we ended up with the title":* Stacey Lindsay, "Gillian Anderson Asked Women to Share Their Sexual Fantasies: The Result Is a Riveting Bestseller," *Maria Shriver's Sunday Paper*, October 12, 2024, mariashriversundaypaper.com/gillian-anderson-want-sexual-fantasies-by-anonymous/.

156 *While a long and dated:* Lisa Diamond, *Sexual Fluidity: Understanding Women's Love and Desire* (Harvard University Press, 2009), 2.

160 *To do this, they suggest:* Betty Martin and Robyn Dalzen, *The Art of Receiving and Giving: The Wheel of Consent* (Luminare, 2021), 117.

160 *originally developed by bodyworker:* Betty Martin, "Wheel of Consent," accessed October 19, 2025, wheelofconsent.org/wheel.

162 *In* Sex When You Don't*:* Cyndi Darnell, *Sex When You Don't Feel Like It: The Truth About Mismatched Libido and Rediscovering Desire* (Rowman & Littlefield, 2022), 180.

163 ***It reads, "I guess my":*** Anderson, ed., *Want,* xiii.

164 ***In 2022, the United Kingdom's:*** Jamie Lennox, "7 in 10 Women Blame Menopause for Divorce, Research Finds," Today's Family Lawyer, October 22, 2022, todaysfamilylawyer.co.uk/7-in-10-women-blame-menopause-for-divorce-research-finds.

165 ***"What we wanted was to":*** Lenz, *American Ex-Wife,* 13.

168 ***Franco, whom I interviewed:*** Stacey Lindsay, "Science Says Making New Friends Is Good for Your Health (and It's Never Too Late): Marisa G. Franco Shows Us How," *Maria Shriver's Sunday Paper,* January 28, 2023, mariashriversundaypaper.com/how-to-make-new-friends.

169 ***"So many of us":*** Stacey Lindsay, "In Our Lonely World, Comedian Lane Moore Is Helping Us Find Our People," *Maria Shriver's Sunday Paper,* August 12, 2023, mariashriversundaypaper.com/lane-moore-find-your-people.

171 ***Humans have a negativity:*** Amrisha Vaish, Tobias Grossman, and Amanda Woodward, "Not All Emotions Are Created Equal: The Negativity Bias in Social-Emotional Development," *Psychological Bulletin* 134, no. 3 (2013): 383–403, doi.org/10.1037/0033-2909.134.3.383.

CHAPTER FIVE: OUR MATERNAL UNFOLDING

182 ***"You are born to one":*** Clarissa Pinkola Estés, *Women Who Run with the Wolves: Myths and Stories of the Wild Woman Archetype* (Ballantine Books, 1996), 193.

189 ***As Sheila Heti writes:*** Sheila Heti, *Motherhood* (Henry Holt, 2018), 21.

192 ***The average age of a first-time:*** Andrea D. Brown et al., *Trends in Mean Age of Mothers: United States, 2016–2023 National Vital Statistics Reports* 74, no. 9 (2025): 1–7, stacks.cdc.gov/view/cdc/174598.

192 ***Data from the CDC also shows:*** Anne K. Driscoll and Brady E. Hamilton, *Effects of Age-Specific Fertility Trends on Overall Fertility Trends: United States, 1990–2023, National Vital Statistics Reports* 74, no. 3 (2025): 1–11, stacks.cdc.gov/view/cdc/174576.

192 ***There's been a steady:*** Max Roser, "Until the Late 1960s, the Total Fertility Rate Was Five—Since Then, It Has Halved," Our World in Data, September 3, 2019, ourworldindata.org/global-fertility-has-halved.

193 ***For women who choose not to:*** Rachel Minkin, Juliana Menasce

Horowitz, and Carolina Aragao, "Reasons Adults Give for Not Having Children," Pew Research Center, July 24, 2024, pewresearch.org/social-trends/2024/07/25/reasons-adults-give-for-not-having-children/.

193 ***Among all high-income nations:*** Munira Gunja, Evan Gumas, Relebohile Masitha, and Laurie Zephyrin, "Insights into the U.S. Maternal Mortality Crisis: An International Comparison," The Commonwealth Fund, June 4, 2024, commonwealthfund.org/publications/issue-briefs/2024/jun/insights-us-maternal-mortality-crisis-international-comparison/.

193 ***and racial and ethnic inequities:*** Donna L. Hoyert, *Maternal Mortality Rates in the United States, 2023*, Health E-Stats Series (National Center for Health Statistics, 2025), stacks.cdc.gov/view/cdc/174577.

193 ***Researchers from the University:*** Caroline Hickman et al., "Climate Anxiety in Children and Young People and Their Beliefs About Government Responses to Climate Change: A Global Survey," *The Lancet Planetary Health* 5, no. 12 (2021): e863–73, thelancet.com/journals/lanplh/article/PIIS2542-5196(21)00278-3/fulltext.

194 ***"Understanding climate anxiety":*** Jade S. Sasser, *Climate Anxiety and the Kid Question: Deciding Whether to Have Children in an Uncertain Future* (University of California Press, 2024), 10.

194 ***Approximately 11 percent of women:*** "How Common Is Infertility?" Eunice Kennedy Shriver National Institute of Child Health and Human Development, last modified February, 8, 2018, nichd.nih.gov/health/topics/infertility/conditioninfo/common.

197 ***Essayist and journalist Meghan Daum:*** Meghan Daum ed., *Selfish, Shallow, and Self-Absorbed: Sixteen Writers on the Decision Not to Have Kids* (Picador, 2016), 2.

199 ***She coined the term:*** Ruby Warrington, *Women Without Kids: The Revolutionary Rise of an Unsung Sisterhood* (Sounds True, 2023), 10.

201 ***In America, the age of:*** Gretchen Livingston, "They're Waiting Longer, but U.S. Women Today More Likely to Have Children Than a Decade Ago," Pew Research Center, January 18, 2018, pewresearch.org/social-trends/2018/01/18/theyre-waiting-longer-but-u-s-women-today-more-likely-to-have-children-than-a-decade-ago.

201 ***More women over forty:*** Brady Hamilton, Joyce Martin, and Michelle Osterman, *Births: Provisional Data for 2024* (National Vital Statistics System Rapid Release Quarterly Provisional Estimates

data series, report no. 38, 2025), cdc.gov/nchs/data/vsrr/vsrr038.pdf.

201 ***Just as the reasons:*** Jamie Ducharme, "Why So Many Women Are Waiting Longer to Have Kids," *Time,* April 10, 2024, time.com/6965267/women-having-kids-later/.

202 ***And for some mothers:*** "Caregiving and the Sandwich Generation," Mental Health America, mhanational.org/resources/caregiving-and-the-sandwich-generation.

209 ***the paths we do not:*** Cheryl Strayed, "The Ghost Ship That Didn't Carry Us," *The Rumpus,* April 21, 2011, therumpus.net/2011/04/21/dear-sugar-the-rumpus-advice-column-71-the-ghost-ship-that-didnt-carry-us.

CHAPTER SIX: OUR HEALTH

216 ***"You must take":*** Sharon Malone, *Grown Women Talk: Your Guide to Getting and Staying Healthy* (Crown, 2024), 8.

222 ***During perimenopause, our ovaries':*** "Perimenopause," The Menopause Society, last reviewed October 20, 2025, menopause.org/patient-education/menopause-topics/perimenopause.

223 ***Research has shown the mid-forties:*** "Perimenopause," Cleveland Clinic, last reviewed August 8, 2024, my.clevelandclinic.org/health/diseases/21608-perimenopause.

224 ***a bevy of symptoms:*** Adam C. Cunningham et al., "Perimenopause Symptoms, Severity, and Healthcare Seeking in Women in the US," *npj Women's Health* 3, no. 12 (2025), doi.org/10.1038/s44294-025-00061-3.

224 ***Women going through perimenopause:*** Nazanin E. Silver, "Mood Changes During Perimenopause Are Real: Here's What to Know," American College of Gynecology and Obstetrics, last reviewed February 2025, acog.org/womens-health/experts-and-stories/the-latest/mood-changes-during-perimenopause-are-real-heres-what-to-know.

227 ***Eating fresh, whole foods:*** Eva Selhub, "Nutritional Psychiatry: Your Brain on Food," *Harvard Health* blog, September 18, 2022, health.harvard.edu/blog/nutritional-psychiatry-your-brain-on-food-201511168626.

227 ***Often referred to as "the happiness":*** "Serotonin," Cleveland Clinic, last reviewed March 18, 2022, my.clevelandclinic.org/health/articles/22572-serotonin.

228 ***Fatty fish, such as:*** Ibrahim M. Dighriri et al., "Effects of Omega-3

Polyunsaturated Fatty Acids on Brain Functions: A Systematic Review," *Cureus* 14, no. 10 (2022): e30091, doi.org/10.7759/cureus.30091.

228 ***Chia seeds, flaxseeds, and:*** "Know the Flax (and the Chia): A Little Seed May Be What Your Diet Needs," American Heart Association, July 19, 2019, heart.org/en/news/2019/07/19/know-the-flax-and-the-chia-a-little-seed-may-be-what-your-diet-needs.

228 ***They also contain zinc:*** Uma Naidoo, "What to Eat for Optimal Mental Health," *Culinary Psychology,* January 26, 2021, umanaidoomd.com/blogs/blog/what-to-eat-for-optimal-mental-health.

228 ***The golden spice turmeric:*** Javad Sharifi-Rad et al., "Turmeric and Its Major Compound Curcumin on Health: Bioactive Effects and Safety Profiles for Food, Pharmaceutical, Biotechnological and Medicinal Applications," *Frontiers in Pharmacology* 11, no. 01021 (2020), doi.org/10.3389/fphar.2020.01021.

228 ***She also loves fresh:*** Andrew Pengelly et al., "Short-Term Study on the Effects of Rosemary on Cognitive Function in an Elderly Population," *Journal of Medicinal Food* 15, no. 1 (2012), doi.org/10.1089/jmf.2011.0005.

228 ***"Extra-dark natural chocolate":*** Thea Magrone, Matteo Antonio Russo, and Emilio Jirillo, "Cocoa and Dark Chocolate Polyphenols: From Biology to Clinical Applications," *Frontiers in Immunology* 8, no. 677 (2017), doi.org/10.3389/fimmu.2017.00677.

229 ***Green tea. My personal favorite:*** Jackson L. Williams et al., "The Effects of Green Tea Amino Acid L-Theanine Consumption on the Ability to Manage Stress and Anxiety Levels: A Systematic Review," *Plant Foods for Human Nutrition* 75, no. 1 (2020): 12–23, doi.org/10.1007/s11130-019-00771-5.

231 ***women in perimenopause:*** Megan Marsh, Marta Novaes Oliveira, and Victoria Vieira-Potter, "Adipocyte Metabolism and Health after the Menopause: The Role of Exercise," *Nutrients* 15, no. 2 (2023): 444, doi.org/10.3390/nu15020444.

231 ***Exercise is crucial:*** Steriani Elavsky, "Physical Activity, Menopause, and Quality of Life: The Role of Affect and Self-Worth Across Time," *Menopause* 16, no. 2 (2009): 265–71, doi.org/10.1097/gme.0b013e31818c0284.

231 ***Further research suggests:*** Sarah Witkowski et al., "Physical Activity and Exercise for Hot Flashes: Trigger or Treatment?" *Menopause* 30, no. 2 (2023): 218–24, doi.org/10.1097/GME.0000000000002107.

231 ***More and more research:*** Aishwarya Vasudevan and Elizabeth Ford, "Motivational Factors and Barriers Towards Initiating and Maintaining Strength Training in Women: A Systematic Review and Meta-Synthesis," *Prevention Science* 23, no. 4 (2021): 674–95, doi.org/10.1007/s11121-021-01328-2.

231 ***It can help offset:*** Hongwei Ji et al., "Sex Difference in Association of Physical Activity with All-Cause and Cardiovascular Mortality," *JACC* 83, no. 8 (2024), doi.org/10.1016/j.jacc.2023.12.019.

232 ***But simple, accessible practices:*** MaryCarol R. Hunter, Brenda W. Gillespie, and Sophie Yu-Pu Chen, "Urban Nature Experiences Reduce Stress in the Context of Daily Life Based on Salivary Biomarkers," *Frontiers in Psychology* 10, no. 722 (2019), doi.org/10.3389/fpsyg.2019.00722/.

232 ***Still, some experts:*** Marty Velasco Hames, "Why Alcohol and Menopause Can Be a Dangerous Mix," *Mayo Clinic News Network*, May 5, 2023, newsnetwork.mayoclinic.org/discussion/mayo-clinic-minute-why-alcohol-and-menopause-can-be-a-dangerous-mix.

233 ***Eighty percent of women under:*** Carly Munn et al., "Menopause Knowledge and Education in Women Under 40: Results from an Online Survey," *Women's Health* 18 (December 2022), doi.org/10.1177/17455057221139660.

233 ***Many perimenopausal and postmenopausal:*** Mary Kathryn Dahlgren et al., "Identifying Variables Associated with Menopause-Related Shame and Stigma: Results from a National Survey Study," *Journal of Women's Health* 32, no. 11 (2023): 1182–91, doi.org/10.1089/jwh.2023.0185.

235 ***"Menopause—that baggy term":*** Susan Dominus, "Women Have Been Misled About Menopause," *The New York Times Magazine*, February 1, 2023, nytimes.com/2023/02/01/magazine/menopause-hot-flashes-hormone-therapy.html.

235 ***hormone therapy is a treatment:*** "Hormone therapy," The Menopause Society, menopause.org/patient-education/menopause-topics/hormone-therapy.

235 ***The therapy dates:*** Marcia Stefanick, "Estrogens and Progestins: Background and History, Trends in Use, and Guidelines and Regimens Approved by the US Food and Drug Administration," *American Journal of Medicine* 118, no. 12 (2005): 64–73, doi.org/10.1016/j.amjmed.2005.09.059.

235 ***The Women's Health Initiative (WHI):*** JoAnn E. Manson et al., "The Women's Health Initiative Hormone Therapy Trials: Update

and Overview of Health Outcomes During the Intervention and Post-Stopping Phases," *JAMA* 310, no. 13 (2014): 1353–68, doi.org/10.1001/jama.2013.278040.

235 ***This study showed only:*** James H. Clark, "A Critique of Women's Health Initiative Studies (2002–2006)" *Nuclear Receptor Signaling* 4 (October 30, 2006): e023, pmc.ncbi.nlm.nih.gov/articles/PMC1630688.

235 ***In the time since, further:*** JoAnn E. Manson et al., "The Women's Health Initiative Randomized Trials and Clinical Practice: A Review," *JAMA* 331, no. 20 (2024): 1748–60, doi.org/10.1001/jama.2024.6542.

236 ***When she was thirty-nine:*** "BRCA Gene Changes: Cancer Risk and Genetic Testing," National Cancer Institute, reviewed July 19, 2024, cancer.gov/about-cancer/causes-prevention/genetics/brca-fact-sheet.

236 ***She said the surgery:*** Amanda Nitschke et al., "Long-Term Non-Cancer Risks in People with *BRCA* Mutations Following Risk-Reducing Bilateral Salpingo-Oophorectomy and the Role of Hormone Replacement Therapy: A Review," *Cancers* 15, no. 3 (2023): 711, doi.org/10.3390/cancers15030711.

240 ***Before 1993, clinical:*** "NIH Inclusion Outreach Toolkit: How to Engage, Recruit, and Retain Women in Clinical Research," National Institutes of Health, Office of Research on Women's Health, last modified April 24, 2024, orwh.od.nih.gov/toolkit/recruitment/history.

241 ***In 2024, President Biden:*** National Institutes of Health, "NIH, ORWH Named to New White House Initiative for Women's Health," *NIH Record* 75, no. 25 (2023), nihrecord.nih.gov/2023/12/08/nih-orwh-named-new-white-house-initiative-women-s-health.

241 ***The news was stunning:*** Maria Shriver, "Maria Shriver at the White House: Women's Health Research Initiative," December 13, 2024, YouTube, 8 min., 7 sec., youtube.com/watch?v=NDdmXBrUvXw.

242 ***Black women are up to:*** Anuli Njoku et al., "Listen to the Whispers Before They Become Screams: Addressing Black Maternal Morbidity and Mortality in the United States," *Healthcare* 11, no. 3 (2023): 48, doi.org/10.3390/healthcare11030438.

242 ***A 2024 study from Deloitte:*** Kulleni Gebreyes et al., "What's Causing Women to Skip or Delay Medical Care?" Deloitte Center for

Health Solutions, September 10, 2024, deloitte.com/us/en/insights/industry/health-care/why-women-skip-or-delay-health-care.html.

242 ***The greater propensity to seek:*** Charlotte Edmond, "US Women Are Paying Billions More for Healthcare than Men Every Year," World Economic Forum, October 18, 2023, weforum.org/stories/2023/10/healthcare-equality-united-states-gender-gap.

243 ***Growing research underscores:*** Lea Merone et al., "Sex Inequalities in Medical Research: A Systematic Scoping Review of the Literature," *Women's Health Reports* 3, no. 1 (2022): 49–59, doi.org/10.1089/whr.2021.0083.

243 ***A 2024 systematic review:*** Kianaat Khan, Noor Tariq, and Saima Majeed, "Psychological Impact of Medical Gaslighting on Women: A Systematic Review," *Journal of Professional and Applied Psychology* 5, no. 1 (2024): 110–25, doi.org/10.52053/jpap.v5i1.249.

243 ***"This past is a presence":*** Elizabeth Comen, *All in Her Head: The Truth and Lies Early Medicine Taught Us About Women's Bodies and Why It Matters Today* (Harper Wave, 2024), xiii.

244 ***Since 1995, Boston University:*** Slone Epidemiology Center, Black Women's Health Study, "About the Black Women's Health Study," Boston University, accessed October 21, 2025, bu.edu/bwhs.

244 ***Medical schools have perpetuated:*** Kelly M. Hoffman et al., "Racial Bias in Pain Assessment and Treatment Recommendations, and False Beliefs About Biological Differences Between Blacks and Whites," *Proceedings of the National Academy of Sciences* 113, no. 16 (2016): 4296–301, doi.org/10.1073/pnas.1516047113.

248 ***Approximately 11 percent of all:*** Colleen Moriarty, "Too Young to Screen: Breast Cancer in Younger Women," Yale Medicine, April 30, 2024, yalemedicine.org/news/breast-cancer-younger-women.

248 ***And Black women are 41 percent:*** "More Black Women Die from Breast Cancer Than Any Other Cancer," American Cancer Society, February 14, 2022, cancer.org/research/acs-research-news/facts-and-figures-african-american-black-people-2022-2024.html.

248 ***Cervical screenings. Medical guidelines:*** US Preventative Services Task Force, "Cervical Cancer: Screening," August 21, 2018, uspreventiveservicestaskforce.org/uspstf/recommendation/cervical-cancer-screening.

248 ***Colonoscopies. Plan to get one:*** US Preventative Task Force, "Colorectal Cancer: Screening," May 18, 2021, uspreventiveservicestaskforce.org/uspstf/recommendation/colorectal-cancer-screening.

248 ***Dr. Ashita Gehlot underscored:*** Cancer Research Institute, "Colorectal Cancer Rates Are Skyrocketing in Young Adults—Is Your Lifestyle Putting You at Risk?" *CRI Blog*, March 5, 2025, cancerresearch.org/blog/colorectal-cancer-awareness-month.

253 ***A 2024 report revealed:*** "Solera Women's Health Study Reveals Women Silently Endure Non-Critical Health Conditions," Solera Health, May 9, 2024, soleranetwork.com/latest-news/solera-womens-health-study.

CHAPTER SEVEN: BEING 40

256 ***"I'm just saying, I guess":*** Pam Houston, *Deep Creek: Finding Hope in the High Country* (W. W. Norton, 2020), 96.

257 ***"These words,* wild *and* woman*":*** Clarissa Pinkola Estés, *Women Who Run with the Wolves: Myths and Stories of the Wild Woman Archetype* (Ballantine Books, 1995), 7.

265 ***"It will never get easier":*** Stacey Lindsay, "It Will Never Get Easier, but You Will Handle Hard Better: Coach Kara Lawson on the Message Behind Her Inspiring Viral Video That Everyone Should Hear," *Maria Shriver's Sunday Paper,* July 16, 2022, mariashriversundaypaper.com/it-will-never-get-easier-but-you-will-handle-hard-better-duke-coach-kara-lawson-on-the-message-behind-her-inspiring-viral-video-that-everyone-should-hear.